Virginia Woolf

Virginia Woolf

by

Michael Rosenthal

Routledge & Kegan Paul
London and Henley

To my parents

First published in 1979
by Routledge & Kegan Paul Ltd
39 Store Street,
London WC1E 7DD and
Broadway House,
Newtown Road,
Henley-on-Thames,
Oxon RG9 1EN
Set in 10 on 12pt Bembo
and printed in Great Britain by
Lowe & Brydone Printers Ltd,
Thetford, Norfolk
© Michael Rosenthal 1979

British Library Cataloguing in Publication Data

Rosenthal, Michael

Virginia Woolf.
1. Woolf, Virginia—Criticism and interpretation
823'.9'12   PR6045.072Z/

ISBN 0 7100 0189 4

Contents

Preface and acknowledgments

Ideally, the reader of this book is someone who has already encountered the pleasures and difficulties of Virginia Woolf's novels and wants to know more about them. At the same time, there are large numbers of people who, while fascinated by all they hear about Woolf and her Bloomsbury friends, have been reluctant to undertake what they consider to be the daunting experience of actually reading her work, and I am hoping that this book will be useful to them as well: it is intended to enhance the understanding of those already familiar with her achievement, and encourage those rather more diffident readers to appreciate the extraordinary accomplishment of a great artist. In stressing the primacy of form for Woolf I have tried to provide a focus which is not only central to her development as a writer but also honors the complexity and merits of each individual work.

While the strategy of my book is perfectly straightforward, I would like to suggest that the three chapters preceding my chronological treatment of Woolf's work should properly be thought of as constituting one single introductory discussion. Woolf's life, the realities of Bloomsbury, and the nature of her work are obviously all connected, and the division into three separate chapters merely represents a convenient way of approaching a unified subject. I should add that the biographical chapter makes no claim to original research; the emphasis and interpretations are mine, but the basic facts of her life have already been definitively told by Quentin Bell. I am, as anyone who writes on Woolf must necessarily be, indebted to his biography.

In the course of writing I have benefited from the critical insight of many friends and colleagues, at Columbia and elsewhere, who have freely shared their ideas with me. I would particularly like to thank Professor George Stade, Professor Peter R. Pouncey, and Professor

Herbert Leibowitz, all of whom read earlier versions of the book and helped me to improve them. A portion of Chapter 2 originally appeared in the New York *Times* Book Review, and a somewhat different form of Chapter 3 in the *Partisan Review*, and I am grateful to both for permitting me to include them here. I was extremely fortunate to have Peggy Humphreys and Phyllis Katz as typists, each of whom worked heroically from illegible manuscript. Finally, I wish to thank Erik, Stephen, and Noah, for encouraging me to work at the expense of other responsibilities (and joys). My fiercest critic and staunchest supporter from the beginning has been my wife, Judith. She and I both know how futile it would be for me to try publicly to thank her for what she has contributed to the completion of this book.

Excerpts from the following books by Virginia Woolf are reprinted by permission of the Author's Literary Estate and the Hogarth Press; and Harcourt Brace Jovanovich, Inc.: *The Diaries of Virginia Woolf, The Letters of Virginia Woolf, A Writer's Diary, A Haunted House and Other Stories, The Voyage Out, Night and Day, Jacob's Room, Mrs. Dalloway, To the Lighthouse, Orlando, The Waves, The Years, Between The Acts, Flush, Roger Fry, A Room Of One's Own, Three Guineas, Collected Essays*; copyright 1920 by George H. Doran and Company; copyright 1928 by Virginia Woolf; copyright 1922, 1925, 1927, 1931, 1937, 1941 by Harcourt Brace Jovanovich, Inc. Page references to the works of Virginia Woolf are to the uniform edition by the Hogarth Press, unless otherwise indicated. References to the *Letters* and *Diaries*, and to Leonard Woolf's autobiography are to the American editions.

1

The Life

To say that Virginia Woolf was the daughter of Sir Leslie Stephen is not only to begin at a logical starting point with an indisputable historical fact—he was after all her father—but also to suggest a great deal about the world in which she grew up. For Sir Leslie, in addition to being a complex, prodigiously productive man, has taken on a kind of metaphoric meaning as well, embodying a recognizable strain of agnostic, literate, late nineteenth-century culture shared by a number of great Victorian families. If not exactly *eminent* in the particular sense with which Lytton Strachey has invested that word, Stephen was at the very least august, a presence of formidable moral energy who earned for himself a legitimate place in the inner circle of the intellectual aristocracy that developed in England during the nineteenth century. A literary critic and historian who longed to be accepted as a serious philosopher, Stephen produced hundreds of articles and over a dozen books during his lifetime, ranging in subject from George Eliot to the science of ethics. His most significant achievement was undertaking in 1882 the editing of the monumental *Dictionary of National Biography*, a project on which he spent nine exhausting years until his health finally dictated he give it up.

Stephen's first wife, Harriet Marian (Minny), Thackeray's youngest daughter, died in 1875, leaving him with one emotionally unstable child who would eventually have to be institutionalized. Bereft at 43 of the wife he loved, Stephen soon found himself comforted by the friendship of Julia Duckworth, a young widow who had been very close to the Thackeray family. The untimely death of her husband in 1870 had left Julia feeling there was little in the world other than taking care of her three young children—and anyone else who seemed to need her ministrations. In his desolation, Stephen was certainly one of the latter—as the portrait of Mr Ramsay in *To the Lighthouse* makes clear,

1

he was to remain emotionally dependent all his life—and Julia found in comforting him a partial antidote to her own unhappiness. Over the course of three years the need of each for the other deepened, and in 1878 they officially renounced their respective states of misery by getting married. To Julia's three children, George, Stella, and Gerald, Stephen soon added four more: two girls, Vanessa and Virginia, and two boys, Thoby and Adrian. Virginia, the third, was born in 1882.

Life in the Stephen nursery was intense, competitive, and full of all those sibling jealousies necessarily present when four children are busy discovering themselves. While frequently struggling, the children were at the same time immensely affectionate with one another, forming close ties that were to endure throughout their lives. In spite of their inevitable rivalry, this was especially true of Virginia and Vanessa who from the start shared an intimacy that was not eroded by time. It was decided early between them that Virginia would be a writer and Vanessa a painter. Virginia's designation as a writer was not arbitrary: although she apparently did not start talking until relatively late—about three years old—she rapidly became absorbed in the fascinations of language. As a very young child Virginia was the family story-teller, weaving tales in the nursery for her brothers and sister until sleep finally interrupted the episode of the evening. In 1891 she began publication of the weekly family newspaper, the *Hyde Park Gate News*, an enterprise which at first included the talents of brother Thoby but soon fell almost entirely to Virginia alone. Maintained for roughly five years, it combines family reporting with an occasional venture into fiction. Altogether, the *Hyde Park Gate News* gives an interesting view of the domestic routine of the Stephens as well as the early imaginative fancies of the aspiring artist. The prose is about what one would expect in a child beginning to explore the power of words. The reunion of two brothers is worthy of a proper grandiloquent style: 'How sweet it was to see him bend down with eyes expressing worlds of joy! (O how much can eyes express!) and kiss the rosy frontispiece turned up to him.'[1] But however exaggerated the language, Woolf was as anxious about her work then as she was to be years later when awaiting the critical reception of each new novel. Placing the freshly produced issue of the *News* on her mother's sofa in the drawing room while her parents were at dinner, Virginia would remain in a state of agitated concern until it was finally read and

---

[1] Quentin Bell, *Virginia Woolf: A Biography* (Harcourt Brace Jovanovich, 1972), 28.

received the appropriate commendation. Her need for approval, as her mature career testifies, did not diminish as she grew older.

While Stephen was a certified Victorian free-thinker, there was nothing emancipated or radical about his view of the family structure or the future of his children. He shared all the unthinking, patriarchal assumptions that Woolf was later to excoriate in *A Room of One's Own* and *Three Guineas*: his boys would go to public schools and Cambridge in preparation for their careers; his girls would receive a proper education at home in preparation for their marriages. These were assumptions that Woolf came bitterly to resent, depriving her as they did of the formal educational opportunities open to her brothers. But within the confines of an ethos that never for a moment considered alternatives to this blatantly unjust system, Woolf had the unique intellectual advantages of being the daughter of Leslie Stephen. Exposure to the heavy-handed tutorial efforts of Leslie and Julia, however, was very definitely not one of them. Their determination to impart to the children the rudiments of Latin, French, history, and mathematics was matched by their complete inability to understand the difficulties a small child might have in trying to learn difficult things. There was no pedagogy and even less patience: Virginia remained counting on her fingers throughout her life and what both sisters learned of history and modern languages they acquired totally on their own. But the failure of her parents as teachers constituted only a small part of the educational experience of growing up in the Stephen household. More important was an atmosphere always charged with ideas and intelligent conversation frequently generated by the presence of England's leading intellectuals, and the resources of a great library. Initially recommending specific volumes to Virginia, Leslie soon gave her the complete freedom of his library, only suggesting with some discretion that there might be particular books not quite appropriate for her. But otherwise no attempt was made to restrain her curiosity, and Virginia roamed at will through his enormous collection, reading prodigiously in every area which interested her. Although she always felt cheated by being denied the university education unquestioningly available to her brothers, free access to a rich and varied library at least made up for some of the loss. Encouraged by her father's own love of literature, Virginia became addicted to books early; it was a habit she never felt any inclination to break.

The busy urban routines of 22 Hyde Park Gate always gave way in the summer to the marvellous refuge of St Ives in Cornwall, where

Leslie owned a house situated right above the bay. The annual retreat to Talland House was undoubtedly the high point of the year for the Stephen children, who adored the beauty, the access to the sea, and the general excitement and freedom they could experience far away from London. For Virginia in particular, as Bell writes, it was 'the Eden of her youth, an unforgettable paradise' (Bell, *Virginia Woolf*, 32), which remained fixed in her imagination as an enclave of nourishment and happiness. In the wind-swept island of the Hebrides in *To The Lighthouse* Woolf celebrates not only the splendor of St Ives itself but the quality of rich family life she came to associate with it. The feelings generated by the warm presence of Mrs Ramsay and the vulnerable but courageous man she loves speak eloquently to what Talland House meant to Woolf (*To the Lighthouse*, 151–2):

> For the night was not shut off by panes of glass, which, far from giving any accurate view of the outside world, rippled it so strangely that here, inside the room, seemed to be order and dry land; there, outside, a reflection in which things wavered and vanished, waterily . . . They were all conscious of making a party together in a hollow, on an island; had their common cause against that fluidity out there.

With Julia's sudden death in May 1895, the order and dry land she had helped create were totally inundated by waves of chaos and dissolution. Not only was Virginia deprived of a mother whom she deeply loved and who was primarily responsible for the emotional sustenance an adolescent needs, but equally important Leslie Stephen lost the wife who had dutifully catered to his inexhaustible demands. Life without Julia was an insufferable prospect for Stephen, and instead of nursing his children through their trauma, he became a drain on whatever resources they had left, miring himself helplessly in grief and self-pity. At a time when the children looked for comfort and guidance, the father stayed gloomily immersed in his own despair, seldom able to surface long enough to make any significant contact with them. Stephen, in fact, never did recover; until the end of his life he remained essentially in mourning, oppressing all around him with those needs that Julia was not available to satisfy.

Although mental illness can certainly not be traced to any single event in a person's life, it is clear that the death of Virginia's mother and the accompanying collapse of her father short-circuited an already fragile system, triggering, by that summer, the first of four break-

4

downs Woolf was to experience during her life. Little is known about the exact nature of her condition. The physical symptoms—which were present at each successive breakdown as well—included intense agitation, spells of auditory hallucination, and a deep and almost completely incapacitating depression. Throughout these short interludes of sickness it was the symptoms alone that were treated, either by exercise or rest or sipping milk in darkened rooms. In this case, exercise was prescribed by the family doctor, and it fell to Stella, Virginia's half-sister, to help keep her outside the required four hours a day, walking and taking bus rides.

While she soon emerged from this first onslaught, she was never again totally free from the spectre of recurring illness. It was a threat she had to endure all her life. Never able to penetrate to any of the emotional roots of her precarious health Woolf could do no more than scrutinize herself carefully for signs of collapse and then take those primitive evasive measures of rest (or exercise) which were the only ones available to her. As her total distrust of psychoanalysis ruled out any radical attempt at cure, all her efforts were devoted simply to resisting. And with Leonard's help (following her marriage) she was remarkably successful in her struggle. Invariably brought to the edge of the abyss with every book she finished, Woolf managed to cling to her equilibrium with what can only be thought of as a kind of heroic tenacity. In the midst of all her self-doubts and anguish, the luminous sanity of her fiction with its steady, uncompromised humanity suggests the extent of her triumph. But the cost was terrible. The alternating rhythm of health and sickness had the cumulative effect of draining Woolf's psychic reserves dry; in 1941, depressed by the war and sensing the imminence of another collapse from which she might not have the strength to recover, Woolf chose to escape altogether by drowning herself in the Ouse.

In his biography, Bell reveals that about the time of Julia Stephen's death in 1895, both Virginia and Vanessa became subject to the rather unfraternal embraces and gropings of their half-brother George. Always warm and demonstrative by nature, the twenty-seven-year-old George apparently went well beyond the bounds of brotherly endearments, oppressing both sisters with a sexual interest they could only perceive as terrifying and obscene. Bell's view is that this kind of incestuous exploitation was sufficiently traumatic to ensure that severe distaste of sexuality, particularly male sexuality, Woolf was to harbor all her life: 'Naturally shy in sexual matters, she was from this

5

time terrified back into a posture of frozen and defensive panic.'
(Bell, *Virginia Woolf*, 44).

It is difficult to know what to make of the rather scanty evidence or
how to evaluate the seriousness of George's fumblings. Bell argues
that the girls could not actually tell anybody about George's behavior
because of their extreme shyness, and because in their innocence it
must have taken them a long time even to realize precisely what was
happening, at which point it was too late to object. In addition, given
George's good-nature and popularity, who would believe them?
Bell's argument is not entirely convincing. If it is true that George's
conduct was such that 'it would have taken a very knowing eye' (Bell,
Virginia Woolf, 43), to perceive that anything was wrong, then it is
hard to imagine that it was quite as traumatic as Bell claims. And
certainly some vocal protest, if only to George himself, was possible
even for girls as pure and as shy as Virginia and Vanessa.

Whatever the exact truth of George's involvement with the two
sisters, it is clear that Virginia detested him; and if Bell's estimate of his
effect on her is correct (Vanessa seems more or less to have escaped
unscathed), he unquestionably contributed to her frigidity and the
general emotional instability which plagued her from the time of her
mother's death. The loss of a love object, the deterioration of the
father, and the entanglement in some kind of unwanted relationship
with an older brother were not a salubrious combination for an
adolescent confronting impulses and anxieties difficult to handle even
in the best of circumstances. That Virginia responded one way and
Vanessa in quite another to the same realities speaks to those mysteries of personality for which there are no simple explanations.

The years between her mother's death in 1895 and her father's in
1904 were neither eventful nor particularly happy for Virginia. While
Vanessa concentrated on her drawing and Stephen, who became Sir
Leslie in 1902, grew ever more self-indulgent in his complaining and
self-pitying, Virginia fought to maintain her health, managing at the
same time to study a variety of subjects, especially Latin and Greek.
During this period one of the most significant developments in her life
in fact occurred when Thoby went up to Trinity College in 1899. It
was here that he met Lytton Strachey, Clive Bell, Leonard Woolf,
Saxon Sydney-Turner and the others who, with the Stephen sisters,
were to provide the nucleus of Bloomsbury. Finding a group of
friends who not only supplied husbands (Leonard and Clive) for his
sisters, but also went on to constitute a social and intellectual ambience

that has earned a permanent place for itself in the history of the twentieth century, Thoby had, by any standards, a rather auspicious first year. Virginia always loved her visits to Cambridge, relishing the world of cultured leisure from which she was excluded by virtue of her sex. Jacob's university experience in *Jacob's Room* speaks pointedly to the quality of her feelings about Cambridge, and to how much of the university's atmosphere she absorbed through her brother, her husband and their friends.

Leslie Stephen's death in 1904, after a long and painful illness, produced an array of conflicting responses in his children. Attached to him in various ways—Virginia perhaps more closely than any of the others—all felt at the same time, and not without some guilt, a certain sense of relief at escaping from his tyranny. It would be difficult to have Leslie Stephen as a father and not have a great many confused feelings about him. He commanded grand love with the same ease that he created bitter resentment: whatever people felt about him, they felt is strongly. Certainly Virginia was deeply affected by his loss (*Letters*, vol. 1, 129). She writes immediately after his death,

But how to go on without him. I don't know. All these years we have hardly been apart, and I want him every moment of the day. But we still have each other—Nessa and Thoby and Adrian and I, and when we are together he and mother do not seem far off.

A trip to Italy was decided upon as a general recuperative measure, and at the beginning of April the four Stephens left for Venice, accompanied by George Duckworth. While the holiday was pleasant enough, particularly for Vanessa, who clearly relished her new freedom, it did nothing at all to relieve the nervous tension Virginia felt building within her. Returning to England in May, Virginia fell almost immediately into the throes of her second serious breakdown. This one was far more acute than the first, involving a suicide attempt in which she threw herself from a window. It was at this time also that she heard the sparrows singing in Greek which Septimus Smith was later to hear in *Mrs. Dalloway*. During the most severe phase of her illness she was cared for at the home of Violet Dickinson, the dear old friend with whom Virginia had an intense relationship as a young woman. Together, Violet and Vanessa, with the aid of a devoted nurse, managed to bring her through her manic storms of accusations and hallucinations so that by early September she was able to leave the Dickinson home at Burnham Wood and live peacefully—if still shakily—with Vanessa in Nottinghamshire.

Even while Leslie Stephen was alive the children had all recognized the necessity of escaping from the dark and melancholy 22 Hyde Park Gate; and his death set in motion a search for new quarters that would not be cluttered with any cobwebs of the past. The place they chose, distressingly enough for their respectable relatives, was 46 Gordon Square in Bloomsbury, an area not considered proper for children of Sir Leslie. But it was light, inexpensive, and, most important, represented a total break from the oppressive confines of family and conventions they had previously known. Staying with relatives and friends throughout the fall and early winter while Thoby and Vanessa made the house ready, Virginia did not permanently settle into Gordon Square until early January of 1905.

Symbolically as well as practically the move to Bloomsbury initiated what we can think of as the adult phase of Woolf's life. Freed from the protective—and necessarily limiting—control of her father, and having regained her sanity after the prolonged spell of debilitating illness, she came to a new house prepared to begin a new kind of independent existence. Even before she arrived, and partly out of the recognition that she was now obliged to start earning money, she had begun sending reviews to the *Guardian*, a weekly newspaper the editor of whose Women's Supplement was a friend of Violet Dickinson's. Mrs Lyttleton was impressed with her work, and on 14 December 1904 Virginia's first piece was published, an unsigned review of W. D. Howell's *The Son of Royal Langbrith*.

Establishing herself at 46 Gordon Square, then, as a fully certified book reviewer, Woolf commenced the journalistic career that she was to maintain throughout her life. Writing reviews and articles were activities that Woolf clearly saw as less significant than writing novels but to which she devoted a substantial amount of time anyway. For one thing, they were a steady source of income for her, particularly before the Hogarth Press and the sale of her own novels provided the financial security she always sought. Along with her writing, Virginia also began teaching. Morley College, an evening institute for working men and women did not exactly provide the kind of students with which she was familiar, but nevertheless she took to instructing them in a variety of subjects—literature, history, composition—with great enthusiasm and much diligence. She found contact with a social class hitherto unknown to her a fascinating experience. Although depressed at the mediocrity of the institution itself and its determined unwillingness to try to educate people adequately, she enjoyed her students sufficiently to continue teaching there for three years.

Perhaps more important to Virginia's development than even the writing and teaching was the rich social life that rapidly sprang up around 46 Gordon Square. However precocious and gifted intelectually, Virginia was still in 1905 the kind of thoroughly innocent daughter that every dominating Victorian father could be proud of. Despite the enormous amount of reading and traveling (and even suffering) she had done, Virginia remained at twenty-five a rather conventional young woman, a product of a home and culture that took care to protect its daughters from the contamination of experience. All this was to change dramatically with the infusion of Thoby's friends into London. Anxious to keep in touch with all his Cambridge acquaintances while reading for the bar, Thoby made it clear that he would be at home on Thursday evenings for anyone who wanted to stop by. Bell assigns the first of these evenings, which as the origins of Bloomsbury have since been invested with a vast mythic significance, to 16 February 1905. The cultural importance of the event was probably not felt by the participants, who consisted of Thoby, Saxon Sydney-Turner, and Gurth, the Stephens's dog. But the evenings quickly grew larger as the availability of good company at 46 Gordon Square became known, and it was not long before Virginia and Vanessa themselves began to attend. Virginia by no means found the gatherings exhilarating at first. The people seemed odd, and talked about art and literature and beauty with an intensity she had never before encountered. As her own reserve melted, however, she became more and more involved with them, discovering ideas and attitudes in their idiosyncratic conversation which helped liberate her from the restricted premises of her own upbringing. Thoby's friends were soon her own as well, and she was seen to be as much a part of the attractiveness of the evenings as anybody else who might appear.

The writing, teaching, and talking occupied Virginia until her life was again painfully disrupted, in November of 1906, by another shattering death. This time it was Thoby, who shortly after returning from a trip to Greece developed a fever that the doctor originally claimed was an attack of 'something or other,' and then changed to a diagnosis of malaria. Ten days later it was finally decided that he was

9

in fact afflicted with typhoid fever, but by this time nothing could be done; Thoby died on 20 November.

Virginia was devoted to Thoby, and his death was something from which she was never entirely to recover. She continued to think of him always; twice he enters her fiction, the first time as Jacob in *Jacob's Room*, where the search for the elusive Jacob can be seen in part as Woolf's own attempt to locate the missing Thoby; and again in *The Waves*, where he stands behind the mythic Percival, whose early and senseless death represents for all of the voices in the novel the first onslaught of mortality. The immediate circumstances surrounding his dying were made even more excrutiating by the Stephens's vow to spare Violet Dickinson, also desperately ill with typhoid, news of Thoby's death until she was out of danger herself. Virginia was thus forced to dissemble (although it is difficult to think that there were not, at the same time, considerable elements of fantasy involved), writing cheery, gossipy letters to Violet, speaking about domestic routines of all the Stephens, and particularly the recuperation of Thoby. Five days after Thoby died, for example, we find Virginia explaining to Violet that (*Letters*, vol. 1, 250)

> Thoby is going on splendidly. He is very cross with his nurses, because they won't give him mutton chops and beer; and he asks why he can't go for a ride with Bell, and look for wild geese. Then nurse says 'won't tame ones do' at which we laugh.

In addition to the devastation wrought on its own, Thoby's death had the further upsetting effect on Virginia's life of precipitating Vanessa's marriage to Clive Bell. Looking for solace at a time of enormous despair, Vanessa, having previously refused him, agreed to marry Clive two days after Thoby died. Besides losing a sister to a man about whom she had serious doubts, Virginia was also forced to give up her residence at 46 Gordon Square, as it was decided that the Bells should remain there while Adrian and Virginia found other accommodation. Clive and Vanessa were married in February and at the end of March Adrian and Virginia moved into what had formerly been G. B. Shaw's house, at 29 Fitzroy Square.

The splitting of the Stephen nucleus into two flourishing centers had the effect of intensifying and extending the friendships that had grown up around Gordon Square. Thursday evenings soon opened at Fitzroy Square as well, and it was possible in a single evening to visit both the Bells and the Stephens—a practice in which many engaged.

At the same time that she became increasingly caught up in the network of personal relationships that remained Thoby's most precious legacy to her, Virginia continued to write. Reviews for the *Times Literary Supplement* provided a steady if minute source of income for her while she began work on her first serious piece of fiction, *Melymbrosia*, which eventually evolved into *The Voyage Out*. But absorption in her work did not obscure the gaiety and marvelous sense of absurdity that were always very much a part of her. It was while living with Adrian in Fitzroy Square that she participated in the superb hoaxing of the British navy conceived by her friend, Horace Cole. Dressing up in grease-paint and beards, Virginia, Adrian and three friends, posing as the Emperor of Abyssinia and entourage, and escorted by Horace as a Foreign Office official, managed to get a guided tour of the British navy's newest battleship, the HMS *Dreadnought*. Perhaps the most exquisite moment for Virginia came when she very solemnly shook the hand of her cousin William Fisher, the flag commander of the *Dreadnought*, without having him recognize her.

Although by no means a prank, another extraordinary episode which occurred in Virginia's life during this same period (1901–1916) after the move to Fitzroy Square involved a proposal of marriage from her dear friend Lytton Strachey. Unambiguously homosexual, as well as temperamentally unfit in any number of ways, Strachey was the least likely of Virginia's friends ever to get married. Nevertheless, feeling depressed himself, and casting about to find some way of investing his life with significance, Lytton settled upon the solitary Virginia as the solution to his worthlessness. By rescuing her from her loneliness, Lytton would find meaning in his own life. The improbability of the notion notwithstanding, Lytton actually proposed to her on 17 February 1909, convinced as he was of her love for him, and was accepted. Following the proposal, he was overcome with the horror of what he had done, fearing that as a man of honor he would be obliged to carry through with what had obviously been a severely mistaken impulse. 'It was an awkward moment,' he wrote to his brother James of her acceptance, 'especially as I realised, the very minute it was happening, that the whole thing was repulsive to me.' [1] His anguish was happily resolved by Virginia who, recognizing his terror, assured him that she did not love him and would not consider

[1] Lytton Strachey to James Strachey in *Virginia Woolf and Lytton Strachey: Letters*, ed. by Leonard Woolf and James Strachey (Hogarth Press and Chatto & Windus, 1969), 32.

marriage. No rejected suitor ever felt more relief than Lytton.

Despite the implausibility of the whole incident, it did not leave Virginia unscarred. For however far-fetched a relationship with Strachey might appear, it still underscored the reality that Virginia was twenty-eight, unmarried, and very much in need of the kind of emotional sustenance she could expect from a devoted husband. Spinsterhood and Adrian were both wearing thin on her.

Fortunately Virginia's marital prospects were not to depend solely upon Lytton's caprices. In 1911, Leonard Woolf, one of Thoby's Cambridge friends, returned to London for a leave after a six-and-a-half-year stint with the Civil Service in Ceylon. On 3 July he had dinner with Clive and Vanessa in Gordon Square, eating in the same rooms he had dined in several days before he had left for Ceylon in 1904. After the meal Virginia, Duncan Grant, and Walter Lamb came to visit. In the midst of the vast social and intellectual changes he felt had occurred since he left England, Leonard comments, 'almost the only things which had not changed were the furniture and the extraordinary beauty of the two Miss Stephens' (L. Woolf, *Beginning Again*, 26–7). He was captivated not only by Virginia's beauty but by her vulnerability, and by a quality for which he could find no other word than 'genius.' Spending a great deal of time with her, Leonard was soon very much in love. His feelings for Virginia were complicated by the need to make a decision about his career: should he stay on in the Civil Service, returning to Ceylon or some more remote district, or should he give up his comfortable salary and predictable future and launch out on a precarious journalistic career? If she would agree to marry him, he resolved, he would have no difficulty resigning from the Service. Virginia, however, did not make things easy: her response to his first marriage proposal, early in 1912, was a claim of uncertainty and a plea for more time. Although hardly satisfying, her indecisiveness was at least hopeful enough to move Leonard to write to the Colonial Office requesting an extension of his leave. When it was refused, he had no choice but to resign. Having made his decision, he continued to work on his novel *The Village in the Jungle* and to see Virginia; his perseverance was rewarded on 29 May when Virginia finally consented to be his wife. The Woolfs were married in August.

In choosing to marry her 'penniless Jew' as she described him to her friends, Virginia selected a man who while understanding her needs would at the same time ask very little from her as a woman. Whether it was the result of brother George's detested caresses or, as is more likely, a series of complex factors we cannot fully understand, Virginia was never able to engage fully the sexual side of her nature, either with men or women. Although Vita Sackville-West, her friend and some-time lover, speaks of Virginia's aversion to the tyranny of male sexuality, the fact is that an intense physical relationship of any sort was impossible for her. In a letter to Leonard written several months before their marriage, she makes clear the quality of her sexual feelings for him (*Letters*, vol. 1, 496):

> I sometimes think that if I married you, I could have
> everything—and then—is it the sexual side of it that comes
> between us? As I told you brutally the other day, I feel no
> physical attraction in you. There are moments—when you kissed
> me the other day was one—when I feel no more than a rock.

But in spite of—and to some degree no doubt even because of—the lack of sustained sexual involvement, theirs was a gratifying and tender, if slightly disembodied, marriage. Understanding flourished in the place of passion; released from the threat of having any serious sexual demands made on her, Virginia was free to give to Leonard what she was capable of giving, to love him for his gentleness, his intelligence, his concern. In return, she drew heavily on his emotional strength, relying on him to help get her through the various crises that continually buffeted her during their lives together. Leonard's good-ness to her was crucial to her survival, as she well knew. The depth of her feeling for him is revealed in the last words she ever wrote—the final note to Leonard before she drowned herself (Bell, *Virginia Woolf*, vol. 2, 226):

> You have given me the greatest possible happiness. You have
> been in every way all that anyone could be . . . . What I want to
> say is I owe all the happiness of my life to you. You have been
> entirely patient with me and incredibly good. I want to say
> that—everybody knows it. If anybody could have saved me it
> would have been you. Everything has gone from me but the
> certainty of your goodness.

Any illusions Leonard might have had about the ease of his life with Virginia were dispelled fairly soon after their marriage. In April of 1913, Virginia finally saw *The Voyage Out*, on which she had worked for more than four years, accepted for publication. Virginia was always at her most vulnerable following the completion of a book, the creative exhaustion and the possibility of criticism inevitably stripping her of whatever fragile defences she possessed. Having suffered from headaches and an inability to sleep even before she sent her manuscript off to Duckworth, she grew increasingly depressed as the summer went on. The terrible symptoms recurred—the anxiety, the violent delusions, the fierce resistance to food—and in September, while Leonard was temporarily out of the house, Virginia again attempted suicide, taking a hundred grains of veronal. This effort was far more serious than the earlier one, and only a frantic stomach-pumping managed to save her life. Leonard now had to confront the possibility that his wife might need to be committed to an asylum. His physicians agreed, however, that if Virginia could be looked after by trained personnel provided by Leonard, she would not have to be institutionalized. George Duckworth generously offered his large house in Sussex to Leonard, and on 20 September, accompanied by two nurses and a friend, Leonard and Virginia left London.

Although there were intermittent spells of seeming recovery, Virginia's complete recuperation (if such it may be called) from this protracted siege of illness took roughly two years. As late as April of 1915, following the publication of *The Voyage Out*, Virginia was totally incapacitated, attended by four nurses. By the beginning of 1916, however, she seemed finally to be in control of herself and able to function normally. For both Leonard and Virginia, of course, the experience had been terrifying: the threat of a permanently disabling mental illness had been a very real part of their lives for two years, and they would never again be altogether free from the fear that it might return. But at the same time—and at great cost—they had triumphed over it, an accomplishment which required the total effort of the two of them. If it was clear to Leonard that they could not possibly consider having children, they had nevertheless come through still intact, still committed to one another and to the work they wanted to do. In addition, Leonard now understood the necessity of attending to her health: from this time on he monitored her physical and mental condition unceasingly, insisting on those spells of rest and calm that helped stave off the nervous exhaustion to which she was prone.

There was another, more tangible, consequence of Virginia's illness. During one of the periods of remission, before the serious collapse of 1915, the Woolfs had talked about the pleasures both might have in learning to be printers. By 1916, with Virginia recovered and once again working strenuously on her writing, Leonard decided it

14

would be a good thing for Virginia to have some kind of manual occupation which could absorb her and help for a portion of each day take her mind off her work, a condition she found extraordinarily difficult to achieve. Their initial impulse to learn the art of printing was thwarted by Leonard's wry discovery that it was 'impossible to teach the art of printing to two middle-aged, middle-class persons. Printing could only be taught to trade union apprentices, the number of whom was strictly limited' (L. Woolf, *Beginning Again*, 233). But while they didn't qualify for instruction in printing, there was nothing to prevent them from buying a hand-press, reading a pamphlet, and teaching themselves to do it. They looked through the window of the Excelsior Printing Supply Co. one March afternoon in 1917, and it occurred to them to go in and ask if such an idea were plausible. They left the shop with £19 5s 5d worth of Old Face type, a small hand-press, assorted materials and implements—and the crucial pamphlet. A month's practice and they were ready to launch the Hogarth Press. Their vision was a press that would publish short works which commercial houses might not bother with, and which they would sell by having people become subscribers to the Press. On 3 May the Hogarth Press began its distinguished career with a run of 150 copies of *Two Stories*, 'The Mark on the Wall' by Virginia and Leonard's 'Three Jews'. Illustrated with four wood-cuts by Carrington, one of their friends, the thirty-two-page production was hand-stitched into paper covers by the two of them. All were ready by July, and in a short time subscribers had purchased 134 copies. The net profits for this first effort were £7 1s, the total production costs £3 15s including the 15s paid to Carrington for her four woodcuts. The enormous profits, as well as the pleasure, induced them to go on to a more ambitious project, and in 1918 they produced 300 copies of 'Prelude,' a sixty-eight-page story by Katherine Mansfield. Although Leonard and Virginia had never intended the enterprise to be any other than an amateur one, the success of their publications and the demand for them rapidly turned a happily therapeutic activity into a serious business. In 1919, they had their first book printed for (instead of by) them, and by 1924 they had become a full-scale commercial publishing house. While Leonard handled the major running of the business, Virginia also continued to be involved in its workings, long after its hand-printed origins had become a quaint memory. And it remained a great relief for Virginia not to have to submit her fiction to any editor: from *Jacob's Room* on, all her work was published by the Hogarth Press.

By the time *Night and Day* was published by Duckworth in 1919, the Woolfs' lives had taken on the basic shape they were to retain for the next two decades or so. With Virginia more or less healthy again and the tumult of the war over, the Woolfs found themselves firmly entrenched in the middle of a flourishing set of Bloomsbury relationships. During the war, they had formed friendships with a number of younger people like David Garnett, Raymond Mortimer, Francis Birrell, and Stephen Tomlin, and 'Bloomsbury' as an idea (and ideal) was now becoming sufficiently well known to require little explanation, though frequently much defense. The centers for Bloomsbury activity were expanded in 1919 to include Monk's House, which Leonard and Virginia bought in Rodmell, a small village near Lewes. Having been forced to leave the country house they were renting in Asham, the Woolfs had desperately sought another place where they could escape from the chaos of London. Monk's House proved the perfect refuge, and from the time they bought it Leonard and Virginia generally spent long summers there as well as numerous shorter visits throughout the year. It was a place they both loved.

Whether in London or Rodmell, nothing—except perhaps for the periodic incapacitating spells of depression and illness—could interfere with Virginia's all-consuming absorption with her work. Bloomsbury's personal relationships and the tasks associated with running a publishing house certainly made their demands on her energies, but they were never permitted to distract her from her single-minded commitment to her fiction. When not actively writing or rewriting a book, she was planning what her next effort would be; rarely was there a time that she was not living inside a work of imagination. Although Woolf did massive amounts of book reviewing throughout her life, contributing regularly to periodicals like the *Times Literary Supplement*, *Athenaeum*, and *New Statesman*, she saw all of this work as being of secondary importance, something to do when she was not fashioning novels. By no means immune to the pleasures money can afford (one reason, indeed for her reviewing), Woolf was most fully alive when agonizing between ten in the morning and one in the afternoon over the page she was currently writing. Once she began producing novels regularly, it was the creative activity itself which became the most interesting feature of her life. As she pointed out in her diary (*A Writer's Diary*, 126),

Now that I have £16 to spend before July 1st (on our new

system) I feel freer; can afford a dress and a hat and so may go about a little, if I want. And yet the only exciting life is the imaginary one. Once I get the wheels spinning in my head, I don't want money much, or dress, or even a cupboard, a bed at Rodmell or a sofa.

The real drama of Woolf's life from the publication of *Jacob's Room* in 1922 to the end lies primarily in her effort to capture those unique forms she sought in each new novel. Next to this artistic quest, the routines of her personal and business existence are of relatively little significance. Unlike a writer, say, like Lawrence, whose relationships and physical peregrinations actively inform his fiction, Woolf creates a fictional universe in which biographical detail does not appreciably enhance the critic's understanding. The relevant history of Woolf from 1922 to 1941 is essentially contained in the novels she wrote.

When she was not writing novels she was working on her journalism, tending to the Hogarth Press, occasionally traveling, maintaining an active set of friendships, Bloomsbury and otherwise, and all the while struggling to keep her extremely delicate mental balance. In addition, though Woolf can by no means be construed as a social activist, she was certainly interested in the question of women's rights, lecturing and writing on the subject. If she was not as radical as current feminists would like her to be, she was nevertheless acutely sensitive to the vast social and economic injustices done to women, as both *A Room of One's Own* and *Three Guineas* indicate. In all of her social attitudes, however, Woolf was very much a creature of a privileged class, and there is no point in trying to invest her with a sensibility and sympathy that were alien to her. The protests she lodged were appropriate for a daughter of the intellectual elite; its gestures were more properly symbolic than anything else. Having always resented the sexism and corrupt values of English universities, she steadfastly refused to accept the honors they wanted to bestow on her when she became eminent: in 1932 she rejected an offer to give the prestigious Clark lectures at Cambridge, and later declined honorary degrees from both Manchester and Liverpool.

But no degree of eminence could ease the anxieties and doubts Woolf had about herself, both as a person and as an artist. Her excruciating vulnerability to criticism was never mitigated by the proven successes of the past; awaiting the reception of each new book was a very great ordeal for Woolf, posing real threats to her health.

17

Woolf's sensitivity was the kind to leave her endlessly exposed to suffering of almost every sort: it is difficult to imagine an existence more emotionally exhausting than the one she led. Although since the siege of 1913–15 she had successfully fought off any recurring long-term attacks of mental illness, the various skirmishes had depleted her energies. The deaths throughout the 1930s of her friends—Lytton Strachey and Roger Fry in particular—and the catastrophic death of her nephew Julian Bell in the Spanish Civil War, also took their toll. Fascism not only claimed the life of the Woolfs' nephew, but with the outbreak of the war and the imminent possibility of a German invasion, it clearly was endangering their own as well. Neither Virginia nor Leonard had any illusions as to how, as Jews and intellectuals, they would be regarded in the case of a British defeat. Adrian, now a physician, supplied them with a lethal amount of morphine, should they need it, and Leonard kept a sufficient amount of gasoline on hand so that they could have the option of running the car in the garage and inhaling carbon monoxide. Throughout May and June of 1940 there was much talk of suicide.

Although increasingly distracted, Virginia continued to work, publishing her biography of Roger Fry in July of 1940. And despite the destruction of their London home by German bombs (while they were in Rodmell), Virginia managed to finish, early in 1941, the manuscript of her last novel, *Between the Acts*. By this time Leonard had become sufficiently alarmed at her deterioration to insist that she see a physician, Octavia Wilberforce, a friend who had a practice in Brighton. A consultation was held on 27 March: Virginia was defensive lest she be sent to a rest home, and scared that she might be slipping into a terminal madness from which there would be no escape; Octavia was as reassuring as possible, attempting to give her confidence that the problems could be overcome, just as they had in the past. Both Leonard and Octavia thought that some of her worst anxieties had been assuaged. They were wrong. On the morning of Friday, 28 March, after leaving her tender and moving farewell note to Leonard, Virginia went to the River Ouse, left her walking stick on the bank, and drowned herself.

2

Bloomsbury

While Virginia Woolf has frequently been celebrated as 'the high priestess of Bloomsbury,' there is very little agreement as to precisely what cult—if any—burnt offerings under her directions. The list of disciples differs with each account and, more importantly, the exact nature of the religion remains very much unresolved. It is a curious fact that 'Bloomsbury' as a metaphor rich with social, moral, and literary meaning was to a significant extent invested with reality and imprinted on the popular mind by those strongly opposed to its existence. If it had not been for the fervent hostility of Frank Swinnerton, Wyndham Lewis, Sir John Rothenstein, and most notably F. R. and Q. D. Leavis, Bloomsbury would surely not have achieved the prominent place in the literary and intellectual history of Britain that it has. Bloomsbury's original notoriety can in large part be attributed to the energies of its critics.

As seen by these critics, Bloomsbury is a simple—and highly unappealing—phenomenon, consisting of a tightly organized, snobbish fraternity of men and women, totally removed from the currents of real life, who devoted themselves exclusively to the cultivation of their sterile egos and undeserved reputations. Precious, decadent, and malign, they are charged both in their lives and in their work with standing firmly outside the values of the serious adult world. For Leavis and the others, Bloomsbury was a self-adulation society, ruthlessly condemning those artists and writers deemed unworthy of membership, while at the same time seething with jealousy at their successes. Once an artist incurred the disfavor of the Bloomsberries, there was no place for him to hide. Wyndham Lewis cautions us against the 'malefic "Bloomsberries," who with their ambitious and jealous cabal have had such a destructive influence upon the intellectual life of England' and Sir John Rothenstein paints the grim picture of what happens to those who offended them:[1]

I doubt . . . whether more than a few people are even now aware how closely-knit an association 'Bloomsbury' was, how untiring its members were in advertising one another's work and personalities . . . . They would have been surprised if they had known of the lengths to which some of these people—with their gentle Cambridge voices, their informal manners, their casual unassuming clothes, their civilized personal relations with one another—were prepared to go in order to ruin, utterly, not only the 'reactionary' figures whom they publicly denounced, but young painters and writers who showed themselves too independent to come to terms with the canons observed by 'Bloomsbury' or more precisely, with the current 'party line,' which varies from month to month in accordance with what their leader considered the most 'significant' trends of opinion prevailing in Paris.

At worse, then, a group insidiously intent on controlling the aesthetic values of a whole country—and willing to stop at nothing in order to do so; and at the very least, an effete band of writers, painters, and critics whose self-indulgence and upper-class insulation from the realities of the time make them morally trivial, and finally irrelevant. Bloomsbury is so self-evidently repellent for the Leavises and their fellow *Scrutiny* critics that they are able to refer to Bloomsbury prose or Bloomsbury values or Bloomsbury tone of voice without any apparent qualms about being misunderstood. The pages of *Scrutiny*, the Leavis literary journal, are in fact filled with exhortations against the perils of Bloomsburyism—which is seen as a kind of creeping paralysis gradually deadening the moral and intellectual centers of any writer whom it attacks. E. M. Forster, we are led to understand, is a writer who ought to have been better than he was—and certainly would have been had he not been infected by the inferior social-cultural milieu of Bloomsbury. It is this same milieu, F. R. Leavis reminds us, which played a decisive role in Virginia Woolf's failure to develop as a writer.

Virginia Woolf, of course, was very much part of Bloomsbury, but hardly the supercilious, malevolent Bloomsbury of Leavis or Rothenstein. The word itself used simply as a descriptive epithet, not a term of opprobrium, began innocently enough. According to Clive

---

[1] Wyndham Lewis, *Blasting and Bombardiering* (Calder & Boyars, 1967), 273; Sir John Rothenstein, *Modern English Painters, Lewis to More* (Eyre & Spottiswoode, 1956), 14.

Bell, it was Molly MacCarthy, Desmond's wife, who in a letter of 1910 or 1911, used the term 'Bloomsberries' to refer to that informal circle of friends who lived (or at least some of whom lived), in and around Bloomsbury. If the letter was written after Leonard Woolf had returned from Ceylon in 1911, the Bloomsberries, in addition to Woolf would include Clive Bell, Lytton Strachey, Maynard Keynes, Vanessa and Virginia Stephen, Duncan Grant, Adrian Stephen, the MacCarthys, Roger Fry, E. M. Forster, and three lesser known men who did not contribute to the Bloomsbury image: Saxon Sydney-Turner, Gerald Shrove, and H. T. J. Norton.

The origin of Bloomsbury, however, was not the London of 1911 but the Cambridge of 1899, when Woolf, Bell, Strachey, and Thoby Stephen first came up and encountered the pellucid, luxuriantly intellectual air which was the university's then. After the sterile, restricted, and often brutal experience of public school, Cambridge was a paradise where culture mattered and human beings were left free to develop their minds and souls. Every member of Bloomsbury who attended Cambridge flourished there, and all left ample testimony about the support and emancipation Cambridge offered them. While E. M. Forster's *The Longest Journey* is perhaps the best known account, his biography of G. Lowes Dickinson sums up most succinctly the role Cambridge played in their lives:[1]

> As Cambridge filled up with friends, it acquired a magic quality. Body and spirit, reason and emotion, work and play, architecture and scenery, laughter and seriousness, life and art—these pairs which are elsewhere contrasted were there fused into one. People and books reinforced one another, intelligence joined hands with affection, speculation became a passion, and discussion was made profound by love. When Goldie speaks of this magic fusion, he illumines more careers than his own, and he seems not only to epitomize Cambridge but to amplify it, and to make it the heritage of many who will never go there in the flesh.

The friendships the four young men formed, first among themselves in the Midnight Society, a playreading club, and later as members of the august Apostles Society with people like Fry, Forster, Keynes, and MacCarthy, established the nucleus of what

---

[1] *G. Lowes Dickinson* (Edward Arnold, 1962), 35.

Bell refers to as 'Old' Bloomsbury.[1] These friendships not only provided important sources of emotional satisfaction, they also partook, philosophically, of the highest good—at least according to G. E. Moore, the reigning genius of Cambridge philosophy. For it was Moore in his *Principia Ethica* who asserted what many take—at times rather simplistically—to be the Bloomsbury credo, that the most valuable things a human being can experience are the pleasures of human friendship and the enjoyment of beautiful objects. In maintaining that the highest goods are personal affections and aesthetic enjoyments, Moore was not convincing his followers of anything they did not in fact believe themselves. The book merely served as theoretical justification for beliefs already held. But even more than its specific doctrines, the *Principia* was important for its method—or perhaps better, its *alleged* method—of bringing scientific reasoning to the subject matter of ethics. With its austere numbered propositions systematically dispatching all previous ethical theorists, the book fairly bristles with the logical apparatus needed to uncover objective truth. Exposing the fallacies found in other ethical thinking, fallacies Moore himself guards against by his technique of 'absolute isolation' and his careful distinctions between goods as ends and goods as means, Moore offered his admiring disciples a clear view through the forest of error to the truth glimmering beyond. That the sublimely obvious conclusion of his chapter on 'The Ideal,' that 'the most valuable things which we know or can imagine, are certain states of consciousness, which may be roughly described as the pleasures of human intercourse and the enjoyment of beautiful objects'[2]—is in fact as grandly subjective an assertion of value as anything Moore had himself criticized was no deterrent to those who celebrated not only his message but also his manner of arriving at it. Here was a method, it was thought, which could clear up all the ethical, philosophical muddles that had ever vexed man. Part of the heady arrogance of the young Bloomsberries was a result of their conviction that they alone possessed the instrument which could unerringly ferret out the truth wherever it lay hidden.

Moore's influence on the future Bloomsberries was enormous, but

---

[1]   In his *Old Friends* Bell does not mention the role of the Apostles Society in the formation of 'old' Bloomsbury, but this is less a result of oversight than of the way Bell can best deal with the fact that he was never asked to be a member of the Apostles.

[2]   G. E. Moore, *Principia Ethica* (Cambridge University Press, 1959), 188.

it was perhaps less the *Principia* itself—though Strachey dated the beginning of the Age of Reason from the time of its publication—than the total impression made by the man. Moore overwhelmed all who knew him with the purity of his soul, his saintly indifference to things of this world, his total absorption in the life of the mind. For Leonard Woolf, Moore

had an extraordinary profundity and clarity of thought, and he pursued truth with the tenacity of a bulldog and the integrity of a saint . . . . He had a genius for seeing what was important and what was unimportant and irrelevant, in thought and in life and in persons . . . . The intensity of Moore's passion for truth was an integral part of his greatness, and purity of passion was an integral part of his whole character.[1]

And Bertrand Russell delights in recounting the only time he ever made Moore tell a lie: '"Moore," I said, "do you *always* speak the truth?" "No," he replied. I believe this to be the only lie he had ever told.' His concern for the truth, his horror at sloppy thinking, inspired those around him to strive for the perfection of character they felt he had already achieved.

Believing in the importance of friendship and art, and made confident by Moore's method, young Cambridge came down to London in 1904 where, joined by Virginia and Vanessa in 1905 after the death of Sir Leslie Stephen, Bloomsbury, for all practical purposes, began. The friends who began meeting at 46 Gordon Square and, by 1907, 29 Fitzroy Square as well, at no time thought of themselves as a self-conscious movement or school. Despite the varied charges brought against them, there was no catechism, no dogma, no leader, not even a membership list. There was instead a group of highly sophisticated, cerebral people who frequently met to do one of the things, at least, they liked best: talk. The talk, as one would expect, was witty, glittering, sometimes brilliant, often trivial. But talk it was, and it was this which angered D. H. Lawrence who, after being exposed to their talk for a weekend, was nearly driven mad and dreamt that black beetles were attacking him.

One of the assumptions which these friends did share—and which accounts for a good deal of the animus directed against them—was a sense of the debased, philistine nature of the English culture around them. They clearly did think of themselves as a cultural elite whose

[1] *The Autobiography of Bertrand Russell* (Allen & Unwin, 1967) I, 64.

task it was to resist the forces of mediocrity, conventionality, and commercialism which had engulfed England. When a hostile critic called Virginia Woolf a highbrow, she proudly accepted the label. Where literature was concerned, Woolf felt, there was nothing wrong with being an 'unmitigated snob.' The stance of moral and intellectual superiority Bloomsbury assumed was not calculated to please the benighted world which so often received its scorn, and the accusations that Bloomsbury was clannish and exclusive have their validity. Reacting against a world it found hostile to the creation of real art or the serious use of intellect, Bloomsbury tried to create for itself an enclave where these things could flourish. Friendship provided them with a vital, nourishing context which they needed for their work. If the great modern British writers tend basically to be solitary figures—Conrad, Lawrence, Joyce, and Yeats, for example—Bloomsbury found creative sustenance in a social network. Frank Swinnerton's remark, intended pejoratively, that Bloomsbury was 'the spiritual home of exiles from Cambridge University'[1] is, in fact, a fair assessment for which Bloomsbury need not apologize.

As Bloomsbury did not embrace one homogeneous sensibility, it is difficult to generalize responsibly about the values of that enclave. How, for example, can we discuss the 'Bloomsbury attitude' towards social issues when we have, on the one hand, Clive Bell telling us in *Civilization* (1928) that slavery is necessary if we want civilization, that despotism in itself is neither good nor bad, and on the other, Leonard Woolf writing reports for the Fabian Society on the possibilities of international government, or Maynard Keynes inveighing against the political and economic idiocies of the Versailles Treaty? Or how can we even attempt to define a Bloomsbury aesthetic when Strachey finds Bell's *Art* (1913), which popularized the term 'significant form,' to be utter trash, and thinks Bell and Fry fatuous for admiring Matisse and Picasso?

Having been nurtured in its youth by Moore's method and example, Bloomsbury did share a common faith in the powers of rationality, a belief that there was no problem that the individual human mind, unfettered by dogma or superstition, could not solve. All things inimical to the free play of the intellect were rejected, and the list of rejected claims included conventional moral pieties of any sort, religion, and most notably the nationalistic allure of the First World War.

---

[1] *The Georgian Literary Scene* (Dent, 1951), 251.

Bloomsbury strongly opposed the war, seeing it as a monstrous blunder threatening to destroy a European civilization which was far more important than the petty claims of any single country. At a time when patriotic zeal ran high in England, many of the male Bloomsberries were Conscientious Objectors.

If a belief in an ideal of civilized, rational behavior seems a peculiar quality to attribute to a modernist sensibility, it is nevertheless an important peculiarity which tells us a great deal about the equivocal nature of Bloomsbury's 'modernism.' For Bloomsbury was by no means the aggressively *avant-garde* movement some of its ardent supporters—as well as its reactionary critics—make it out to be. Although Bloomsbury flourished in the midst of the great modernist ferment of the early twentieth century—the world of the first Post-Impressionist exhibition, of Bergson, Freud, Proust, Joyce and Eliot—it did not in any easy way welcome everything that was new. If human character did change 'in or about December 1910,' as Virginia Woolf asserted, it is clear that Bloomsbury, nurtured in the more traditional, more morally comprehensible world before the change, viewed the new character and the new standards with some skepticism. The Bloomsbury response to Freud is an interesting example of this complex attitude. Though Freud was knowingly discussed at parties (as Dora Carrington's letters show) and though Bloomsbury even produced its own analysts in James and Alix Strachey, Adrian and Karen Stephen, psycho-analysis was always regarded with great distrust by literary Bloomsbury. Both Clive Bell and Desmond Mac-Carthy worried about its effects on art, fearing it might be used by young writers as a bogus short-cut to psychological profundity, and more disturbingly, as a justification to obliterate moral standards altogether. Virginia Woolf's references to Freud in her work are few—and invariably sneering. Her mention of the curative value of psycho-analysis in a review of a novel by J. D. Beresford suggests her general feelings: 'A patient who has never heard a canary sing without falling down in a fit can now walk through an avenue of cages without a twinge of emotion since he has faced the fact that his mother kissed him in his cradle.' (*Contemporary Writers*, 152).

Threatening to the moral fabric of a work of art, it was, as a form of therapy, something to be talked about—and laughed about—not experienced. Bloomsbury's peculiar sophistication thus affords us the ironic and painful spectacle of Leonard Woolf, one of the first English reviewers of Freud, publishing Freud's works at the Hogarth Press while Virginian Woolf attempted to combat her recurrent attacks of madness by sipping milk in darkened rooms. Concerned exclusively in her treatment with diet and rest, the Woolfs acted as if they had never heard of Freud. The contrast between the pioneering publisher and the hopelessly ill-treated patient serves as a powerful emblem in helping define the Bloomsbury sensibility.

And while the Hogarth Press published Freud, it did not offer the same opportunity to another great twentieth-century writer, James Joyce. Honoring Joyce as the courageous novelist who broke free from the dessicated assumptions of Edwardian realism, Woolf has nothing but the highest praise for him in 'Modern Fiction' and 'Mr. Bennett and Mrs. Brown.' He emerges from these two essays as the life-giving innovator who dared to turn his back on the rusty novelistic tools bequeathed him by his Edwardian ancestors in order to render 'the flickerings of that innermost flame' which he understood to be reality. As a fellow experimenter in novelistic form, it is perfectly reasonable that Woolf should find Joyce's aims and methods admirable. The problems he and the other Georgian writers encountered of having no viable form with which to express a new vision was, indeed, precisely hers. In claiming importance for what Joyce is doing, she is implicitly saying something about her own work. What is interesting is less the public approbation for *Ulysses* than her intense disgust for the novel which was privately stated. Complaining in a letter to Strachey in 1918 of the physiological functions afforded dog and man in the opening chapters—'there's a dog that p's – then there's a man that forths' (*Virginia Woolf and Lytton Strachey: Letters*, 73)—she concludes that the Hogarth Press will not publish it. And she expresses an almost visceral repugnance for the novel in a diary entry of 1922 (*A Writer's Diary*, 47):

> An illiterate, underbred book it seems to me; the book of a
> self-taught working man, and we all know how distressing they
> are, how egotistic, insistent, raw, striking, and ultimately
> nauseating. When one can have the cooked flesh, why have the
> raw?

It was not only Mrs Woolf who objected to the raw flesh of *Ulysses*. In *Aspects of the Novel*, Forster, though recognizing the uniqueness of Joyce's achievement, censures him for having made 'a dogged attempt to make crossness and dirt succeed where sweetness and light failed'.[1]

[1] *Aspects of the Novel* (Edward Arnold, 1958), 113.

Both these comments suggest that however emancipated the Bloomsberries were in their drawing-room conversation—or even in the conduct of their own personal relations—they brought to the criticism of fiction a stringent and rather old-fashioned kind of propriety. The fact is that the Bloomsberries were neither thoroughly 'modern' nor Victorian, neither revolutionary nor reactionary. In their commitment to creating and maintaining a vital, flourishing art, the Bloomsberries brought to the possibilities of the new a rich sense of the values of the old. Interested in formal experimentation, they nevertheless were concerned at the same time with the deterioration of standards. If the 'proper stuff of fiction' now included the inner life which Galsworthy, Bennett and Wells had overlooked, that inner life still had to have an appropriate decorum about it. Although any technique which broke away from the sterile realism of the Edwardians was affirmed, it was not in itself a good unless it embodied a significant and palatable vision of the human condition. Joyce was too indecent for Woolf, and Dorothy Richardson, another radical experimenter in the novel form, too trivial. The rendering of the inner life is meaningless unless it helps the reader to fathom in a profound way the nature of reality. Reviewing Dorothy Richardson's *The Tunnel*, Woolf finds the inner life it portrays superficial: it fails to shed 'quite as much light as we had hoped into the hidden depths' (*Contemporary Writers*, 120). Her insistence that new fictional methods should provide a coherent and substantial interpretation of the world is the kind of traditional value that all Bloomsbury shared. Richardson's new technique is finally not satisfying (*Contemporary Writers*, 120):

> In particular, the figures of other people on whom Miriam casts her capricious light are vivid enough, but their sayings and doings never reach that degree of significance which we, perhaps unreasonably, expect. The old method seems sometimes the more profound and economical of the two . . . . We want to be rid of realism, to penetrate without its help into the regions beneath it, and further require that Miss Richardson shall fashion this new material into something which had the shapeliness of the old accepted forms.

It is impossible, of course, to read Woolf's comments about *Ulysses* as a book by a self-taught working man without acknowledging that her criticism is responding to something other than a mere violation of

27

standards of propriety. A member of the privileged class is obviously speaking and exhibiting the upper middle class viewpoint which forms an important part of the Bloomsbury mind. That Forster, the Stephens, Strachey, Bell and the others came from a world of reasonable affluence and refinement is a fact that has not easily been forgiven them. Critics like the Leavises seem to find the coal miner's poverty of D. H. Lawrence far more authentic than the leisured Cambridge background of Bloomsbury. But it is pointless to hold someone's advantages against him; it is a fact that Bloomsberries were advantaged and they certainly made no attempt to deny the existence of that fact. Money, says E. M. Forster, is the second most important thing in the world (personal relations being the first), and he admits that if it had not been for the £500 a year left him by his great aunt, he never would have had the opportunity to develop as a writer. And Virginia Woolf is painfully aware, as she attends a working women's guild meeting, of the enormous distance separating her from the working members (*Collected Essays*, vol. 4, 136):

> All those questions, I found myself thinking . . . which matter so
> intensely to the people here, questions of sanitation and education
> and wages, this demand for an extra shilling, or another year at
> school, for eight hours instead of nine behind a counter or in a
> mill, leave me, in my own blood and bones, untouched . . . .
> However hard I clap my hands or stamp my feet there is a
> hollowness in the sound which betrays me. I am irretrievably cut
> off from the actors. I sit here hypocritically, clapping and
> stamping, an outcast from the flock.

Arguing in 'The Leaning Tower' that a writer's background and education necessarily help shape his point of view, Woolf points out that almost all English writers since Chaucer have come from the middle class. The writer 'sits upon a tower raised above the rest of us; a tower built first on his parents' station, then on his parents' gold. It is a tower of the utmost importance; it decides his angle of vision; it affects his power of communication' (*Collected Essays*, vol. 2, 169). Coming from Leslie Stephen's drawing room and public schools and Cambridge, Bloomsbury sat firmly—and quite consciously—on such a tower. Without it there clearly would have been no Bloomsbury. Anyone seated on such a tower, of course, is open to all sorts of attacks, and it cannot be denied that Bloomsbury is vulnerable on various fronts. From Woolf's condescending dismissal of *Ulysses*, to

Strachey's mock horror at finding he has contracted shingles—a working man's disease—to Clive Bell's serious notion that the man of superior cultivation ought to be supported by a slave class so that he will be left free to develop his sensitivity, a vein of self-indulgent superiority can occasionally be detected running through Bloomsbury.

But every point of view has its limitations, and if Bloomsbury was sometimes snobbish, that snobbishness was part of a sensibility which spoke out powerfully on behalf of culture, rationality, the importance of art, and the value of 'a passionate skepticism'[1] which rejected any easy short cut to the truth. Snobbish perhaps—but much more as well.

With the publication of Strachey's *Eminent Victorians* in 1918, Bloomsbury was immediately established under the banner of Strachey's anti-Victorianism. Strachey's was by no means the first work to sever the Victorian umbilical cord—*The Way of All Flesh*, for example, was published in 1903—but coming as it did at the end of the war, it caught—and to a certain degree, no doubt, helped create—the disgust of a young generation for the hypocritical blunderings of its elders. As Cyril Connelly commented, it can be thought of as the first book of the 1920s. In the guise of four Victorian biographies, *Eminent Victorians* is a fiercely moral treatise excoriating the previous age's superstition, self-righteousness, mindless public-schools, attitudes and blatant nationalism which Strachey felt had made the war inevitable. The happy slaughter of 20,000 Arabs with which Strachey ends the life of General Gordon surely struck a resonant note for a country which had recently witnessed the futile massacre of the Somme.

But Strachey's elegant disclosure of Victorian folly does not really permit us the luxury of classifying Bloomsbury as anti-Victorian. If the Victorians had their problems, so did the Edwardians and the Georgians, and there was clearly much in the structured Victorian world that Bloomsbury found admirable. Having inherited their towers from their Victorian ancestors, the Bloomsberries inherited a fair number of genes as well, and both tower and genes ensured that however artfully Strachey disposed of the Victorians, the essential family identification was never totally obscured. The past always remained a functional part of Bloomsbury's baggage.

Perhaps Bloomsbury's most decisively modernist act was the first

---

[1] The term is Leonard Woolf's, found in *Quack, Quack* (Hogarth Press, 1935).

Post-Impressionist Exhibition which Roger Fry organized at the Grafton Galleries in November of 1910. (If Virginia Woolf's sublimely arbitrary dating for the change of human character is to be taken at all literally, it is certainly this exhibition to which it refers.) With Desmond MacCarthy acting as secretary, Fry brought together for the first time in London the works of Manet, Cézanne, Gauguin, and Van Gogh which he had long admired on his trips to the continent. Faced suddenly with astonishingly new kinds of paintings, the public was, predictably enough, outraged. Hysterical laughter at the amateurishness of the artists could barely be heard over the irate charges of indecency and perversion levied against the canvases themselves, the organizer, the secretary, and the whole milieu which had spawned such an offensive travesty. Modern art did not come easily to England, and the ill-feeling generated by the exhibition was immense. After it was over, however—and profitably over, it is interesting to add, Desmond MacCarthy's own share of the profits coming to £460—England had learned to look at art in a new way.

Considering the exhibition's radical undermining of accepted aesthetic canons, it is fascinating to find Clive Bell justifying Post-Impressionist technique by making it part of the central tradition of all great art. Although Bell had been developing his notion of 'significant form' independent of Fry, *Art*, published in 1913, served as a kind of post-facto defense of Fry's Post-Impressionist exhibition. The defense rests simply on the fact that the Post-Impressionist paintings all embody the principle of significant form. The elusiveness of the notion of significant form (significant form being that which conveys to us an aesthetic emotion; when we experience an aesthetic emotion we know we are in the presence of significant form) need not concern us here. What matters is that it is the sole criterion of great art—or even just plain 'art'—from primitive cave paintings to the present. So it is not the 'newness' in itself of the Post-Impressionist method or vision which is valuable but the fact that its articulation of significant form returns us to the age-old function of all art—the communication of aesthetic emotions through such expressive form. The Post-Impressionists have not taught us to see differently; they have taught us to see what we should always have been seeing. For Bell, Post-Impressionism marks a return to the enduring concern of painting—another example of the way Bloomsbury sought to have its newness along with its valued traditions.

Whatever the characteristics—literary, moral, or aesthetic—we are justified in imputing to the abstraction known as the Bloomsbury sensibility, we must recognize that above all the term 'Bloomsbury' is most accurately employed—or perhaps least abused—when applied to the large and heterogeneous group of friends who experienced a good deal together over the better part of three decades. I have already mentioned the founding fathers—and mothers—who began meeting in Gordon and Fitzroy Squares. To these we can add a host of different Stracheys, James, Marjorie, and Olivier, who were fully accepted friends at the start of the First World War. And from 1914 on, a variety of young writers and artists came also to share in their affections, people like David Garnett, Raymond Mortimer, John Lehmann, Ralph Partridge, Francis Birrell, Frances Marshall, F. L. Lucas, George Rylands, Roger Senhouse, and Stephen Tomlin, to name a few.

No two lists are alike, but the discrepancies are not important. Indeed, the lack of any neat consensus about Bloomsbury affiliation emphasizes the fact that it was not a chartered organization but a fluid collection of friends who shared a serious commitment, among other things, to art and friendship. That Bloomsbury also achieved a metaphoric status (though one of shifting value) is not something for which it can be held entirely responsible.

As a discernible if loosely knit social entity, as well as an alleged corporate sensibility, Bloomsbury can more or less be said to have existed from its inception in 1905 to the late 1930s. Its extinction was primarily a result of the laws of erosion and diffusion that affect all groups. The wider the network of contacts and acquaintances, the less distinct the character of any group necessarily becomes. And certainly by the 1930s Bloomsbury's complexion had changed considerably from the early parties in Gordon and Fitzroy Squares. Furthermore, the deaths in 1932 of Lytton Strachey and in 1934 of Rogert Fry deprived the group of two of its most prominent members. Both were beloved figures whose losses dealt an enormous blow to all of them. But beyond the workings of entropy and the diminishings caused by death, there is another less practical reason for Bloomsbury's gradual dissolution in the 1930s. To the extent that Bloomsbury can ever be said to have fashioned for itself an ideal of civilized behavior, such an ideal was made rudely irrelevant by the changing historical scene in Europe. For the beliefs which had sustained Bloomsbury for so long, that the claims of the individual transcended all others, that the creation of art in itself was an important human enterprise, that human reason could be trusted were all made to seem starkly anachronistic in

31

a world of Fascist fears and Communist hopes. Bloomsbury's marvelous pacificism of the First World War had little meaning for the new realities of Guernica and concentration camps. The world was once again going mad and Bloomsbury values no longer seemed to matter. Although Woolf protested against the shrillness, the callow kind of social involvement which she found in Auden, Spender, Isherwood, MacNeice, Day Lewis, and the others, nevertheless it was their voices that now spoke in compelling ways about what was happening. If we want to locate the end of Bloomsbury with a date as sublimely arbitrary as the one Woolf uses to indicate the month when human character changed, it would be 18 July 1937. It was on that day that Julian Bell, one of the younger Bloomsberries whose father, Clive, once wrote that 'there are no qualities of greater moral value than artistic qualities,' and that 'despotism in itself is neither good nor bad,' was killed driving an ambulance for the Republican forces in Spain. Giving his life for a cause that was alien to his father's world, Julian signified just how inappropriate that world had finally become.

Bloomsbury's demise did not mark the termination of its history, however. Although it has long since ceased to exist, Bloomsbury has shown a remarkable capacity to survive in the public's imagination, first as the embodiment of a pathological condition to be avoided at all costs, as diagnosed by the Drs Leavis and their fellow scrutinizers of our moral and literary health, and more recently as the precursor of a new heaven on earth, that divine state of sexual freedom, aesthetic fulfillment, and non-traditional role playing. For reasons that are less literary than cultural, the cloud of moral opprobrium surrounding Bloomsbury's work and activities has lifted, revealing not a horrid group of jejune inverts but an emancipated, highly civilized group of friends leading productive lives free from the taint of pieties and conventions. In their notorious (but finally rather benign) sexual permutations, people find a metaphor for social salvation. No longer viewed as a sign of degeneracy, their legendary polymorphous perversity is taken as a demonstration of an immensely desirable free-wheeling personal and cultural style. Exemplary indeed, not cautionary, as Nigel Nicolson's best-selling portrait of the unusual relationship between his parents, Harold and Vita Sackville-West, indicates.[1] At a time when all instances of traditional sexual stereotyping are being exposed, Bloomsbury's precocious versatility is thought to have much to teach us.

[1] *Portrait of a Marriage* (Weidenfeld & Nicolson, 1973).

The current public enthusiasm for Bloomsbury has been nourished by the scholarly mills which have been producing biographies and volumes of letters and journals with regularity. More remarkable than the sheer number of these is the commercial success they achieve. People await the newest revelations about the personal intrigues with much the same eagerness as Dickens's readers anticipated each new installment by the master. All things bearing the Bloomsbury label have inestimable value as collector's items, so that even the office boy at the Hogarth Press, and the Woolfs' maid, have been enticed to come forth with their reminiscences of what that fabled world was like.

While we can certainly be grateful that Bloomsbury was rescued from the cultural dustbin to which it had been consigned—and if we can tolerate another arbitrary date, I would point to Michael Holroyd's biography of Lytton Strachey, published in 1967, as the first phase of the rescue—it is clear that in the long run adulation is not much more edifying than dismissal. Bloomsbury threatens to collapse altogether beneath the enormous burden of redemptive social and moral thinking attached to it. Or to change the image, to be inflated out of all recognizable proportions by the vast cultural claims made for it. As the abstraction grows in importance, what gets lost is the living reality of a basically unselfconscious group of friends who, whatever the varied nature of their personal lives, were all fiercely absorbed in their work. In generalizing and celebrating, we tend to create cultural movements that satisfy our own needs of the moment. The Bloomsbury of the 1970s speaks in important ways to our current aspirations to break away from traditional sexual and psychological fetters, to develop a society free from constraint and oppression. And to this end we have invented a Bloomsbury which is quite different from the Bloomsbury invented by the 1930s and 1940s, and will no doubt be yet again different from the one invented fifty years hence.

In cautioning against the unqualified acceptance of any of the Bloomsbury myths, I do not mean to suggest that every version is necessarily fictional. Obviously there are certain values and attitudes that Bloomsbury shares—I have tried to discuss some of them here—and it is legitimate to think of Bloomsbury as something more than the sum of its distinguished and diverse parts. Yet it is important to remember the most significant feature of Bloomsbury is not the style it affected but the work it produced. Beyond the cultural uses to which Bloomsbury has been and will be put stands the separate and

33

unique achievements of Forster, the Woolfs, Strachey, Bell, Fry, Keynes, and the rest. They are not achievements on which we can sensibly pin any label, and they are finally what matters most about Bloomsbury.

3

The Problem of the Fiction

It is only relatively recently that Virginia Woolf seems to have emerged from the limbo of polite esteem in which she has generally been held into the forefront of the contemporary social and literary scene. Having languished for decades in the shadow of her august fellow modernists like Joyce, Lawrence, and Conrad, Woolf appears at last to have secured for herself the stamp of the authentic classic that had previously managed to elude her. The obligatory if slightly stale respect invariably accorded her by readers has now given way to a passionate, searching interest in every aspect of her life. The torrent of Newsletters, Quarterlies, Miscellanies, English Institute Conferences, and Modern Language Association Sessions, among other forms of tribute, attest to her arrival. Virginia Woolf is a very hot literary property indeed.

The impulses behind this adulation are worth exploring, particularly as they tell us a good deal more about our world than they do about Woolf. To begin with, it is clear that the rediscovery of Woolf is part of the larger phenomenon of the canonization of Bloomsbury which has been in process for the past ten years. It is a marvelous irony of social history that Virginia Woolf's Bloomsbury associations, which for years had damned her in the earnest eyes of the Leavises and others, now constitute one of her strongest sources of appeal. Riding the crest of the Bloomsbury mania, Woolf has become a cult figure in a way that would certainly have amazed her. It is probably fair to say that the renewed interest in Woolf on the part of the general reader is more a result of her role in the chic, provocative Bloomsbury way of life than of any developing awareness of the inherent merit of her fiction.

If sheer titillation accounts for much of the public's attention, the gradual realization that Virginia Woolf was, in fact, a woman writer

35

(or at least not a man, the androgynous theory having its own advocates) has also played a substantial role. The polemical grinder of the feminist movement has greedily devoured Woolf, spewing her forth as the appropriately committed feminist whose preoccupation with the cause is somehow the key to her fiction. Such a view of Woolf is not particularly useful. It is of course true that she was very much concerned with the economic and social plight of women, and deeply sensitive to the psychic crippling inflicted on them by a male dominated world. *Orlando, A Room of One's Own, Three Guineas,* and assorted essays eloquently testify to her involvement in these issues, as well as to the deft way she can expose the absurdities of our culture. But to focus on her fiction through any sort of politicized feminist lens is seriously to distort it. Woolf herself deplored novels that preach, and hers are conspicuously free from the proselytizing that frequently occupied her when she was not at her desk struggling with her fiction. This is not to argue that Woolf was not conscious of the assumptions of an environment which held for example, that Virginia's brothers, but not Virginia, should go to university; it is simply to protest against the reductionist view, in vogue today, that Woolf's novels speak in some essential and exclusive way to feminist preoccupations. Woolf, in fact, hated the word 'feminist' altogether—'What more fitting than to destroy an old word, a vicious and corrupt word that has done much harm in its day and is now obsolete? The word "feminist" is the word indicated' (*Three Guineas,* 184), finding it divisive and inimical to the overall unity of civilized people she so desired.

The feminist claim on Woolf has lately been joined by the androgynist, which sees Woolf's novels as endorsing the splendors of the androgynous mind as a palliative to all our ills. Taking as a seminal passage Woolf's discussion in *A Room of One's Own* of the flourishing artistic imagination being able to transcend any narrow sexual role, the hunters of androgyny doggedly chase the metaphor through all of Woolf's fiction, hacking out new patterns of meaning as they go. But metaphors are better left in peace to illuminate the specific contexts in which they appear. The illustrative use of anydrogyny to represent the kind of wide-ranging, non-dogmatic, resonant intelligence Woolf finds admirable—and capable of producing great art—cannot be generalized into establishing Woolf's 'androgynous vision.' To discover that Woolf believes that men and women should share a complex view of reality, one as free as possible from the parochialisms of any single sex, is not to discover anything very new about her work.

If Woolf is to survive as other than a precious oddity of the modernist movement, it will be neither as a member of a coterie, a radical feminist, nor a prophetic androgynist. Sexual ideologies and exotic ambiences aside, Woolf's fiction must be able to meet the reservation still shared by many and most recently expressed by Elizabeth Hardwick: acknowledging the richness of Woolf's language and the glow of her genius, Hardwick goes on to say, 'yet in a sense, her novels aren't interesting'.[1] Whatever else novels are, they should at least be interesting, and it is a fact that hers have not always been thought so. Woolf was herself aware that her work posed more than the usual difficulties for readers. Her diary notes with sympathy (and some irritation) the puzzled efforts of critics to comprehend what she is doing. The problems are real, and a passage from *Between the Acts*, her last novel, suggests what they are: 'Did the plot matter? She shifted and looked over her right shoulder. The plot was only there to beget emotion . . . Don't bother about the plot: the plot's nothing' (*Between the Acts*, 109). Isa's reflection on the meaning of Miss La Trobe's pageant at once describes Woolf's own art and points out the greatest obstacle to its appreciation. For plot is indeed nothing in Woolf 's fiction, and character, Isa might have gone on to say—or character traditionally conceived—not much more. Novelists who dispense with both of these staples are going to have difficult times, and Woolf has received her share of critical abuse for writing novels in which, it is argued, nothing happens.

Not, of course, that she is the sole practitioner of the twentieth-century novel to have abandoned established notions of plot and character; the modern novel clearly developed through precisely such liberties, but in many ways her work is the most radical. For despite the formal breakthroughs made by Conrad, Ford, Lawrence, Joyce and others, their work still exhibits a basic narrative interest (perhaps *Finnegan's Wake*, a fictional cosmos unto itself, could be considered an exception) which is almost entirely lacking in Woolf's. However complicated the point of view and richly patterned the symbolic structure, their novels essentially remain part of a story-telling tradition from which Woolf dissociated herself. We are impelled through *Ulysses* less by its dazzling virtuosity than its abiding concern for Leopold and Stephen and what befalls them, just as we are absorbed in the destinies of Paul Morel or Decoud or Lord Jim or Benjy or even Winnie Verloc as they go about their muddled business. Although

[1] *Seduction and Betrayal* (Vintage, 1974), 141.

they do so in a variety of innovative ways, the great modern novels of the twentieth century implicate the reader in the lives of their characters as they confront experience, and in the problems of choice and self-definition that confrontation engenders. 'Yes—oh dear yes,' E. M. Forster writes in *Aspects of the Novel* with bemused resignation, 'the novel tells a story' (*Aspects of the Novel*, 27). Subtilized and internalized though it is, the primitive energy of the story animates most of modern fiction.

Woolf's novels, however, contain no substantial narrative impulse. In a very real sense it is true she does write novels in which nothing happens. It would be impossible, for example, to speak in any serious way about the sustained 'action' of *The Waves* or *Between the Acts*, or even of a more manageable novel like *To the Lighthouse*. Her work contains little humor, passion, or particular dramatic or even ideological tension. Demanding everything and making few concessions to readers, it seems to many hermetically sealed in its austerity and fragility from the vital currents of life. Woolf recognized, of course, that in writing novels that lacked any strong narrative thread she was cutting herself off from one of the enduring appeals of fiction, but she had no difficulty making this choice.

For as an artist Woolf was obsessed with what we can call formal rather than thematic concerns, with finding ways of embodying, as she says, 'the exact shapes my brain holds' (*A Writer's Diary*, 176). That Woolf was absorbed primarily in creating shapes is what makes her such an utterly original voice in modern literature. It is also what makes her such a difficult writer to talk about, for her work does not readily lend itself to critical analysis of character or theme or philosophy. The difficulties are not simply ours: certainly Woolf's own language fails when she tries to formulate for herself her fictional intentions. Reflecting in her diary on Arnold Bennett's criticism that *Jacob's Room* doesn't have characters that survive, Woolf agrees that she hasn't 'that "reality" gift. I insubstantiate willfully to some extent, distrusting reality—its cheapness. But to get further. Have I the power of conveying the true reality?' (*A Writer's Diary*, 57). If distinctions between 'reality' and 'true reality' are seldom satisfying, this at least has the virtue of suggesting what one should *not* expect from a Woolf novel. Other attempts to state positively what she wants her fiction to achieve are no more successful (*A Writer's Diary*, 132):

That is one of the experiences I have had here in some Augusts;

and got there to a consciousness of what I call 'reality': a thing I see before me, something abstract but residing in the downs or sky . . . in which I shall rest and continue to exist. Reality I call it. And I fancy sometimes this is the most necessary thing to me; that which I seek. But who knows—once one takes a pen and writes? . . . Now perhaps this is my gift: this perhaps is what distinguishes me from other people. I think it may be rare to have so acute a sense of something like that—but again, who knows? I would like to express it too.

The reality Woolf wants her fiction to express cannot easily be formulated apart from the particular way it inheres in each novel. It is not a substantive vision of the sort J. Hillis Miller finds in Conrad's fiction, whose 'aim is to make the truth of life, something different from any impression or quality, momentarily visible. Not colors or light but the darkness behind them is the true reality'.[1] Woolf's reality has nothing to do with stripping away illusion or penetrating surface phenomena to unearth the grim darkness beneath, but resides in a form which makes comprehensible the way the various impressions and colors and darkness together constitute the texture of human life. It is something which is communicated emotionally rather than intellectually. Woolf writes (*Collected Essays*, vol. 2, 129):

> When we speak of form, we mean that certain emotions have been placed in the right relations to each other; then that the novelist is able to dispose these emotions and make them tell by methods which he inherits, bends to his purpose, models anew or even invents for himself.

Endlessly evolving new techniques to dispose these emotions, Woolf succeeds in making out of the chaos and disharmony she found in the world marvelously coherent shapes. One of the best descriptions of what she tries to do in her novels was written by Roger Fry, not about Woolf at all but about the Post-Impressionist painters he so loved. Interestingly, Woolf quotes the passage herself in her biography of Fry (*Roger Fry*, 177–8):

> Now these artists . . . do not seek to give what can, after all, be but a pale reflex of actual appearance, but to arouse the conviction of a new and definite reality. They do not seek to imitate form, but to create form, not to imitate life, but to find an

[1] *Poets of Reality* (Harvard University Press, 1966), 27.

equivalent for life. By that I mean that they wish to make images which by the clearness of their logical structure, and by their closely knit unity of texture, shall appeal to our disinterested and contemplative imagination with something of the same vividness as the things of actual life appeal to our practical activities.

The center of a Woolf novel, then, does not reside in any of those several themes frequently singled out for critical investigation—the workings of consciousness, the perception of time, the quality of personal relationships—but in her effort to orchestrate these in such a way as to make us feel how together they constitute part of the experience of living. The quest is always for the form that will embody Woolf's sense of what that experience is. From *Jacob's Room* to *Between the Acts*, every one of Woolf's novels originated not with any notion of theme or character but with some notion of the form the novel might take. As she indicates in her diary, *Jacob's Room* developed out of three short pieces she was working on even as she was struggling through to the end of her second novel, *Night and Day* (*A Writer's Diary*, 23):

> I'm a great deal happier . . . today than I was yesterday having this afternoon arrived at some idea of a new form for a new novel. Suppose one thing should open out of another—as in an unwritten novel—only not for 10 pages but 200 or so—doesn't that give the looseness and lightness I want . . . Conceive(?) 'Mark on the Wall,' 'K. G.' ['Kew Gardens'] and 'Unwritten Novel' taking hands and dancing in unity. What the unity shall be I have yet to discover; the theme is a blank to me; but I see immense possibilities in the form I hit upon more or less by chance two weeks ago.

Similarly, her first intuitions about *The Waves* were purely formal ones (*A Writer's Diary*, 104):

> Why not invent a new kind of play; as for instance:
> Woman thinks . . .
> He does.
> Organ plays.
> She writes.
> They say.
> She sings.
> Night speaks.

They miss.
I think it must be something on this line—thought I can't now
see what. Away from facts; free; yet concentrated; prose yet
poetry; a novel and a play.

Or consider her early sense of *Between the Acts* (*A Writer's Diary*,
287):

Will another novel ever swim up? If so, how? The only hint I
have towards it is that it's to be dialogue: and poetry; and prose
all quite distinct. No more long closely written books . . . .
It came over me suddenly last night as I was reading . . . that I
saw the form of a new novel. It's to be first the statement of the
theme; then the restatement; and so on: repeating the same story:
singing out this and then that, until the central idea is stated.

Before there is theme there is already a vision of form, and even after
the substance of the novel has been thought out the commitment is
always to the design.

Such a commitment does not make her, as many have claimed, a
theoretician of the novel. Intuitions about form affect her in much the
same way as a fresh image will stimulate a poet's creative process.
Neither an abstract nor purely intellectual fascination, formal considerations provide Woolf with the emotional and imaginative impetus
for each new book. Her absorption with formal problems makes the
thematic content of her novels relatively unimportant to her fictitional
inspiration, and it is a fact that such content does not alter radically
over the course of her lifetime. Although intended somewhat flip-
pantly, her note that *To the Lighthouse* contains 'all the usual things I
try to put in—life, death, etc.' (*A Writer's Diary*, 76–7)—is very much to
the point and might well have been written about any of her works. It
is less the things themselves than the different patterns they achieve in
each novel, the relationship she fashions between them that matters.
The challenge in every work is always to find a new method for
rendering her sense of experience: once a form has been fully worked
out, Woolf moves on to a different attempt. Each experiment is 'a shot
at my vision—if it's not a catch, it's a cast in the right direction' (*A
Writer's Diary*, 173)—and represents a shot she will not repeat a second
time. A London day in the life of Clarissa Dalloway, the passage of ten
years on an island in the Hebrides, the makeshift, harried performance
of Miss La Trobe's pageant—each constitutes a unique version of

Woolf's remarkably steady perception of the world. The extraordinary structural diversity of *Jacob's Room*, *Mrs. Dalloway*, *To the Lighthouse*, *The Waves*, *The Years*, and *Between the Acts* paradoxically attests to the underlying singleness of purpose Woolf held to throughout her career.

Woolf's own quest as an artist—to create shapes that will make lasting sense of the fluidity of life—is reflected within her novels by people who are engaged in the same kind of search. 'Odd how the creative power at once brings the whole universe to order,' she notes in her diary (*A Writer's Diary*, 220), speaking to the impulses both behind and within her fiction. In so far as it is possible to generalize about the meaning of the human activity in Woolf's fictional world, we can say that the characters in her novels constantly try, through widely different means, to establish for themselves from the chaos around them a coherent grasp of their world. What Woolf attempts to accomplish through her fiction, that is, Lily Briscoe attempts with her painting, Bernard with his novel, Miss La Trobe with her pageant. And although these are the specific aesthetic endeavors which most closely approximate to Woolf's own, the instinct to bring things together is not limited to painters and writers. Certainly it is the animating principle behind the soliloquies of all the voices in *The Waves*, not just Bernard's, and is what impels that superficially least creative of souls, Clarissa Dalloway, to give her parties. Most memorably, of course, it is Mrs Ramsay's particular genius, possessing as she does the ability to 'choose out the elements of things and piece them together and so, giving them a wholeness not theirs in life, make of some scene, or meeting of people (all now gone and separate), one of those globed compacted things over which thought lingers and love plays (*To the Lighthouse*, 295–6).

The workings of the creative imagination shaping different visions of order, then, is the single great theme which appears in Woolf's fiction. The importance of that imagination in her work comes directly out of the overwhelming sense of human isolation in which every novel is steeped. Whether it is Jacob searching for himself, or Septimus and Rezia unable to talk to each other, or Giles and Isa struggling in their tempestuous marriage, or even Mrs Ramsay, giving of herself to exhaustion, the people in Woolf's fiction invariably feel cut off, not only from other human beings but from the world around them. The fact of isolation and the possibility of fleeting transcendence and communion—these are the two poles of Woolf's fictional universe. Rooted in one, characters can earn, through their own arduous efforts, brief contact with the other. Scratching out its monotonous 'Unity-Dispersity . . . Un . . . dis,' the gramophone of *Between the Acts* (235) actually lays out the psychic contours of all of Woolf's mature work. 'Scraps, orts, and fragments,' (*Between the Acts*, 220), as Miss La Trobe's pageant insists, the isolated selves in Virginia Woolf's world grapple not only with their own inadequacies and fears but with the uncertainty of personal relationships, the intractableness of language, the fact of death, to achieve their completed visions. The battle is difficult—filled with the same kind of loneliness and pain Woolf experienced in her own life as she fought her way through the demons of madness and despair that constantly assailed her to the lucid forms of the fiction—and the successes transient, but there is nothing else. Whatever the suffering involved, all the novels from *Mrs. Dalloway* on manage to end on a final note of affirmation: a party is given, a lighthouse reached, a pageant produced. Such accomplishments, however trivial they might appear, suggest the basic commitment to living made by the fiction. As Lily Briscoe understands after she has finished her painting, it does not matter in the least whether the canvas is ultimately destroyed or rolled up in some dusty attic. In Woolf's universe to be able to say, 'I have had my vision,' is the consummate human achievement, and Lily's words, which close *To the Lighthouse*, speak not only to her particular feat in completing her canvas but to the successes of the other protagonists as well and finally, of course, to those of Woolf.

They could not be reasonably applied, however, to Woolf's first two novels, *The Voyage Out* (1915) and *Night and Day* (1919). If D. S. Savage is perhaps unduly harsh in finding *Night and Day* to be the dullest novel in the English language, it is nevertheless true that her first two books are not particularly distinguished. Lacking any kind of formal originality, both are lamentably tedious, dragging on far longer than they should in a thoroughly pedestrian manner.

Although Terence Hewet's notion in *The Voyage Out* that he would like to write a 'novel about silence,' about 'the things people say,' seems to anticipate Woolf's later development, neither of these initial efforts suggests the unique things to come. What they do make clear is how uncongenial the realistic—or what Woolf might call the Edwardian—method of fiction was to her genius. For Woolf, conventional techniques could produce only conventional fiction. It was not until the publication of *Jacob's Room* in 1922 that she felt, as she notes in her diary, that she has finally learned 'how to begin (at 40) to say something in my own voice' (*A Writer's Diary*, 47). Irrevocably turning away with *Jacob's Room* from the established tradition within which *The Voyage Out* and *Night and Day* were written, Woolf devoted the next nineteen years of her life to exploring the different possibilities of that newly discovered voice.

Jacob's Room is the first of her novels which tries to dispense with what Woolf calls the 'appalling narrative business of the realist: getting on from lunch to dinner.' Her well-known rejection of the realist method—enunciated most emphatically in two essays, 'Mr Bennett and Mrs Brown' and 'Modern Fiction'—claims that in its attention to the superficial and mundane, realism fails to catch the vital experience of living itself. Trotting out her favorite trio of Edwardian villains—Wells, Bennett, and Galsworthy—in both essays, Woolf demonstrates how they frittered away their talent 'making the trivial and the transitory appear the true and the enduring' (*Collected Essays*, vol. 2, 105). In a word, they are *materialists*, devoting themselves with varying degrees of success to the pursuit of the unimportant. Opposed to these are writers who, like Joyce, are spiritual, who understand that life is a far more curious and fluid affair than the stolid materialists would have us believe. The mind does not function according to rigidly defined patterns, Woolf declares, but rather receives 'an incessant shower of innumerable atoms' (*Collected Essays*, vol. 2, 106), so that if a writer were not constrained by convention and forced to follow prescribed directions, 'if he could base his work upon his own feeling . . . there would be no plot, no comedy, no tragedy, no love interest or catastrophe in the accepted style, and perhaps not a single button sewn on as the Bond Street tailors would have it.' Neither unique to Woolf nor by any means a theoretical principle she holds to in her own criticism, such an argument is primarily an intensely personal assertion of what her own fiction will be. Implicitly, we cannot help but feel, it is also a way of absolving herself from continuing to labor in the direction that the rather dismal *Night and Day* and *The Voyage Out* suggest she could not manage very happily.

Employing techniques of point of view and organization in *Jacob's Room* that she had tentatively experimented with in 'Mark on the Wall,' 'Kew Gardens,' and 'Unwritten Novel'—three short pieces she published between 1917 and 1920—she attempts to embrace the 'unknown and uncircumscribed spirit' of life by writing a novel that steadfastly avoids much of the prosaic connective tissue necessary to narrative fiction. *Jacob's Room* is technically very different from *The Voyage Out* and *Night and Day*. Instead of the consecutive narrative movement of these books, it progresses by a series of discrete jumps through Jacob's life. Moving without apology—or much serious transition—from incident to incident, the novel is compounded of specific, isolated moments strung together relating to Jacob, his friends, his family. But if Woolf manages to liberate herself from some of the formal conventions under which she wrote her first two novels, such liberation is not in itself a recipe for fictional success. A freer form is not necessarily a fully expressive form, and while *Jacob's Room* has been purged of narrative dross, the result is not altogether satisfying. The novel's episodic organization does not find in the discontinuities of existence significant patterns that imprint themselves on the imagination. If the novel succeeds in documenting the isolation and the fragmentariness of existence, at the same time it does not embrace them in an affecting, substantial form. An important new direction which helped Woolf break free from the confines within which she had been working, *Jacob's Room* is finally a sterile form, one not capable of the resonance of her mature work.

But Woolf learned her lessons well and her next effort, *Mrs. Dalloway*, achieves a formal coherence and power altogether absent from *Jacob's Room*. In place of the flaccid chronological organization covering all of Jacob's life, *Mrs. Dalloway* effectively focuses on the events of one day in the lives of Clarissa Dalloway and Septimus Smith. Digging 'caves and tunnels' beneath her characters, Woolf creates a densely structured texture in which a June day in London is constantly informed by pressures and vestiges of the past. The novel is complexly organized both spatially and temporally. Physical meetings of characters in the street—and finally in Clarissa's home—merge with a web of intersecting memories and reveries to create a form that succeeds brilliantly in conveying Woolf's sense of the isolation, ironies, and ecstasies of life. Implacably tolling out the passage of time throughout the book, Big Ben punctuates the reflection of individual characters with its unyielding insistence on the passage of time. In addition to the mundane purpose of announcing a shift of narrative focus from one character to another, the gonging serves to emphasize the restricted framework of a single day which Woolf's imagination exploited continually during her career for her best work. It is significant that Woolf's four most distinguished novels—*Mrs. Dalloway*, *To the Lighthouse*, *The Waves*, and *Between the Acts*—essentially take place, either metaphorically or actually, within a twenty-four hour period. *Mrs. Dalloway* and *Between the Acts*, of course, do so explicitly. Although ten years elapse between parts One and Three of *To the Lighthouse*, the novel imagistically follows the movement of an entire day from the late afternoon of the first part, through the dark night of the second, to the early morning which opens the third section. And the nine poetic interludes of *The Waves*, describing the progression of the sun across the sky, clearly set the different dramatic soliloquies within the natural rhythm of a single day. However startlingly varied in form they are, the fact that all four play variations on the basic structure of a day indicates the degree to which Woolf's imagination flourished within the security of strict limitations. When she deserts these confines, as the difficulties of *Jacob's Room* and *The Years* reveal, her work loses considerably in power.

Woolf's feelings about *Mrs. Dalloway* as she was still completing it in 1924—'if this book proves anything, it proves that I can only write along those lines [of *Jacob's Room*] and shall never desert them, but explore further and further and shall, heaven be praised, never bore myself an instant' (*A Writer's Diary*, 63)—were prophetic about the course all of her fiction was to follow. The process of formal exploration, haltingly begun in *Jacob's Room*, continues until her death in 1941. It is an open-ended search, each new novel struggling with formal problems totally alien to everything preceding it. For too long it has been a critical commonplace to see *The Waves* as the teleological fulfillment of Woolf's genius. Such a view not only leaves critics hard pressed to explain what came after—*The Years* and *Between the Acts*—it seriously distorts the nature of what came before. For Woolf's novels do not follow a linear path, the discoveries of one leading to the production of the next, but rather constitute a series of discrete forays in altogether different directions into unknown territory. *The Waves* no more represents a culmination of her work than does *Orlando* or *To the Lighthouse*. Even *The Years*, with its superficially realistic trappings is not, as frequently thought, a renunciation of experiment. Moving from the sustained internality of *The Waves* to the strict 'externality' of *The Years*, from the novel of vision to the novel of fact, was as daring an innovation for Woolf as was the extraordinary conception of *The Waves* itself. What matters in each novel is that Woolf was able to force herself 'to break every mould and find a fresh form of being, that is of expression, for everything I feel or think' (*A Writer's Diary*, 220). Just as *The Waves* is an entirely different book from *Orlando*, published three years earlier, so with *The Years*, Woolf comments in her diary, 'I am breaking the mould made by *The Waves*.'

Common to all her novels is the attempt to create a texture for them of the sort Lily Briscoe seeks for her painting (*To the Lighthouse*, 264):

> Beautiful and bright it should be on the surface, feathery and evanescent, one colour melting into another like the colours on a butterfly's wings; but beneath the fabric must be clamped together with bolts of iron. It was to be a thing you could ruffle with your breath; and a thing you could not dislodge with a team of horses.

The centrality of such a conception for Woolf is also suggested, in language strikingly similar to Lily's, by a 1925 diary entry. Musing on the greatness of Proust, Woolf praises him for qualities she unmistakably wants to achieve in her own work: 'The thing about Proust is his combination of the utmost sensibility with the utmost tenacity. He searches out those butterfly shades to the last grain. He is as tough as catgut and as evanescent as a butterfly's bloom' (*A Writer's Diary*, 72).

The delicacy of her sensibility, of course, is granted her even by her most vehement detractors; indeed, it is frequently used as a reason for dismissing her as a serious artist, on the grounds that her exquisiteness (the epithet most generally attached to her) leads only to sterile exercises in preciosity. In fact, highly patterned and sensitive though the surface of her novels is, there is nothing exquisite in the least about her fiction. From the bewildered Mrs Flanders, standing dumbly in Jacob's room after his death, holding out his shoes, to the curtain rising at the end of *Between the Acts* on the confrontation between Isa and Giles, her work deals with enduring human concerns without solace of illusion or sentimentality. Woolf looks unflinchingly at a world that offers very little in the way of easy gratification. Death and the anguish of isolation are the inescapable pressures felt in every book; it is always in the face of these that her characters attempt to fashion their precarious visions of order, and their fleeting successes never obscure our sense of the difficulty of the battle or the knowledge that the dangers remain. In affirming the possibility of order, she never falsifies the chaos threatening it. 'Nothing was ever one thing,' *To the Lighthouse* (286) insists, and James's discovery as he nears the lighthouse that it is not just the 'silvery, misty-looking tower' (*To the Lighthouse*, 286) that gleamed at him when he was a child, but also something stark, solid, and forbidding, is precisely the kind of complex view Woolf holds to throughout her life.

Despite her tough-mindedness and complexity, it is still not clear that Woolf will ever quite luxuriate in the unquestioned eminence accorded a Conrad or a Joyce or a Faulkner. As long as the cult of Bloomsbury worship flourishes, of course, Woolf's reputation will continue to grow. But even Bloomsbury's mythic stature will one day erode and we will once again have to confront an enigmatic writer whose novels lack the narrative interest and overt social and psychological concerns of the other great twentieth-century writers. Such a confrontation will always be difficult for a large number of readers. Woolf's uncompromising effort to convey 'the exact shapes my brain holds' is an enterprise whose basically subjective character has frequently been thought to ensure its ultimate insignificance. As I have tried to indicate, however, the explicitly personal nature of her attempt is neither precious nor self-indulgent. Developing out of Woolf's urgent need to get to the heart of the reality she felt was somehow available to her, the novels are at the same time informed by a strict artistic integrity which prevents them from degenerating into the narrowly private. In rendering that vision of reality, Woolf provides us with a rich variety of compelling shapes that speak in immediate ways to all of us, revealing her special truth that[1]

> behind the cotton wool [of daily life] is hidden a pattern; that we—I mean all human beings—are connected with this; that the whole world is a work of art; that we are parts of the work of art. *Hamlet* or a Beethoven quartet is the truth about this vast mass that we call the world. But there is no Shakespeare, there is no Beethoven; certainly and emphatically there is no God; we are the words; we are the music; we are the thing itself.

[1] *Moments of Being: Unpublished Autobiographical Writings,* ed. J. Schulkind (Harcourt Brace Jovanovich, 1976), 72.

4

The Voyage Out

First novels of great writers always have about them the particular fascination of being first. Whatever their merits, we read them with enthusiasm, eager to discover any incipient manifestations of greatness. If successful, we marvel at their precocity; if not, we still have the satisfaction of having encountered the very beginnings, of perhaps gaining from a misbegotten initial effort increased respect for an artist's mature achievement. Although not without its virtues, *The Voyage Out* (1915) largely affords these latter sorts of pleasures. No amount of critical legerdemain can turn it or its successor, *Night and Day* (1919), into compelling works of fiction. That Woolf had to make her way through two rather pedestrian novels before discovering the life-giving experimental possibilities of *Jacob's Room* in 1922 is not, however, a moral blemish that requires apology. It was part of her artistic evolution which obviously worked according to an inner chronology that could neither be interrupted nor speeded up. Woolf had to begin in the realist tradition in order finally to purge herself of it and create those new forms demanded by her vision.

But if we need not be defensive about *The Voyage Out*, at the same time there is no point pretending it is an especially impressive book. It is not—and for several good reasons. In the first place, as we have seen, Woolf was simply not capable of producing great fiction as long as she remained under the tyrannies of the realist form. Employing in her first fictional effort the basic conventions available to all aspiring writers of the time, Woolf cannot achieve any version of those resonant shapes characteristic of her genius. The novel's straightforward linear chronology, unfolded through the agency of the omniscient third-person narrator, ensures that Woolf can do little more than render rather pallidly—and somewhat tediously—those same concerns which make up the living tissue of her later novels. 'Life, death,

49

etc.'—these are all here too, but unlike *To the Lighthouse*, essentially talked at, not effectively embodied in the book's structure. Without the pressure of the form to create patterns of significance, the ordinariness of existence which Woolf's novels explore remains flat.

In addition to the lack of any original, sustaining form, *The Voyage Out* suffers from considerable uncertainty as to its overall focus. Liberally sprinkled with a variety of interesting thematic possibilities, it never manages to blend them together successfully. The book functions more as a splendid repository for embryonic Woolf concerns and motifs than as a totally self-contained, expressive fiction in its own right. Too much material remains undigested for the novel ever really to arrive anywhere. It is tempting, in fact, to see in the open-endedness of the title some sense of Woolf's own doubts about where the book was heading, as compared, for example, to the specific destination—and successful realization—of *To the Lighthouse*.

The novel's most specific destination is the growth into experience of Rachel Vinrace, a stultifyingly cosseted young woman who has reached the age of twenty-four without showing any evidence of the slightest contamination at the hands of life. As cut off from her own inner self as she is from the outer world, she boards her father's freighter, the *Euphrosyne*, knowing little about anything that matters. Sailing away from the sterile confines of her secure London existence to Santa Marina, a small town somewhere on the coast of South America, Rachel encounters vast new continents of emotional and intellectual possibilities. She becomes alive for the first time not only to others, particularly men, but to herself as well, understanding as she never had before her own resources and needs. Rachel's gradual expansion into a complex, sensitive woman also functions, in large part, as a kind of organizing principle in the novel, uniting the common interest of a variety of disparate characters. Altogether, Rachel's voyage out into life, which ends as such symbolic literary voyages frequently do, in death, provides Woolf with a viable—if somewhat unsteady—vessel with which to begin to chart the waters of her own imagination.

Certainly no one is more in need of some kind of emancipation at the start than Rachel. A victim of the most limited and trivializing sexist education available to women at the end of the nineteenth century, Rachel has been intellectually groomed to a bland indifference by the 'kind doctors and gentle old professors' (31) engaged by her father for her instruction. Carefully led past the difficult or the controversial, Rachel was permitted all manner of pleasant study, failing to be informed only about 'the shape of the earth, the history of the world, how trains worked, or money was invested, what laws were in force, which people wanted what, and why they wanted it, the most elementary idea of a system in modern life—none of this had been imparted to her by any of her professors or mistresses' (31). Her ignorance about life is matched by her total insulation from it—a beatific condition deftly managed by her father and two aunts, Lucy and Eleanor, who raised her after the death of her mother. Feeling that it is best not to feel strongly, Rachel channels most of her energy into the piano, grateful for the sensuous absorption provided by music. At the outset of her voyage it is music alone which offers her satisfaction and a means of expression.

Rachel's aunt, Helen Ambrose, is initially appalled at the sight of her niece, finding her distressingly immature and uninformed. Dreading the three weeks she will have to spend on board with her on the way to her brother's house in Santa Marina, Helen soon discovers that Rachel is far more substantial than she first appeared. Her diffidence, she learns, is not an indecisiveness; beneath her mildness there lurks a sensibility and intelligence that need only be properly cultivated in order to flourish. Helen rapidly falls under the spell of her goodness, realizing that most of her limitations were imposed upon her by forces of father and aunts (not to speak of an entire culture) which she had little opportunity to resist. To rescue her from the cocoon of propriety in which she had been forcibly wrapped becomes Helen's mission: she resolves to take over the task of re-educating Rachel.

Helen's commitment to Rachel's growth is clearly fueled by Woolf's own resentments against the sexist assumptions of an educational system which attempted for so long to keep women in a state of happy blankness. Although Woolf was herself particularly fortunate to have her father's library in which to roam, her good fortune never went so far as to extend to her the same opportunity of a university education granted her brothers. Rachel's exploitation at the well-meaning hands of her family provides Woolf with a paradigmatic instance of all the suffocating paternalism she detested throughout her life and most notably protested against in *A Room of One's Own* and *Three Guineas*. Helen's anger at the shackles Willoughby has permitted Rachel to live with—she 'could hardly restrain herself from saying out loud what she thought of a man who brought up his daughter so that at the age of twenty-four she scarcely knew that men desired women and was terrified by a kiss' (90)—anticipates by some fourteen years the first of Woolf's broader cultural treatments of essentially the same issue in *A Room of One's Own*.

Rachel's education is one portion of a wide-ranging concern in *The Voyage Out* about the rights of women and the nature of the relationship between the two sexes. From Richard Dalloway's smug conviction that women can never be taken seriously as political beings and ought never to have the vote, to Terence Hewet's instinctively feminine point of view, a good deal of attention in the novel is devoted to a topic obviously very close to Woolf's own heart. In *A Room of One's Own* Woolf argues for the importance of the 'incandescent' imagination in literature, the imagination that can consume all personal grievance, 'all desire to protest, to preach, to proclaim an injury, to pay off a score, to make the world the witness of some hardship' (*Room*, 86) in the all-encompassing integrity of the work of art. While Woolf certainly does not engage in any shrill polemic here, it is fair to say that the intrusive nature of some of this material and her heavy-handed way of dealing with it, indicates that she had by no means achieved at the start of her career the incandescence of her later fiction. Terence's ironic celebration of the male world—'What a miracle the masculine conception of life is—judges, civil servants, army, navy, Houses of Parliaments, lord mayors—what a world we've made of it!' (235)—is a perception which is perhaps more properly at home in the didactic *Three Guineas* than in the fictional *The Voyage Out*.

Helen's ambition to see Rachel grow into a complex, self-sustaining adult is unwittingly—if traumatically—abetted by the egregious Dalloways' arrival in Lisbon. Snobbish, sententious, and filled with the worst kind of nationalistic and paternalistic cant, the Dalloways are pilloried with great relish by Woolf. In large part they represent all that is complacent and sterile about the English upper class: Clarissa, the daughter of a peer; Richard, the recently defeated but still actively aspiring Member of Parliament. From their very first appearance Woolf exposes them in all their essential triviality, catching particularly the self-congratulatory flavor of their dedication to the life of public service which is the privilege of the rich and the powerful. Richard is redeemed by his commitment to English civilization, just as Clarissa is redeemed by her belief in him:

> I often wonder whether it is really good for a woman to live
> with a man who is morally her superior, as Richard is mine. It

makes one so dependent. I suppose I feel for him what my mother and women of her generation felt for Christ' (55).

For all their fatuousness, however—and at times they border on sheer caricature—the Dalloways do have an energy and even a charm which Rachel finds appealing. Providing her with an alternative to the deadly pedantries of William Pepper and Ridley Ambrose, the two dons, who along with Helen and Willoughby make up the company on the ship, Richard and Clarissa both bring new interest to Rachel. She finds Clarissa oddly sympathetic and eager to befriend her; Richard, full of the fascination invested in those who have actually made things happen. Flourishing in the stimulating presence of the Dalloways, Rachel suddenly experiences the most severe shock of her life in the form of a kiss—the first of her life—impulsively bestowed upon her by Richard in a passionate moment. It affects Rachel with a power belied by its relative innocuousness. At once frightening and pleasing, it succeeds in tearing from Rachel the serene innocence in which she had been luxuriating. The terrifying nightmare it generates, complete with oozing damp and the gibberings of a deformed man with pitted face and long nails, suggests not only the extent of her fear of sexual contact but also heralds the beginning of her painful but necessary confrontation with the new demands of an adult identity. As difficult as she finds dealing with it, even she can understand that 'something wonderful had happened' (85). For the first time, 'Life seemed to hold infinite possibilities she had never guessed at' (85).

It is ironically appropriate that Richard is the person to precipitate much of Rachel's lurch into the initial throes of self-discovery, as there is no one less sensitive to the needs of other people than he. Totally oblivious of the substantial psychic legacy he has left behind, Richard departs the next day with Clarissa not only from the *Euphrosyne* but from the entire novel as well. Neither is heard from again. During their brief but compelling stint in the novel the Dalloways earned for themselves a sufficient portion of Woolf's imaginative energies to ensure their return (in modified form, to be sure) in *Mrs. Dalloway*. Indeed they are in many ways far too interesting for the brief roles they are allotted here. The sheer force of their depiction threatens to violate the texture of the rest of the novel, for they are immediately and endlessly absorbing in the completeness of their folly as no other characters are. While exposing them, Woolf has also created them to perfection, an accomplishment which an uncertain novel like *The*

Voyage Out cannot handle with ease. Part of that perfection is Woolf's ability, without falsifying what is basically unacceptable in their characters or values, to make them vulnerable and even curiously attractive human beings. Their spirit and the seriousness with which they take their ideals of service, however flawed those ideals may be, are admirable qualities which cannot be dismissed. And for all their public bluster, there is the pang of envy shooting through Clarissa's heart at the mention of Helen's son which hints at a private anguish endured beneath the façade. In addition, anyone who reveres Jane Austen possesses for Woolf a not altogether negligible moral sensibility, and the Dalloways understand her genius full well. Richard's assessment, in fact, that she is our greatest female writer because 'she does not attempt to write like a man' (66), is precisely the estimate of Austen that Woolf herself makes in *A Room of One's Own*. Dalloway's literary judgment is clear proof that he is by no means entirely without virtue.

With the passing of the Dalloways, Rachel returns to Helen's tutelage to work out the implications of all that happened. If Helen thinks Richard to be a second-rate spirit, she is not unhappy in the least with his behavior, as it gives her the opportunity to explore with Rachel the unknown tracts of her feelings. Encouraged by Helen, Rachel suddenly achieves for the first time a 'vision of her own personality, of herself as a real everlasting thing, different from anything else, unmergeable like the sea or the wind . . . and she became profoundly excited at the thought of living' (94–5). It is to help nourish this vision that Helen persuades Willoughby to let Rachel remain with her when they arrive in Santa Marina instead of continuing to travel inland with her father.

Once the *Euphrosyne* discharges its passengers at Santa Marina, Rachel is immediately absorbed into the social network of English vacationers quietly living in the small town. An odd conglomeration of wealthy old ladies, young barristers, dully married couples, an aspiring novelist, a Fellow of King's, and a smattering of other souls, together they constitute the human framework within which Rachel's growth into selfhood—with all its attendant implications for the novel as a whole—will take place. As in all of Woolf's novels, the quality of life in that framework is, to say the least, uneventful. Much desultory talk and the occasional mild permutation of a relationship is the basic fare, although *The Voyage Out* also includes more exotic events like a picnic, a dance, and even a brief trip to a native village. The inconsequential nature of the action, of course, is not a failure of narrative impulse but the deliberate method employed by an artist trying to suggest certain kinds of truths about human experience. The problem with *The Voyage Out* is not its surface blandness but the fact that it lacks the tension of form necessary to vitalize the material. To say that the novel explores matters of life, love, and death without any pervasive conflict or drama is not to speak of its success or failure but merely of its aim.

Stumbling out of the confusion and exhilaration of her embrace at sea with Dalloway, Rachel moves on land towards a coherent sense of self largely through the agency of her successful relationship with Terence Hewet, the young novelist. The course of her progress towards a viable maturity is very much the course of their love. Ironically, it is not Terence but his friend St John Hirst whom Helen thinks at first is the most appropriate person to help her complete Rachel's education. Enormously bright—believing, perhaps with justification, that he will be 'one of the people who really matter' (189)—St John, however, is woefully inexperienced with women. Whereas Helen wants someone to speak to Rachel about the emotional facts of life, all he can manage is to recommend to her that she read Gibbon. He is far happier confiding in Helen as the wise, receptive older women than he is awkwardly struggling to communicate with Rachel, attractive though he finds her. The formidably intellectual Hirst, in fact, becomes increasingly dependent emotionally on Helen, finally leaving it up to her to decide if he should continue as a Fellow of King's or leave to read for the bar. Despite his intelligence and general goodness, he is prevented by his emotional ineptitude from actively pursuing the serious commitment with a woman that part of him at least can fantasize about. His undemanding friendship with Helen, 'the only woman I've ever met who seems to have the faintest conception of what I mean when I say a thing' (189), is all that he can achieve at this point.

Terence does not have Hirst's difficulties. Open to his feelings and able to talk easily about those of others, he is as at home in personal relationships as Hirst is out of his element. 'People like you better than they like me,' Hirst admits, adding somewhat reluctantly, 'Women like you, I suppose' (124). Although by no means as intellectually gifted as his friend, Terence has an extraordinarily rich human understanding, one capable of rendering far more penetrating assessments of people and experience than Hirst can make. His intelligence, indeed,

55

is precisely the intelligence of the novelist he seeks to be. It is generally true that creative artists in Woolf's fiction, whether Lily Briscoe in *To the Lighthouse* or Bernard in *The Waves* or Miss La Trobe in *Between the Acts*, are invested with special insight which, if not explicitly endorsed by their creator, at least speaks to concerns very close to her own. And although Terence has yet to produce anything, he is no exception. In a number of ways his vision of life corresponds closely to Woolf's.

Unlike Hirst, who thinks people can be rigidly classified according to certain types, Hewet shares Woolf's more complex view of the uniqueness of each individual soul and the enormous difficulty of ever getting to know it. The tight circles that Hirst argues can be drawn around groups of people give way, in Terence's metaphor, to bubbles of selfhood—'You can't see my bubble; I can't see yours; all we see of each other is a speck, like the wick in the middle of that flame' (125)—through which people negotiate the world. Conferring an absolute separateness upon each human being, Terence's bubble image also permits the possibility of merger, of two souls bursting together upon one another, thus establishing that condition of isolation and communion basic to Woolf's fictional universe. At once separate and part of the whole, the truth is, as Terence points out, 'that one is never alone, and one is never in company.'[1]

None of this is easy for Hirst, whose rather more desiccated intelligence demands far neater categories than his friend needs, but he is able nevertheless to recognize the peculiar strength of Terence's creative imagination when he grudgingly acknowledges, 'I don't think you altogether as foolish as I used to, Hewet . . . . You don't know what you mean but you try to say it' (125). Terence's attempt to express what he can only imperfectly articulate for himself is, of course, very much Woolf's own, and leads him to imagine writing a novel which can be thought of as an extraordinarily prescient anticipation of those poetic, experimental forms Woolf herself goes on to evolve (262):

'I want to write a novel about Silence,' he said; 'the things people don't say. But the difficulty is immense . . . . However, you don't care . . . . Nobody cares. All you read a novel for is to see what sort of person the writer is, and, if you know him, which of his friends he's put in. As for the novel itself, the whole conception, the way one's seen the thing, felt about it, made it stand in

[1] The bubble metaphor remains intact throughout Woolf's career. It is also used by North in *The Years* to express his vision of isolation and unity.

relation to other things, not one in a million cares for that. And yet I sometimes wonder whether there's anything else in the whole world worth doing.'

Suggesting the kinds of enterprise to come, beginning with *Jacob's Room* in 1922, Terence's ideal novel at once approximates what Woolf wanted her fiction to achieve as well as ironically underlines the difficulties of *The Voyage Out*. For it is only through the formal brilliance of her later fiction—totally lacking here—that she succeeds in taking the thing and making it stand in harmonious, effective relation to other things. But if Terence is not fortunate enough to be included in such a novel, his commitment to orchestrating a total vision of human experience which goes well beyond the bog of mere personal relationships interesting to most readers (and most writers) engages him in the same aesthetic quest on which Woolf was soon to embark. Both understand that the most important things are not necessarily what people say, just as both share Hewet's reflection that the really important questions are those one never asks.

Although it is not clear that Terence will in fact ever write his book, it would certainly, were it finished, not only have the same highly conscious form of Woolf's mature novels but their same unyielding assumption that we 'live in a state of perpetual uncertainty, knowing nothing, leaping from moment to moment as from world to world' (147). In the midst of all the polite chatter and genteel hypocrisy of Santa Marina, Terence penetrates to the stark truth at the heart of all Woolf's novels, that the world is a difficult, fragmented place through which we stumble at our own peril, without anything to sustain us beyond ourselves. Terence's response to a minor instance of emotional dishonesty gives rise to a despairing question which sounds throughout Woolf's own fiction (262):

'Why is it that they *won't* be honest?' he muttered to himself as he went upstairs. Why was it that relations between different people were so unsatisfactory, so fragmentary, so hazardous, and words so dangerous that the instinct to sympathise with another human being was an instinct to be examined carefully and probably crushed?

In Terence's company, Rachel begins to emerge from the layers of timidity and conventional belief which had previously restricted her. Exploring the developing impulses of her own self, she

57

starts to question things she had formerly accepted out of an essentially mindless reflex. The demand for honesty, both emotional and intellectual, becomes of pressing importance to her now; scrutinizing Christianity carefully for the first time, for example, she finds all that she had blithely affirmed to be hypocritical and life-denying, and with 'the violence that now marked her feelings, she rejected all that she had implicitly believed' (279). Above all else, of course, her contact with Terence plunges her into a state of emotional flux, buffeted by feelings and thoughts she only dimly understands.

The relationship between Rachel and Terence progresses slowly. Although they are mutually attracted to each other from the beginning, her gradually dissipating confusion and his reluctance to commit himself definitively require some time to resolve themselves. Spending a good deal of time together exchanging ideas and feelings, they grow inexorably closer to one another, needing only some kind of catalyst to stimulate explicit avowals of love. The irrepressible Mrs Flushing and her expedition to the native village provide precisely that. Moving into the primitive interior on a journey which is fraught with all manner of Conradian overtones, Rachel and Terence disengage themselves from the rest of the group for a walk in the jungle. Terence knows the time has come and in the solitary intensity of the moment explains to Rachel that they love each other, a solemn declaration which she solemnly repeats. They embrace; Terence cries. Returning to the boat they remain wrapt in the grip of powerful feelings neither can really understand, feelings which rapidly open the way to a new intimacy and honesty between them: 'With every word the mist which had enveloped them, making them seem unreal to each other, since the previous afternoon melted a little further, and their contact became more and more natural' (344). By the next day so much has happened between them that Helen, detecting the extraordinary change, realizes that Rachel at last 'had passed beyond her guardianship. A voice might reach her ears, but never again would it carry as far as it had carried twenty-four hours ago' (351). Translated into the prosaic terms of civilization, the overwhelming personal experience in the heart of the jungle is seen by Santa Marina as 'not anything unusual that had happened . . . they had become engaged to marry each other' (355).

If the occupants of Santa Marina are quite right in finding nothing unusual in an engagement, they completely miss the point of how uniquely rich and alive the relationship is. Particularly when compared to their own sodden, sterile ones, Rachel and Terence pursue theirs with a passion and integrity which is indeed unusual. Eagerly responding to every nuance of the other's personality, the two continually stimulate their mutual appetite for intimacy. The more they learn about one another, the greater the admiration and the need to know. Their engagement marks not the beginning of the slide into a safe routine but the start of a relationship that promises growth and nourishment for both of its partners. Such relationships do not abound in Santa Marina, as Terence's dispassionate analysis of the human condition there suggests (156):

> They are not satisfactory; they are ignoble . . . . Amiable and modest, respectable in many ways, lovable even in their contentment and desire to be kind, how mediocre they all were, and capable of what insipid cruelty to one another! There was Mrs. Thornbury, sweet but trivial in her maternal egoism; Mrs. Elliot, perpetually complaining of her lot; her husband a mere pea in a pod; and Susan—she had no self, and counted neither one way or the other; Venning was as honest and as brutal as a schoolboy; poor old Thornbury merely trod his round like a horse in a mill; and the less one examined into Evelyn's character the better he suspected.

In the midst of these and others like them as well, Rachel and Terence stand out as a tribute to the possibility of life and love.

However admirable Rachel and Terence are in the texture of the novel's values, they are aesthetically not altogether successful in their rendering. Romantic love is not a particularly congenial subject for Woolf, and it must be admitted that the description of Rachel and Terence in love suffers from a portentousness which strikes a jarring note. This is particularly true of them on Mrs Flushing's trip. Attempting to invoke the presence of intense emotion through a proliferation of 'murmurings' and weighted silences, Woolf resorts to strained language reminiscent of some of the excesses of early Yeats. The breathy, contrived dialogue between the two—and Terence's tears—demonstrate how alien to Woolf any such effort is to handle explicit emotional material of this sort. As Terence somehow knows already, Woolf's genius lies in shaping the things people don't say into expressive patterns in which every part figures in the whole, not in

[handwritten marginalia: "agreeable", "pompously bleak"]

59

narrowly focusing in any conventional way on a romantic attachment between man and woman. It is hard not to compare Woolf's awkward treatment of them with her masterful portrayal of Isa and Giles, the married couple in *Between the Acts* (1941), who remain entangled throughout the book in a complex and anguished relationship without uttering a single word to one another. From the explicit to the powerfully spare and suggestive: such is the distance Woolf was to travel as an artist.

Secure in her happiness with Terence, Rachel ponders the curious, at times seemingly aimless ways in which lives assume their shape and significance (384–5):

> For the methods by which she had reached her present position, seemed to her very strange, and the strangest thing about them was that she had not known where they were leading her. That was the strange thing, that one did not know where one was going, or what one wanted, and followed blindly, suffering so much in secret, always unprepared and amazed and knowing nothing; but one thing led to another and by degrees something had formed itself out of nothing, and so one reached at last this calm, this quiet, this certainty, and it was this process that people called living.

Rachel is absolutely right in her understanding of the essentially random quality of life in Woolf's universe. It is the same condition Terence acknowledges earlier when he claims we ' live in a state of perpetual uncertainty, knowing nothing, leaping from moment to moment as from world to world,' a condition basic to all of Woolf's fiction. Where Rachel is crucially wrong, however, is in assuming that all the suffering, stumbling, and ignorance necessarily lead to the goal of calm certitude she feels herself finally to have achieved. Such a benign principle of order is not to be found in Woolf's novels. Like everything else, happiness too is uncertain and fleeting; if it seems to emerge mysteriously from the chaos, it disappears with equal capriciousness. A temporary state, in short, not the inevitable reward awaiting all those who endure. In Rachel's case, her fulfillment with Terence is no more rightfully hers than the sudden fatal illness which takes it all away is undeserved. Both, as Terence realizes, are part of living.

Although at the first hint of Rachel's illness he experiences an overwhelming 'sense of dismay and catastrophe . . . . all round him he seemed to hear the shiver of broken glass' (399–400), he is at least intellectually prepared to deal with the fact of death, even if he is betrayed emotionally by his own vulnerability. For Terence there is nothing horrible or unnatural about death, the protests of Evelyn Murgatroyd, Mrs Thornbury, and others notwithstanding. Lying 'back with the hands clasped upon his breast and his eyes shut' (170), he even goes so far early in the novel as to demonstrate how easy it is to imagine being dead. It is not so easy, of course, to accept the death of Rachel; however great his understanding, no amount of preparation could adequately equip him to deal with his anguish at the impending loss of his love (420–1):

> He could not get used to his pain, it was a revelation to him. He
> had never realised before that underneath every action,
> underneath the life of every day, pain lies, quiescent, but ready to
> devour; he seemed to be able to see suffering, as if it were a fire,
> curling up over the edges of all action, eating away the lives of
> men and women.

Rachel's senseless death and Terence's pain constitute an important part of the novel's fabric, the other side, as it were, of Rachel's satisfying vision of harmony and meaning. Together they help define that process that Woolf herself calls living. Beyond ecstasy and despair, of course, and more enduring than both is the daily business of life, with its pleasures and sadnesses, relationships and routines. It is not accidental that with the death of Rachel, some twenty-five pages from the end of *The Voyage Out*, Terence and Helen, the two people closest to her, also disappear from the book, leaving the rest entirely to that host of innocuous vacationers—Elliotts, Thornburys, Flushings and the like—who are not substantially affected by the death. Reflecting on what happened, they continue to eat their meals, pursue their relationships, and play their chess as always. Life, indeed, goes on, as Mrs Thornbury instinctively knows when she pauses in her knitting, as Mr Elliott knows when he checkmates William Pepper. Giving the last pages over to the idle gossip and amusement of the survivors, Woolf makes sure we know this too. The novel ends with St John, half-asleep, seeing 'the figures of people picking up their books, their cards, their balls of wool, their work baskets, and passing him one after another on their way to bed' (458), seeking their sleep in preparation for the next day.

5

Night and Day

If *The Voyage Out* falls short of Terence's vision of a novel that might succeed in conveying 'the way one's seen the thing . . . made it stand in relation to other things,' *Night and Day* (1919) is even more demonstrably not the kind of book Terence would have had any interest in writing. It represents Woolf's most complete immersion into the realm of personal relationships, a realm Woolf later recognized as consummately Jane Austen's, not her own. There is no attempt made here to set the human interaction into the broader context of those impersonal concerns which together make up the 'reality' her mature experimental novels seek to articulate. In form and substance it is thoroughly conventional—E. M. Forster thought of it as a 'strictly formal and classical work' (*A Writer's Diary*, 20)—as it investigates the complicated web of feelings entangling the four major characters of the novel: Katharine Hilbery, Ralph Denham, William Rodney, and Mary Datchet. In their bumbling, at times comically convoluted efforts to make some sense out of the confusion of their emotions, to find 'a true feeling among the chaos of the unfeelings or half-feelings of life, to recognize it when found, and to accept the consequence of the discovery' (331), they provide Woolf with a rich sampling of human behavior, its perils and possibilities. Their struggles to perceive reality accurately—and then to adjust themselves productively to it—embrace all varieties of insight and self-delusion, cravenness and determination, jealousy and generosity of spirit which are part of the fallible human condition.

   Their efforts do not meet with facile success. Beset by loneliness and undermined by their own longings, the characters thrash about in considerable turmoil, unable to penetrate to their own needs or, when they do, to act upon them effectively. The problem of achieving a true feeling, difficult in the best of times, is compounded by the unsettling

62

nature of the different relationships. Individual quests for a sustaining order are threatened by the chaos that all of the characters, in spite of themselves, generate in each other. Much in the novel depends, as Katharine understands, 'upon the interpretation of the word love; which word came up again and again, whether she considered Rodney, Denham, Mary Datchet, or herself' (331). Love is the common spectre plaguing the four of them, spreading the seeds of disarray everywhere: that Mary loves Ralph who loves Katharine who is engaged to William (whom she does not love) is not a situation conducive to the well-being of any of them. In the dense human network of *Night and Day*, one person's doubt is the next's torment. And although each finally works out some reasonably viable accommodation, it is the erratic, uncertain process by which people negotiate the treacheries of their own conflicting impulses as well as the obstacles posed by others which primarily interests Woolf.

The four major characters whom she chooses to follow come from widely different backgrounds: the daughter of a distinguished literary family who has herself no aptitude for literature; a clerk of great promise in a solicitor's office who for a time entertains the notion of retiring to a cottage to write a history of the English village; an enthusiastic suffragette, daughter of a country rector; and a government clerk with a passion for Elizabethan literature and a lamentable need to write bad dramas himself. Their intricate patterns of decisions and indecisions, retractions and resolves not only constitute the basic substance of the novel but provide the form as well. Meeting repeatedly in each other's rooms, offices, and on the street as their relationships come together and fade apart, the characters engage in what can be thought of as a kind of emotional—and physical—minuet throughout *Night and Day*. It is perhaps this quality Forster had in mind when he referred to the novel's formal and classical nature.

While Katharine's recognition that much depends on love is central to the novel, love is by no means the sole problem the characters must confront on their way to achieving a complex identity. Certainly this is true for Katharine herself. Grand-daughter of the great nineteenth-century poet Richard Alardyce, Katharine has grown up in the sophisticated drawing rooms of one of England's intellectually elite families. A family, it goes without saying, that is not altogether unrelated to Virginia Stephen's own. Although proud of the Hilbery tradition and culture, Katharine at the same time has been severely confined by them and the life they circumscribe. She yearns to escape from the tea parties and polite literary chatter to a world where she can follow her own interests. In place of her required allegiance to literature she wants to be free to indulge her fascination with mathematics and astronomy without the guilt she currently feels in violating family expectations. Studying mathematics surreptitiously at night or in the early morning, Katharine is constrained to conceal from all her perfidious love of numbers, for (40–1)

> in her mind mathematics were directly opposed to literature. She would not have cared to confess how infinitely she preferred the exactitude, the starlike impersonality, of figures to the confusion, agitation, and vagueness of the finest prose. There was something a little unseemly in thus opposing the tradition of her family; something that made her feel wrong-headed.

Most particularly, she wants to be rid of the oppressive reverence of the past Alardyce glories exacted by her mother, whose never-to-be-finished biography of her poet-father Katharine is obliged to help her write. Her daily stint through the poet's life with the hopelessly disorganized Mrs Hilbery fills Katharine with rage at the cruel waste of her time. With all her charm and good intentions, Mrs Hilbery is in fact extremely manipulative, playing on Katharine's sympathies and draining her resources in the interests of a project which can have little meaning for her daughter. Buried under the weight of her grandfather's image, Katharine resents her bondage to the great spirit that was Alardyce, feeling at times that it 'was necessary for her very existence that she should free herself from the past; at others, that the past has completely displaced the present, which, when one resumed life after a morning among the dead, proved to be of an utterly thin and inferior composition' (38). In either case, it is inimical to her fulfillment in the present, and points to the kind of exploitation to which, as a dependent woman living at home she is necessarily vulnerable. 'She lived at home' (39): the words describe precisely the state of cultural and economic slavery Woolf is protesting against in *Three Guineas*.

Brought up to do nothing and without any formal education (like Sir Leslie, Mr Hilbery feels universities were not intended for women), Katharine is a prime representative of that extraordinarily ill-paid, undervalued, overworked group of women which exists solely to serve others and which Woolf so deplored: 'the daughters of educated men' (Woolf's term in *Three Guineas*). As a member in good

64

standing of such a group, Katharine has two options: to live at home, following the whims of mother or father (in her case, primarily the mother), or to escape by marriage. Neither in itself is satisfactory, as neither speaks to the question of what sort of person Katharine is and what she can become. Cut off from any kind of productive work other than the stultifying Alardyce worship she is obliged to perform with her mother, Katharine lacks entirely the sustaining self-definition she seeks. Taking refuge in clandestine mathematical calculations early in the morning can perhaps make an intolerable situation endurable, but it cannot provide answers for a woman of sensitivity and intelligence who has been forced to do nothing all her life. 'I want to assert myself, and it's difficult, if one hasn't a profession' (54), she argues, more or less correctly diagnosing her plight. And as Mary accurately—if somewhat cruelly—replies for her when Katharine is asked by one of Mary's colleagues if she is looking for a job, 'Marriage is her job at present' (379).

Katharine's involvement in the genteel but none the less fiercely manipulative Hilbery household makes it difficult for her not only to make contact with herself, but also to perceive external reality clearly. Visiting Mary's cluttered suffragette office, for example, where she encounters people actually working for a cause in which they believe, she sees a magical world of exotic presences (92):

> Shut off up there, she compared Mrs. Seal, and Mary Datchet, and Mr. Clacton to enchanted people in a bewitched tower, with the spiders' webs looping across the corners of the room, and all the tools of the necromancer's craft at hand; for so aloof and unreal and apart from the normal world did they seem to her, in the house of innumerable typewriters, murmuring their incantations and concocting their drugs, and flinging their frail spiders' webs over the torrent of life which rushed down the streets outside.

'Life isn't altogether real to her yet' (215), as her cousin Henry points out, suggesting the distance she will have to travel from the emotionally thwarting Hilbery atmosphere. Her path to reality is made more complicated by the debilitating effect her phantasies have upon her ability to deal constructively with her emotions. Investing her life with richness when there is so little actually around her, her excursions into an imaginary world of emotional fulfillment are always marked, upon her return, 'by resignation and a kind of stoical

65

acceptance of the facts' (145). Among others, the 'facts' she is led to embrace by looking around her concern the illusoriness of passion, the doubtful nature of love, and the limited opportunity in life for any real satisfaction. Together they all conspire to make marriage with the first candidate, loveless and passionless though she knows it will be, seem perfectly reasonable. 'In a world where the existence of passion is only a traveller's story brought from the heart of deep forests' (226), there is no reason to insist upon such niceties. Although Katharine harbors aspirations for a different kind of union, she is led to see these impulses as self-indulgent and altogether unrealistic. Seeing how little happiness her mother and aunt had insisted upon in their lives, she is encouraged to renounce such a goal for herself. If it is true, as Mrs Hilbery suggests, that marriage is not the happiest, but rather the most *interesting* life for a woman, then Katharine might as well get on with it. She, too, 'could pretend to like emeralds when she preferred diamonds' (225).

Such at least is the logic that brings her to accept a proposal of marriage from William Rodney. Certainly it would be difficult to find many other reasons for contemplating a life with William. Although endowed with some sweetness and intelligence, there is at the same time something unyieldingly absurd about him. Self-important in a silly way, rigid, and in general a rather flaccid personality, William does not offer very much in the way of masculine appeal. 'Half poet and half old maid' (64), Katharine herself calls him, giving him more credit for his artistic abilities than he deserves. His initial appearance at the discussion club to which he has come to read his paper on the Elizabethan use of metaphor suggests rather accurately the essential man (470):

> The first sight of Mr. Rodney was irresistibly ludicrous. He was very red in the face, whether from the cool November night or nervousness, and every movement, from the way he wrung his hands to the way he jerked his head to right and left . . . bespoke his horrible discomfort under the stare of so many eyes. He was scrupulously well dressed, and a pearl in the centre of his tie seemed to give him a touch of aristocratic opulence. But the rather prominent eyes and the impulsive stammering manner . . . drew no pity, as in the case of a more imposing personage, but a desire to laugh, which was, however, entirely lacking in malice. Mr. Rodney was evidently so painfully conscious of the oddity of

his appearance, and his very redness and the starts to which his body was liable gave such proof of his own discomfort, that there was something endearing in this ridiculous susceptibility, although most people would probably have echoed Denham's private exclamation, 'Fancy marrying a creature like that!'

A man, in short, about whom it is difficult to have strong feelings of any sort. Generous and even thoughtful at times, William nevertheless lacks any of the jagged edges of selfhood that make people interesting. His blandness, the distance he lives from his feelings, render him more of a well-intentioned figure of fun than anything else. His response to Katharine's announcement that she would in fact marry him is typical of his inability to function in personal relationships (146):

> William made no answer. She waited stoically. A moment later he stepped briskly from his dressing-room, and observed that if she wanted to buy more oysters he thought he knew where they could find a fishmonger's shop still open.

Not that Katharine confuses her intention to marry William with any thought of being in love with him. Even when directly beseeched by William she cannot bring herself to proclaim that she cares for him in a serious way. But having been sufficiently disabused about the possibilities of happiness in marriage, she effectively can find no grounds on which to resist.

Her capitulation to William is complicated by the appearance of Ralph Denham, the ambitious, aggressive clerk whose vision of the future includes a seat in the House of Commons, a modest fortune, and perhaps even an insignificant office in a Liberal Government. Ralph has all the fibre and assertiveness William lacks. Enjoying intellectual combativeness, he is candid and quick to offend. His initial hostility to Katharine, based in part on how inappropriate he feels himself to be in her parents' drawing rooms, for example, leads him to excoriate the ease and insulation of her life, accusing her of never doing anything herself or knowing anything first hand. He claims none of the civilities that make life endurable for the Hilberys, concerned with establishing for himself the privileges they were fortunate to inherit. He is perceived by others—not incorrectly—as a 'hard and self-sufficient young man . . . who was consumed by a desire to get on in the world' (130).

Beneath his dogged commitment to work, however, there is

another part of him which only his sister knows, an untamed spirit which has nothing to do with success or worldly achievement, but exists in an entirely different realm. Here self-glorification is not the only motive (129):

> It sometimes seemed to him that this spirit was the most valuable possession he had; he thought that by means of it he could set flowering waste tracts of the earth, cure many ills, or raise up beauty where none now existed; it was, too, a fierce and potent spirit which would devour the dusty books and parchments on the office wall with one lick of its tongue, and leave him in a minute standing in nakedness, if he gave way to it.

To resist its promptings is not easy; as Ralph's sister alone recognizes, it requires enormous effort on his part to continue to function productively in his professional role. Indeed, it is only by the 'constant repetition of a phrase to the effect that he shared the common fate, found it best of all, and wishes for no other' (129) that he manages to subdue his extravagant impulses to the sober interests of his current career. By sheer power of the will he has created for himself at the start of the novel a life 'rigidly divided into the hours of work and those of dreams' (130).

Mary Datchet's life has no such neat divisions. In many ways the opposite of Katharine, she is totally absorbed in her suffrage and reform work, work which includes her dreams for a better world. While Katharine has grown up with all the benefits—as well as the disadvantages—of Hilbery eminence, Mary has enjoyed the freedom of social insignificance. Full of energy and intelligence, she has left her father's country parsonage, obtained a college education, and forged a rich existence in London—all through her own determination. Katharine's malaise of aimlessness is not an affliction she knows. The range of her interests, her active involvement in social causes shape her life in a way Katharine can only envy. Clarity of vision and understanding is everything to Mary; while Katharine is prepared to opt for emeralds rather than diamonds, Mary insists on facing up to the facts, however unhappy they may be. 'I mean to have no pretences in my life' (279), she maintains, even if the cost of such honesty, for example, is to refuse Ralph, whom she desperately loves, when she knows that in spite of his offer of marriage he basically loves Katharine.

These are the four, then, out of whose muddled dealings with each other Woolf constructs the novel. In recognizing that the only truth available to her is the precarious illumination of her own feelings, Katharine comments not only on her plight but on Woolf's novelistic strategy as well (331):

> For the more she looked into the confusion of lives which,
> instead of running parallel, had suddenly intersected each other,
> the more distinctly she seemed to convince herself that there was
> no other path save the one upon which it threw its beams.

The intersection of four lives, plunging people into a welter of perplexing and at times contradictory feelings, initiates the process of self-discovery from which, in one form or another, the characters emerge with some sharpened sense of the limitations and possibilities of their lives. In its tightly structured way, *Night and Day* charts the uncertain growth into maturity the four experience. Although the obstacles to such growth vary in each case, the challenge all the characters face is to see life steadily and whole without the distortions produced by their own fantasies or the intrusive needs of other people. Unsullied perceptions are not easily come by in this novel, as long as the tyrannies of love and loneliness remain as potent as they are. The establishment of a realistic sense of self in the face of all that discourages it is seen as a creative act of major significance. Anticipating the image of the globe in *To the Lighthouse*, which embodies Mrs Ramsay's ability to create moments of order which endure ('a globed, compacted thing over which thought lingers and love plays'), Woolf similarly employs the image here to suggest the goal of completeness which can at least be fleetingly achieved. Having worked through the snares of her own weaknesses to a significant relationship with Ralph, Katharine feels that 'she held in her hands for one brief moment the globe which we spend our lives in trying to shape, round, whole, and entire from the confusion of chaos' (333). And even if mildly threatened by Ralph's desire to see Mary, once again at the end of the novel, Katharine overcomes her own hesitation, 'anxious for him to do what appeared to be necessary if he, too, were to hold his globe for a moment round, whole, and entire' (333).

The globes, of course, are by no means the same. For Katharine, the globe she holds suggests her unwillingness to settle for the convenience of William and the emotionally dishonest life to which her mother resigned herself years before. Refusing to honor the insidious promptings in her that happiness is illusory and any efforts to seek it ultimately foolish, Katharine manages to find the strength to reject the bogus solution William offers. Escape from the Hilbery household is no answer if it promises no larger kinds of fulfillment than those already available (or not available) to her as the dependent daughter without any work to sustain her. Katharine's struggle—which is not as easy as it might sound—is to believe that life can be more than what the Hilberys have experienced, that reality need not be that desiccated thing one returns to after the ecstasy of dreams has subsided. Between her mother's dedication to the past and her own excursions into the pleasures of an imaginary world, her problem is to locate a viable present, one which has within it the possibilities of fruitful relationships and constructive work. In so far as she is finally able to act on the recognition that she need not be condemned to William, Katharine embraces life without any of the self-imposed fetters with which we first see her bound. Although her choice of Ralph is no simple answer to the problem of what she will do in this world (her secret love of mathematics does not in itself provide a career definition), it does clearly represent a healthy step into a reality in which emotional satisfaction is not a fantasy but a genuine option.

If Katharine's equivocations about the inappropriate William suggest her difficulties in perceiving herself and others accurately, Ralph's obsession with Katharine similarly points to his own. Their distorting lenses work differently. While Katharine tries to gloss over William's shortcomings in order to make a life with him appear plausible, Ralph torments himself with the utter perfection of Katharine. For him there is no one so beautiful or good or wise as Katharine. She slips neatly into the division he maintains in his life between dreams and work, and he is careful to preserve the fantasy of her intact (150):

> All down the street and on the door step, and while he mounted the stairs, his dream of Katharine possessed him; on the threshold of the room he had dismissed it, in order to prevent too painful a collision between what he dreamt of her and what she was.

Adulation is an onerous burden to endure, but despite her best efforts Katharine cannot chip away at the image of her Ralph chooses to worship. '"You call that, I suppose, being in love,"' she chides him; '"as a matter of fact it's being in delusion"' (404). The convenience of living with an ideal more than outweighs its disadvantages, even if the disadvantages include among them the anguish of not being able to achieve union with the beloved. It structures and justifies the lover's existence, as the troubadour poets knew. Indeed, Ralph feels much more comfortable with illusion than with opening himself to the complex range of emotions that attach to real relationships. '"You can force me to talk as if this feeling for you were an hallucination,"' he argues, '"but all our feelings are that. The best of them are half illusions"' (316). Despite the pain, or even because of it, Ralph feels at ease with his idealization of Katharine; besides investing his life with an unalterable—if unattainable—source of meaning, it enables him to sustain the split, which is clearly important to him psychologically, between the mundane concerns of his everyday existence and the special realm in which the exalted Katharine dwells.

Ralph's growth is marked by his ability to merge the two parts of his life into one, to accept the splendor of Katharine without the extravagant illusion he has always attached to her. He moves out of his emotional impotence when he realizes that 'The partition so carefully erected between the different sections of his life had been broken down' (514), and he is able to function as a whole man in the real world. No longer requiring the support of his fantasies, Ralph brings Katharine—not the vision of her—into the mainstream of his life, finding at last in reality the emotional satisfaction and meaning which for most of the novel he is content to limit to dreams and delusions. Although they come at it in different ways, both Katharine and Ralph end by fashioning their globes out of the stuff of a living human relationship firmly rooted in the world.

Every bit as real as theirs, Mary's satisfactions are not to be found in personal relationships. This is less the result of conscious preference than of the failure to win the love of Ralph. Her recognition that Ralph adores Katharine is not an easy one for her to accept, as her feelings for him are intense. Furthermore, although at the start of the novel she is certainly absorbed in the work her suffragette society is doing, she has none of the true believer's passion in the cause she finds in her colleagues, Mr Clacton and Mrs Seal. What Mary construes as 'personal happiness' still matters to her in a way that no longer seems to affect—if it ever did—her associates. She sees Mr Clacton and Mrs Seal as somehow 'not in the running' for life, 'shadow people, flitting in and out of the ranks of the living—eccentrics, undeveloped human beings, from whose substances some essential part has been cut away' (279). Such at least is her view immediately following her loss of Ralph. The despair which initially assails her provokes the heretical thought that she would gladly give up all of her political activity and 'be content to remain silent for ever if a share of personal happiness were granted her' (271).

But Mary has a resilience and depth which soon carry her well beyond this limited—if emotionally comprehensible—position. While Ralph and Katharine move from their different but equally constricting fantasies into an acutely felt personal involvement with each other, Mary gradually moves out of the narrow absorption with herself and into a place in the larger scheme of things, a development described as a 'transformation from the particular to the universal' (275). Outside of the private concerns of self Mary discovers 'there remained a hard reality, unimpaired by one's personal adventures, remote as the stars, unquenchable as they are' (275), and it is to this realm that she finally commits herself. Renouncing the merely personal, Mary ends not in a state of bitter resignation but rather with a rich sense of the meaning of her life, a meaning to be found in work instead of love (471):

A stage in her life had been accomplished in the last months which had left its traces for ever upon her bearing. Youth, and the bloom of youth, had receded, leaving the purpose of her face to show itself in the hollower cheeks, the firmer lips, the eyes no longer spontaneously observing at random, but narrowed upon an end which was not near at hand. This woman was now a serviceable human being, mistress of her own destiny, and thus, by some combination of ideas, fit to be adorned with the dignity of silver chains and glowing brooches.

Like Lily Briscoe of *To the Lighthouse*, Mary finds fulfillment without the nourishment of human relationships necessary to Katharine and Mrs Ramsay. Her vision of a society reformed by her energies takes her beyond herself and constitutes her final triumph. Looking at the light in her window at the end of the novel, both Mary and Ralph understand the way in which it expresses 'something impersonal and serene in the spirit of the woman within, working out her plans far into the night—her plans for the good of a world that none of them were ever to know' (536).

Although *Night and Day* cannot be read in any way as auto-biography, it is nevertheless hard not to see in the opposition between Katharine and Mary a kind of imaginative split between a version of the person Woolf imagined herself to be—the pampered, slightly priggish, passive daughter of the middle class, opting for the security of marriage—and a fantasy projection of her exotic antitype, the aggressive, crusading activist, immersed in her toil for the good of society. While Mary appears as unlike Woolf as it is possible to be, she is connected to her (and Katharine) as any counter-image is connected to its opposite. In their different ways, both Mary and Katharine constitute fragments of the complex truth of how Woolf regarded herself at this point in her life.

Of the four major characters in *Night and Day*, William Rodney is without doubt the slightest, teetering always on the edge of the ridiculous. Serving, among other things, as the false choice from which Katharine must disentangle herself, William is treated with markedly less sympathy than the others, occasionally invested with an emotional ineptitude that renders him almost a purely comic figure. His inappropriate responses and lack of any significant self-awareness are distinguishing characteristics which no one else in the novel shares. At the same time that he cannot avoid being foolish, he too is permitted the happiness that Woolf grants freely to everybody in her second book. If Katharine cannot love him, at least Cassandra, her younger and more impressionable cousin, might, and accordingly William shifts his affections to a place where they can be returned. While William and Cassandra comprise a no more likely couple than William and Katharine did, it can be argued that Cassandra's inexperience (she is only twenty-two) and enthusiasm make all things plausible. But plausible or not, what matters is that like Ralph, Katharine, and Mary, William works his way through the false directions (for him a relationship with a woman who does not cherish him) to arrive at a state of personal fulfillment represented in his case by Cassandra. William's benign silliness is not sufficient to prevent him from experiencing the satisfactions that love, when properly understood and shared, is capable of producing in *Night and Day*. Whether it is achieved through love or, as with Mary, dedication to a cause, the novel celebrates the possibility of completeness and self-discovery Woolf conscientiously extends to all.

Shifting her focus from one character to the next as they move, singly and together, through the streets and rooms of London, Woolf tries to create out of their separate (but interconnected) lives a sustaining vision of the whole. The problem with the book is that the characters are not really sufficiently compelling to command our interest on their own, nor are they in any way redeemed by the novel's form. Without the transforming energies of an original form, the characters plod on in their emotional skirmishing in a way Woolf herself came to see as interminable (Bell, *Virginia Woolf*, vol. 2, 42). E. M. Forster's judgment, noted in her diary, that the characters were not particularly lovable and that 'he did not care how they sorted themselves out (*A Writer's Diary*, 20), suggests the difficulty Woolf faced when encasing pedestrian characters in a pedestrian form. But if *Night and Day* is not particularly successful, it at least had the salutary effect of helping Woolf understand the inadequacies, for her artistic needs, of the conventional techniques she employed in her first two novels. In this sense, the tedium of *Night and Day* was instructive, stimulating the prose experiments that in 1922 led to the publication of *Jacob's Room*. Certainly this is one of the lessons Woolf had in mind when she comments, while struggling with *The Years* in 1933: 'I can take liberties with the representational form which I could not dare when I wrote *Night and Day*—a book that taught me much, bad though it may be' (*A Writer's Diary*, 193).

6

Jacob's Room

'There's no doubt in my mind that I have found out how to begin (at 40) to say something in my own voice,' Woolf writes in her diary after completing *Jacob's Room*, the first of her novels to break with Edwardian convention. She did not discover her unique voice accidentally. It evolved, rather, out of the experimental short stories she wrote during—and after—the composition of *Night and Day*. As she suggests herself, *Jacob's Room* is the product of ' "Mark on the Wall," "K.G." [Kew Gardens] and "Unwritten Novel" taking hands and dancing in unity' (*A Writer's Diary*, 23). Although not of great interest in themselves, these three prose pieces are important in understanding how and why *Jacob's Room* came to be written, for they show Woolf working with possibilities of point of view and structure radically different from anything she had attempted in her first two novels. The tentative discoveries made through these short pieces clearly provided Woolf with the impetus to employ the new techniques on a full-length work of fiction.

None of the three is in any simple sense a short story. Lacking any traditional notion of plot, character, or action, they can best be thought of as experiments in different methods of organizing material, experiments that would eventually free her from the restrictions within which she was content to write *The Voyage Out* and *Night and Day*. The earliest of them, 'The Mark on the Wall' (1917), traces the workings of a narrator's mind as it ponders a black circle on the wall several inches above the mantelpiece. Anchored always to the physical point on the wall, the mind wanders through time in a largely associative manner moving easily between personal memories, historical reflections, and philosophical speculation. Although diffuse, the ramblings are neither chaotic nor arbitrary. Patterns of meaning emerge from the reverie, and it is clear that Woolf is not documenting

75

the shower of atoms upon the human brain but writing a kind of meditation on the nature of time, the fact of death, the precariousness—and final futility—of human understanding. Lodged in one single mind, Woolf is free to treat these themes without the harassment of narrative obligations: the flow of the narrator's consciousness releases her from any concern with 'the appalling narrative business of the realist.'

The randomness of the narrator's mind serves to embody Woolf's vision of 'the mystery of life; the inaccuracy of thought! the ignorance of humanity!'[1] (*Haunted House and Other Stories*, 23). The more the mind examines something, the more elusive it becomes. Life is very definitely an odd affair for Woolf, as the narrator's perambulations emphasize again and again. Nothing can be known; nothing can be fixed. Perhaps the most striking image of this sense of life in all of Woolf's work is the narrator's observation that life can be compared to 'being blown through the Tube at fifty miles an hour . . . . That seems to express the rapidity of life, the perpetual waste and repair; all so casual, all so haphazard . . . .' (*Haunted House and Other Stories*, 38).

The stops and starts of the human mind, of course, are a splendid means of rendering the casual, haphazard sense of life, and 'The Mark on the Wall' shows Woolf beginning to realize the formal possibilities of the interior monologue. In addition, the interior life of the individual is, in Woolf's terms, more 'real' than the life the Edwardian realists sought: by placing herself in another's mind, Virginia Woolf takes the first step that leads some fourteen years later to *The Waves*, her most elaborate attempt to embrace the significance of human life through a completely internalized world.

'Kew Gardens' (1919) poses challenges of an entirely different sort from those Woolf sets herself in 'Mark on the Wall.' If in the earlier story a snail (which is what the spot above the mantelpiece turns out to be) is used to unify the workings of a single mind, here a snail is used to organize a spatial scene. Its painstaking efforts to traverse a few inches of flowerbed provide a focus for an otherwise unrelated series of people who pass the snail while they stroll through Kew Gardens on a Sunday afternoon. Simply from a structural point of view, 'Kew Gardens' can be regarded as an exercise in ordering random activity into coherent patterns. For an artist who sees the world, in one aspect at least, as being totally fragmented, such an exercise is useful, for the

[1] All references to Woolf's short stories are to the Harvest edition of *A Haunted House and Other Stories* (Harcourt, Brace & World, 1949).

problem Woolf will face throughout her career is how to present in a satisfying, ordered way a vision of disorder and human isolation. To stay entirely within a single mind, as she does in 'Mark on the Wall,' is one solution, but obviously a severely limited one which does not permit Woolf to deal with very much of the world. In 'Kew Gardens' the narrator's vision, fixed on the microcosmic struggle of the snail, establishes an arbitrary frame that momentarily organizes the haphazard human scene as it moves past the snail.

Although totally different from each other, the four couples—the happily married pair, the two men, the two elderly ladies, and the young lovers—immediately achieve a kind of unity merely by passing across the narrator's stationary field of vision. But the connection among them is more than simply their progression past the snail. Foraging in their individual pasts and wrestling with the inadequacy of language, the isolated couples are seen finally as comprising part of a basic human pattern which causes them to lose their individualities and be absorbed into the very texture of nature itself (*Haunted House and Other Stories*, 35):

> Thus one couple after another with much the same irregular and aimless movement passed the flower-bed and were enveloped in layer after layer of green blue vapour, in which at first their bodies had substance and a dash of colour, but later both substance and colour dissolved in the green-blue atmosphere.

The kind of perception Clarissa Dalloway has— and which Septimus in his insane way shares—that behind the diversity of things there lies an essential oneness, is here articulated for the first time. Establishing order out of random activity, 'Kew Gardens' treats in miniature the kinds of formal problems all of Woolf's larger fictions go on to confront.

Of the three transitional pieces, 'An Unwritten Novel' (1920) is thematically the most directly relevant to *Jacob's Room*. Employing her favorite paradigm of two people in a railway carriage, which she is to use again in *Jacob's Room* as well as in 'Mr. Bennett and Mrs. Brown,' Woolf explores the difficulty of knowing people which forms such a central concern of the novel. Sitting in the carriage across from a nervous lady, the narrator, carefully reading the text of the unknown woman's face and gestures, creates for her a name (Minnie Marsh), a spinsterish past, a set of hopes, fears and frustrations. Like an artist, the narrator fabricates a character out of her own imagination, a character

77

whose fictional reality we finally come to accept. By the time she leaves the train she has indeed become Minnie Marsh, the lonely woman with the unloving sister-in-law, the guilt for having been responsible for the death of her baby brother, her obsession with punctuality. And when the fiction is shattered by the young man who comes to greet 'Minnie' when she steps off the train, we share the narrator's shock at the destruction of her carefully constructed universe: 'Well, my world's done for! What do I stand on? What do I know? That's not Minnie. There never was Moggridge. Who am I? Life's bare as a bone' (*Haunted House and Other Stories*, 21). The fictions that sustain us, the story makes clear, are not very sustaining, but they are all that we have. For Woolf, the narrator's creation of Minnie is the way we create the world—and the people—around us. Unable to grasp them directly, we gather together the various shreds of evidence and attempt to generalize from those. Certainly it is the method by which we 'know' Jacob Flanders.

As she says in her diary, *Jacob's Room* marked a necessary step, for Woolf, 'in working free' (*A Writer's Diary*, 52). With the experimental discoveries of the short stories fresh in her mind, Woolf was ready to attempt a whole novel in the new manner, leaving behind her the secure conventions that went into *Night and Day*. Although her third novel, *Jacob's Room* is in a sense Woolf's first, with all the many defects of most first novels.

There is nothing particularly startling (there never is in Woolf) about the subject of the novel: *Jacob's Room* is about Jacob Flanders, vaguely modeled after Virginia's brother, Thoby, whose life we follow from infancy through his years at Cambridge, his abortive love affairs, his travel in Greece, his work, and finally to his death in the First World War. But of course the story, such as it is, does not absorb Woolf's energies any more than it does ours. The interest of the novel lies in the way Woolf presents the story of Jacob, in her efforts to find a form that would adequately express her vision of reality without falling prey to the deadness and waste of the realist method. Her attempt, it should be admitted at the outset, is not entirely successful, but if *Jacob's Room* fails as a novel, it nevertheless has the virtue of failing in ways that point neatly to the success of her later work.

Although strictly chronological, moving from childhood to death, the chronology of *Jacob's Room* has nothing to do with the linear chronology, for example, of *The Old Wives' Tale*. For rather than giving us a story moving smoothly and continuously through time,

Woolf presents us with a series of discrete moments, one following another, with little concern for the connective tissue between them. The chapters, though proceeding in a linear way to record Jacob's development, exist primarily as separate entities, each focusing on specific moments in Jacob's life or in the life of his friends. Remove a chapter and you would simply widen the gap between the previous moments and the ones to come; you would not in any way impair the coherence of the narrative. And what is true of the succession of the chapters is true also of the organization within the chapters themselves. Transitions are generally non-existent as the narrator jumps from character to character and from incident to incident without hesitation or apology. The basic unit of organization is the isolated moment, and each chapter consists of a number of these, dealing with Jacob, or his acquaintances, or even passing strangers who make one brief appearance and then leave the novel entirely. Time moves forward in this novel, but in an extremely discontinuous, choppy manner.

The jaggedness of the narrative is deliberate, not a thwarted effort to write a smoothly flowing lyric novel. It represents Woolf's first attempt at creating an expressive form which would in itself reflect the nature of life as she understood it. The form of *Jacob's Room* is clearly designed to parallel the 'form' of living: a fragmented, discontinuous world demands a fragmented, discontinuous shape. A world in which people experience time as a succession of distinct moments strung together must be embodied, aesthetically, in a fictional world similarly constructed. Such a notion of form, of course, is painfully rudimentary; just how rudimentary can be seen by considering the kinds of rich, complex forms Woolf goes on to evolve in *The Waves* and *Between the Acts* to deal with essentially the same kind of world *Jacob's Room* is treating. Although managing for the most part to avoid the realist dead end Woolf abhorred, *Jacob's Room* nevertheless fails to achieve an aesthetically satisfying shape. Discontinuity is not in itself a particularly useful structural principle for a novel, and the different techniques Woolf borrows from her experimental short pieces are not able to provide an extended fiction with the compelling form necessary to her successful work.

But if the form of the novel is ultimately self-limiting, it does at least serve as a consistent vehicle for the themes. A fragmented world of disparate souls cut off from one another is obviously a place of loneliness, of uncertainty, a place where it is difficult to know oneself or anybody else; and these are exactly the concerns which animate the novel. All converge in the character of Jacob, the second of Betty Flanders's three sons. For those who take Woolf's 'shower of atoms' metaphor in 'Modern Fiction' as a literal description of her own fictional technique, reading *Jacob's Room* must constitute an enormous shock: one can think of no character more tenaciously portrayed from the outside than Jacob is. We learn about Jacob from every conceivable source—from letters he writes, the books he reads, the Greece he loves, from fragments of phone conversations overheard by a dim-witted servant, from the impressions of a fifty-year-old woman who sits across from him in a train carriage going to Cambridge, from the mother who adores him, the women who disappoint him, the friends who miss him. From every conceivable source, that is, except his own mind, which the narrator is at pains not to violate. 'Whether we know what was in his mind is another question' (93), the narrator cautions after describing the look on Jacob's face at a point of emotional crisis in his life. It is a question the narrator deliberately leaves unanswered, for in the world of *Jacob's Room* there is no way we can gain access to the mind of another. Jacob is seen exclusively from the outside, from the way he impresses himself on others, because this is precisely the way people are known in this life. We are all in the position of the narrator in 'An Unwritten Novel', creating Minnie Marsh. Our inability to know others—a basic assumption about human existence which remains constant during Woolf's artistic career—is insisted upon throughout *Jacob's Room*; her aims in the novel are perhaps best summed up by this twice-repeated phrase, 'It is no use trying to sum people up. One must follow hints, not exactly what is said, nor yet entirely what is done' (29, 153). We grope after Jacob from the evidence available about him because such, for Woolf, 'is the manner of our seeing. Such the conditions of our love' (71). Jacob, of course, finally eludes our search—as all characters in Woolf's world must. There is a kind of epistemological despair in Woolf's fiction which is strongly felt here: 'Life is but a procession of shadows' (70)—we can really know nothing.

Although Jacob remains always the subject of the novel, we might say that the book is less about Jacob, than the difficulties, or perhaps better the manner, of knowing him. It is not in any conventional sense a character 'study' of Jacob, and Woolf is completely justified when she expresses indignation, in her diary, over those (like Arnold Bennett) who complain of her inability to create characters who survive. Jacob certainly does not have the fictional reality of a Becky Sharp or a Heathcliff or a Stephen Daedalus, and that is precisely what Woolf intends. The novel, after all, is entitled *Jacob's Room, not Jacob Flanders*. It is not Jacob so much as the process of putting him together which is important, and it becomes clear as we follow Jacob through the different rooms he inhabits—the rooms of London, of Cambridge, of Greece—that our method of experiencing Jacob is intended to serve as a kind of model for our method of experiencing the world. For it is finally the universe at large which is Jacob's room, and we are left as impotent before its mysteries as Mrs Flanders is when, in the last lines of the novel, she numbly holds up a pair of Jacob's old shoes and asks Bonamy, one of his close friends, what she should do with them.

Jacob's shadowy presence, then, forms the appropriate center of a novel that deals with the difficulty of formulating coherent impressions of people or of life. We know the world the same way we know Jacob: through indirections, and darkly. But if in his elusiveness Jacob suggests the elusiveness of life itself, in his mundane, corporeal body he provides Woolf with a structural center to help organize the randomness of the novel. He acts, in a sense, like the mark on the wall, serving as a convenient focal point around which Woolf can build the life of the novel. Woolf is as explicit about this as she is about almost everything else she does in *Jacob's Room* (94):

> The march that the mind keeps beneath the windows of others is queer enough. Now distracted by brown panelling; now by a fern in a pot; here improvising a few phrases to dance with the barrel-organ; again snatching a detached gaiety from a drunken man; then altogether absorbed by words the poor shout across the street at each other (so outright, so lusty)—yet all the while having for centre, for magnet, a young man alone in his room.

Functioning both as an organizational device as well as a character whom we only know imperfectly, Jacob is not a memorable literary creation—nor was he meant to be. Jacob's insubstantiality is part of the book's meaning; to invest him with the weight of a Mr Ramsay would be to muddle the novel entirely. E. M. Forster's criticism that Woolf created characters who could not be remembered afterwards on their own account—'What wraiths, apart from their context, are the wind-sextet from *The Waves*, of Jacob away from *Jacob's Room*! They speak no more to us or to one another as soon as the page is turned'.[1]

---

[1] E. M. Forster, *Two Cheers for Democracy* (Harcourt Brace, 1951).

250)—actually speaks to the very purpose behind those characters, particularly Jacob. For he satisfies perfectly the demands Woolf makes on him, even if these demands preclude his attaining an important place in our literary imagination.

The world Jacob moves through is, as I have suggested, the archetypal world of all of Woolf's fiction: random, fragmented, lonely. A sign of the immaturity of her technique in *Jacob's Room* is the rather heavy-handed way she insists on documenting these facts of existence. Woolf's uncertainty here produces a novel filled with its own justification and explanation. All too often the novel is transparently schematic, teeming with incidents which self-consciously call attention to their importance to Woolf's method and vision. One such moment concerns Mrs Norman's perception of Jacob in the train carriage to Cambridge. The impulse behind the scene, of course, comes straight out of 'An Unwritten Novel,' with Mrs Norman playing the role of the unnamed observer of the story and Jacob the creature we know only as Minnie Marsh. It is a veritable *locus classicus* of human perception according to Woolf, and the narrator makes sure we understand its significance: 'Nobody sees any one as he is, let alone an elderly lady sitting opposite a strange young man in a railway carriage. They see a whole—they see all sorts of things—they see themselves . . . .' (28). Having contributed her partial perceptions to our sense of Jacob—his loose socks, his shabby tie, his firmness and indifference—Mrs Norman promptly forgets him as soon as they arrive in Cambridge, so that Jacob's image 'was completely lost in her mind, as the crooked pin dropped by a child into the wishing-well twirls in the water and disappears for ever' (29). And just as Jacob disappears from Mrs Norman's life, so Mrs Norman disappears from the novel, called into being for one brief scene to testify how transient our encounters are with people and how little we know of them.

Mrs Norman is not the only character who makes a single appearance in the novel to demonstrate some axiom of perception or human behavior basic to Woolf's universe. The novel is filled with isolated vignettes of people who, though utterly superfluous to the unfolding of Jacob's life, illustrate some essential truth either about Jacob's room or Jacob himself. The looseness of the novel's structure, of course, permits an endless variety of people and incidents to pop up whenever and wherever the narrator pleases. Nothing can be out of order in a novel where there is no strict order: characters are free to appear and disappear with impunity. Thus we find ourselves reading for a few pages about Miss Marchmont, who prowls through books in the British Museum looking for something she cannot even define for herself; or hearing Rose Shaw, after telling the story of poor Helen Aitken spurned by a man named Jimmy, conclude that 'life is damnable, life is wicked' (96); or following the sad relationship of Cruttendon and Jinny which ends with the two of them apart, he painting orchards in solitude, she living in Italian pensions and cherishing in a small box some pebbles picked from the road. Weaving numerous isolated moments like these into the text, Woolf builds the life of the novel out of material which turns Jacob's personal conviction—'it was not that he himself happened to be lonely, but that all people are' (140)—into a general truth.

The human implications of the jerky narrative structure, then are appropriately, even obsessively embodied by the pervasive nature of these motifs of isolation and despair. Both form and themes suggest a world which does not hold together, a world which cannot finally be understood. As a narrative *Jacob's Room* is really more sequential than causal: incidents don't grow out of other incidents so much as they simply follow them. Although Woolf's commitment to this kind of randomness is in part her deliberate rebellion against the narrative tyrannies of the past, it is also part of a new vision demanding a new form to express it. The most memorable example of contingent behavior in the novel occurs when Mrs Flanders is trying to decide what university Jacob should attend. Captain Barfoot, one of Betty Flanders's admirers, has heard from Mr Polegate that he can only advise that Jacob be sent to one of the universities. Betty remembers that Mr Floyd 'was at Cambridge. . . no, at Oxford. . . well, at one or the other' (27), and then engages in a series of disjointed reflections concerning Archer's report, the start of the cricket season, and the possibility that Captain Barfoot might stand for the Council. The scene—and the chapter—ends with the following statement: 'Jacob Flanders, therefore, went up to Cambridge in October 1906' (27). The marvelously incongruous 'therefore,' suggesting logic and causality where there are none, embodies precisely the kind of arbitrariness that the novel as a whole illustrates. The ironically appropriate use of the word makes clear how far Woolf had traveled not only from the dread Edwardian materialists, but also from her own first two novels, where such deliberate short-circuiting of conventional cause and effect could not possibly exist.

In a world which does not offer any simple connections, human understanding can only be achieved with great diligence. Order, if it is to exist at all, must be man-made, and the need to create one's own order, which the very form of the novel makes imperative, is insisted upon throughout *Jacob's Room*. It implicitly accounts for the stress in the novel on actual moments of physical perception, with characters invariably scrutinizing not just Jacob but each other as well, in an effort to understand something about the world outside of them. *Jacob's Room* is filled with people struggling to formulate coherent perceptions to sustain them through the welter of impressions and experiences constantly assailing them. The wide variety of human testimony we have concerning Jacob's appearance and behavior not only suggests the difficulty of knowing him but also the urgency of such a task.

The human effort involved in bridging the chasms between people is explicitly emphasized by Woolf when she praises letters for courageously attempting to overcome human isolation (91):

> Venerable are letters, infinitely brave, forlorn, and lost.
> Life would split asunder without them. 'Come to tea, come to dinner, what's the truth of the story? have you heard the news? life in the capital is gay; the Russian dancers . . . .' These are our stays and props. These lace our days together and make of life a perfect globe.

Letter writing, for all that it distorts and conceals (Jacob's letters to his mother, for example, are models of omissions), nevertheless constitutes a life-giving instinct to thwart the isolation that Woolf sees inevitably enveloping us. However fragile and ephemeral, letters symbolize the human effort to connect: 'Masters of language, poets of long ages, have turned from the sheet that endures to the sheet that perishes . . . and addressed themselves to the task of reaching, touching, penetrating the individual heart. Were it possible!' (92).

It is, of course, not possible; words are finally too stale and intractable to penetrate the human heart. But people go on writing letters for essentially the same reason they go on reading books: to try to carve out for themselves, from the tumult around them, some coherent vision of the world. Transmuting disorder into ordered, aesthetically satisfying patterns, the completed work of art represents for Woolf the supreme human effort of achieving coherence. It is surely this coherent vision of things that Woolf finds people seeking in books (96):

Shawled women carry babies with purple eyelids; boys stand at
street corners; girls look across the road—rude illustrations,
pictures in a book whose pages we turn over and over as if we
should at last find what we look for. Every face, every shop,
bedroom window, public house, and dark square is a picture
feverishly turned—in search of what? It is the same with books.
What do we seek through millions of pages? Still hopefully
turning the pages—oh, here is Jacob's room.

Significantly, the two activities with which the novel begins are
letter writing and artistic creation. The opening words of the novel
come from the letter Betty Flanders is writing to Captain Barfoot; and
at the very moment she is putting these words down on paper, Betty is
actually comprising—unbeknownst to her—part of the landscape that
the painter Charles Steele is trying to capture on canvas. In their
loneliness—Betty's letters are tear-stained; Charles, 'an unknown man
exhibiting obscurely' (6), is gratified if his landladies admire his paintings—and in their efforts to create some kind of order and connection
for themselves, Betty through the mail and Charles on his canvas, the
two provide an appropriate opening for the novel. Waging a battle
against despair and isolation, Charles and Betty introduce not only
Jacob's Room but in fact all of Woolf's fiction, for it is essentially this
battle that is being fought by every one of her characters, from Mrs
Dalloway to Miss La Trobe.

It is a battle that can never finally be won. In Woolf's novels, sorrow
is everywhere (47):

Yes, the chimneys and the coast-guard stations and the little bays
with the waves breaking unseen by any one make one remember
the overpowering sorrow. And what can this sorrow be? It is
brewed by the earth itself. It comes from the house on the coast.
We start transparent, and then the cloud thickens. All history
backs our pane of glass. To escape is vain.

And the final disorder of death is never far from the surface of
Woolf's fictional world, as it was clearly never far from her own mind.
'Such confusion everywhere!' (176) exclaims Mrs Flanders when she
enters Jacob's room after his death, an exclamation which suggests not
only the chaos of the room but of the survivors as well. Empty-
hearted and bewildered, Bonamy and Mrs Flanders poignantly
embody the vulnerability of the living to the fact of senseless death. In

the face of death, human aspirations for order and meaning are as futile as Bonamy's final cry of 'Jacob! Jacob!' (176). Beginning the novel by mentioning the death of Betty's husband, and ending it with the death of her son, Woolf makes clear just how precarious the whole human enterprise is. Although sudden, Jacob's death is not entirely unexpected. The sheep's skull that fascinated him as a child and the pistol shots that echo through the novel all hint that like Yeats's Robert Gregory, another young man of promise killed in the war, Jacob, too will never live 'to comb grey hair.'

'The strange thing about life,' Woolf writes in *Jacob's Room*, 'is that though the nature of it must have been apparent to every one for hundreds of years, no one has left any adequate account of it' (94). In its experimental form, *Jacob's Room* itself is the first of Woolf's novels to attempt to leave such an account. The ambitiousness of the undertaking, however, is not matched by the requisite artistic maturity: the form of the novel as a whole is not aesthetically satisfying, and Woolf's technique within the novel is, at best, uneven. The problem of narrative focus in this new kind of fiction, for example, remains unsolved, the narration moving awkwardly between the impersonal third-person and intrusive first-person comments belaboring some point of doctrine or even method. All too frequently we are explicitly told what we are watching or what life does (or does not) mean. But however flawed, *Jacob's Room* gave Woolf at once a voice and the confidence that she was embarking in the right direction. What exactly that direction was, of course, she had no way of knowing, although it was clear to her as early as 1924 that *Mrs. Dalloway*, the book she was currently working on, 'proves that I can only write along those lines [of *Jacob's Room*], and shall never desert them, but explore further and further and shall, heaven be praised, never bore myself an instant' (*A Writer's Diary*, 63). Not only *Mrs. Dalloway*, in fact, but all of Virginia Woolf's subsequent fiction testifies to the accuracy of this insight.

7

Mrs. Dalloway

Mrs. Dalloway is Virginia Woolf's most personal book. Not by any means her most autobiographical—that designation clearly belongs to *To the Lighthouse*, with its evocation of Virginia's parents and their summers at St Ives—but her most personal in its articulation of feelings excruciatingly close to her heart. No novel of Woolf's is as saturated with the pain and exultation of living, the obsession with death, the terror of loneliness as is *Mrs. Dalloway*. The sparrows that Leonard Woolf reports sang in Greek to Virginia during her spells of illness sing here to Septimus as well, and the novel as a whole reflects, more poignantly perhaps than does her other work, that anguished sensibility she movingly reveals to us in the pages of her diary. It has a power and richness of feeling absent in *Jacob's Room*.

But it is form as much as feeling which distinguishes *Mrs. Dalloway* from *Jacob's Room*. Always among the most perceptive of her own critics, Woolf herself seemed to feel the formal deficiencies of *Jacob's Room*. 'I expect I could have screwed *Jacob* up tighter, if I had foreseen,' she mentions in her diary (*A Writer's Diary*, 54); and in anticipating what the reviewers would say about it—'a disconnected rhapsody' (46)—she points to what are the very real structural problems in the novel. *Mrs. Dalloway*, published three years after *Jacob's Room*, has none of these problems. It is clearly the product of an artist who has not only discovered her own voice, but has mastered the art of using it. Woolf's new maturity turns the disconnected rhapsody of *Jacob's Room* into the extravagantly organized symphony of *Mrs. Dalloway*. Far more 'tightly screwed up' than *Jacob*, *Mrs. Dalloway* is completely free from the uncertainties, heavy-handedness, and occasional flabbiness that marred her first experimental effort. The single day in June on which Clarissa gives her party serves brilliantly as Woolf's vehicle for rendering the way life is experienced, not merely by Clarissa, Septimus, and Peter, but by everybody.

Unlike *Jacob's Room*, with its loose structure and arbitrary narrative shifts, the day on which Septimus commits suicide and Clarissa gives her party is one of the most minutely connected in all of fiction. Working primarily (although not exclusively) from within the minds of her characters, Woolf creates a tightly unified texture in which almost every change of focus from one character to another occurs through what we might call specific spatial and psychological, or external and internal, hinges. Woolf moves us from consciousness to consciousness, that is, by creating particular moments of immediate physical contact between people on the streets of London, or by having characters intersect in the thinking of one another. Shifting us deftly from one mind to the next, Woolf has written a novel literally steeped in connections and interconnections of all sorts. Instances abound: Peter Walsh, for example, having just finished painfully re-experiencing the breakup of his relationship with Clarissa, watches a little girl running along and stumbling into a lady's legs. The lady is Lucrezia, and as she dusts the child off she begins her meditation on the difficulties of her relationship with Septimus. And some pages later the baton is handed back to Peter as he passes Septimus and Rezia having their dreadful argument: 'And that is being young, Peter Walsh thought as he passed them,' (79) returning to thoughts of his own emotional life.

In addition to the specific contact in space between two characters, Woolf establishes another kind of connection at the beginning of the novel when she charts the responses of a group of disparate characters to a central stimulus occurring in public view. The mysterious limousine driving through central London and the sky-writing plane advertising toffee both serve as the object of speculation by a variety of otherwise unrelated people. Emily Coates, Sarah Bletchley, Mr Bowley, Mrs Dempster, Mr Bentley, Lucrezia, and others who have nothing in common are temporarily brought together by the curiosity they share as to what the plane is spelling as it flies over them at that moment.

The transitions that Woolf devises on the streets of London also take place through the thought processes of the different characters. A subject dwelt on by one person constitutes the bridge into the next person's thoughts. Thus we move easily from Clarissa's meditation on her marriage to Peter's feelings on that same relationship, or simply from Clarissa's response to Peter to the working of Peter's own mind. The absence of any physical proximity is no obstacle to the artfully fashioned narrative connections Woolf gives us in this novel.

Perhaps the most important kind of connection *Mrs. Dalloway* insists upon is that between the present and the past. The actions and thoughts of the people wandering through London on a sunny day in June are continually informed and nourished by the pressures of the past. *Mrs. Dalloway* makes clear, in fact, that an individual's experience of the 'present moment' is always saturated with the residue of the past. Although there obviously are significant events which take place during it—such as Septimus's suicide, for example—the single day in June primarily serves as a surface on which the past crystallizes. Clarissa's memory of the kiss Sally Seaton bestowed on her when they were young has far more immediacy than anything Clarissa actually does herself during the day. Such, for Woolf, is the nature of reality, and such is precisely the sense of living that the novel seeks to express.

The realization that experiencing the present continually involves immersion in the past sets *Mrs. Dalloway* radically apart from *Jacob's Room*. Jacob's experience of life is almost totally in the present; the temporal movement of the novel through a span of years occurs in what we can call a strictly 'horizontal' way. The few hours of *Mrs. Dalloway*, on the other hand, are enriched with pervasive 'vertical' descents into the past. This coalescing of past and present was one of the formal achievements in *Mrs. Dalloway* which most pleased Woolf (*A Writer's Diary*, 60):

> I should say a good deal about *The Hours* [preliminary title for *Mrs. Dalloway*] and my discovery; how I dig out beautiful caves behind my characters: I think that gives exactly what I want; humanity, humor, depth. The idea is that the caves shall connect and each comes to daylight at the present moment.

The fluid nature of consciousness Woolf creates through the network of these caves, in which temporal boundaries and definitions lose their distinctiveness, forms a counterpoint to the inexorable tolling of Big Ben. Impassively sounding out the hour, Big Ben punctuates the reveries, the pain, the pleasures with his dreary announcement that time is passing. Woolf's explorations in the timelessness of the caves is thus effectively juxtaposed to the steady progression of time on the surface, and the two effectively express that

89

dual sense of life—that it is at once eternal and ephemeral—which is so characteristic of Woolf's novels.

From its very inception the formal possibilities of *Mrs. Dalloway* —the densely organized texture of a single day with its minutely controlled transitions, its careful fusion of past and present—fascinated Woolf. 'The design is so queer and so masterful,' she writes in her diary. 'I'm always having to wrench my substance to fit it. The design is certainly original and interests me hugely' (*A Writer's Diary*, 58). Compressing experience into a shape which not only reveals Woolf's vision of reality, but is itself aesthetically and intellectually satisfying, the form of *Mrs. Dalloway* succeeds in a way the form of *Jacob's Room* does not.

The 'design' of a novel (to use Woolf's terms), of course, must finally be judged by its relation to the 'substance,' and it is here—in the interplay between design and substance—that the richness of *Mrs. Dalloway*'s construction can best be understood. The primary impact of the design is ironic, for the web of interactions occurring both physically—in the streets of London—and mentally—in the memories and associations of the characters—provides the formal unity of a novel depicting a world in which people are irrevocably cut off from themselves as well as from one another. Massive structural connections, that is, ironically emphasize the profound sense of disconnectedness experienced by almost everyone in the novel. Thwarted feelings, an inability to express what one does feel, and an inability to act decisively on whatever feelings can be expressed are the emotional realities of the world. The neat transitions make the general incomprehension all the more powerful. Hearing the ambulance and reflecting on the efficiency and communal spirit which it symbolizes, Peter remains unaware that inside it lies Septimus's broken body, a victim of that very civilization he is celebrating. The sense of human isolation, rendered in *Jacob's Room* through a discontinuous narrative form is far more effectively embodied in *Mrs. Dalloway*, a novel firmly and smoothly held together through a series of painstakingly wrought transitions.

But if the intricately connected design ironically underlines the devastating solitude in Virginia Woolf's world, at the same time it is faithful to that other side of Woolf's vision which sees an overriding, almost mystical unity existing not only between human beings, but between human beings and the non-human world. In Woolf's novels people are at once alone and together, 'scraps, orts and fragments,' yet part of a greater harmony. Cut off from one another in any kind of realistic social way, they are yet intangibly linked not only to others but to the universe around them.

The most striking example of this kind of isolated soul is Septimus Smith, the young war veteran who throws himself out of a window shortly before Clarissa gives her party. Spiritually and emotionally eviscerated by the horror of war, Septimus returns to civilian life no longer able to feel. The cost of physical survival, for Septimus, has been severe; obsessed with self-loathing for having escaped while others died, he emerges from the war mad, a product of the universal lunacy around him. His madness insulates him from all human relationships, even that with his wife, Lucrezia, whom he married without any emotional commitment, following his release from the army. Sitting next to Lucrezia on a bench or walking with her through London, Septimus shares a certain physical contact with her, but nothing else. There is no point talking to others, because no one else could possibly grasp the full extent of his guilt, the truth of the world that he has divined—'that human beings have neither kindness, nor faith, nor charity beyond what serves to increase the pleasure of the moment' (75)—or the supreme secret which he alone of all men knows: 'first, that trees are alive; next, there is no crime; next love, universal love.'

Septimus's madness is the madness of an innocence brutally violated by a civilization which cannot understand it, a civilization which sends its young men off to war to be destroyed. His psychopathology—though genuine—is nevertheless infinitely finer than the health possessed by Dr Holmes and Dr Bradshaw, those two apostles of exercise and proportion who hound him to his death. However aberrant his behavior, he retains a kind of inner purity which makes society and its official guardians of mental and moral stability, like Holmes and Bradshaw, seem far more deranged than he. A victim, in large part, of their inadequacies, he remains inescapably locked within himself: 'That was it: to be alone for ever. That was the doom pronounced in Milan when he came into the room and saw them cutting out buckram shapes with their scissors; to be alone for ever' (160).

But although Septimus is indeed doomed to be alone forever, he nevertheless intuits in his madness the degree to which he is part of the larger process around him. His sense that 'trees were alive. And the leaves being connected by millions of fibres with his own body, there on the seat, fanned it up and down; when the branch stretched, he, too made that statement' (26), and his experience of lying 'high, on the back of the world. The earth thrilled beneath him. Red flowers grew through his flesh; their stiff leaves rustled by his head,' (76) are admittedly pathological versions of an insight which is central to the novel and to the rest of Woolf's fiction as well. Fragmented though individuals may be in themselves, they are at the same time seen as belonging to a larger pattern in which their disparate, isolated selves are part of a transcendent unity. From *Mrs. Dalloway* on, all of Woolf's novels are written with this double focus. While solitude remains the dominant note of interpersonal relationships, the novels also suggest the existence of an impersonal realm in which everything is connected and which provides, to use Yeats's phrase, the 'counter-truth' of her fictional world.

Septimus's example, of course, is extreme, but there is a more reliable witness who shares the same kind of understanding. Superficially, no one could possibly be more removed from Septimus than Clarissa Dalloway is. A rich, cossetted member of the upper class, married to a respectable—and Conservative—member of the House of Commons, a giver of parties which the prime minister attends, Clarissa stands at the opposite end of the social and economic scale from Septimus. And yet in her more moderate way, Clarissa articulates almost precisely that same sense of identification with the universe which we hear from Septimus (11–12):

> somehow in the streets of London, on the ebb and flow of
> things, here there, she survived, Peter, survived, lived in each
> other, she being part, she was positive, of the trees at home; of
> the house there . . . part of a people she had never met; being laid
> out like a mist between the people she knew best, who lifted her
> on their branches as she had seen the trees lift the mist, but it
> spread ever so far, her life, herself.

Septimus's insistence that there is no death parallels Clarissa's theory that 'since our apparitions, the part of us which appears, are so momentary, compared with the other, the unseen part of us, which spreads wide, the unseen might survive, be recovered somehow attached to this person or that, or even haunting certain places, after death' (168). Both the poor, insane Septimus and the fashionable, desirable Clarissa share that vision of oneness which is clearly Woolf's own. But it is not simply the substantive nature of the vision which is important so much as the fact that two people as apparently different as Septimus and Clarissa should possess it. The vision is made flesh in the novel through the relationship of Clarissa and Septimus, who not only comprehend, as we have seen, the degree to which they are part of other people but actually constitute, symbolically at least, one common identity. Although they never meet and do not know each other, Clarissa and Septimus are doubles, linked to each other throughout the novel in a number of ways. A similar physical appearance, shared attitudes and psychological responses, and Clarissa's deep, intuitive understanding of the meaning of Septimus's suicide make clear the extent to which the two selves are one.

The physical resemblance of 'beak-nosed' (17) Septimus and Clarissa, with her 'ridiculous little face, beaked like a bird's' (13), of course, is the most rudimentary kind of identification. Far more important are the lines from *Cymbeline*—'Fear no more the heat o' the sun/Nor the furious winter's rages'—which pass through the consciousness of both Septimus and Clarissa at various points in the novel. Foreshadowing the suicide to which Septimus must finally resort to escape his torment, the lines also suggest the attraction such an expedient holds for Clarissa herself. Clarissa's proper societal self never entirely obscures the deep temptations to self-destruction which she finds every bit as compelling as Septimus does. Her relationship with Richard, however sterile in some ways, provides her with the kinds of protection that Septimus cannot get from his bewildered Lucrezia: 'Even now, quite often if Richard had not been there reading *The Times* . . . she must have perished. She had escaped. But that young man had killed himself' (203). Loving life as they both do, Septimus and Clarissa also understand the security and relief offered by extinction. Death is at once a refuge from the terror of loneliness as well as a protest against the oppression of people like Holmes and Bradshaw who make living intolerable. For Septimus realizes even at the end that life is good; it is only people who ruin it. He kills himself reluctantly, unwilling to leave life, yet seeing no other way to avoid 'Human nature . . . the repulsive brute with the blood-red nostrils' (102) who decrees that he must rest, sip milk, take an interest in things outside of himself. It is finally not 'the heat o' the sun' he must escape: 'He did not want to die. Life was good. The sun hot. Only human beings?' (164)

Clarissa—who never learns Septimus's name—hears about his death when the Bradshaws come late to her party. Momentarily resenting

93

the intrusion of death into one of her life-affirming gatherings, Clarissa is quick to empathize with Septimus, feeling her own body plummet to the ground as his did, sensing that same obscure evil lurking in Bradshaw. Immersed in Septimus's self, Clarissa completes the meaning of his act for us (202):

> Death was defiance. Death was an attempt to communicate,
> people feeling the impossibility of reaching the centre which,
> mystically, evaded them . . . . There was an embrace in death.

Performing flawlessly as 'the perfect hostess'—that term of censure applied to her by Peter Walsh—Clarissa nevertheless manages in the midst of the trivial conversation eddying around her to experience the anguish of an unknown young suicide in a manner which would astonish, if they knew, the unsuspecting guests. Clarissa has depths unimagined by those whom she politely charms, and if Peter's diagnosis of her as an incorrigible social being is correct, it is also true, though Peter can never know it, that she 'felt somehow very much like him—the young man who had killed himself' (204).

As Woolf indicates in the preface to the 1929 American edition, *Mrs. Dalloway* was originally to end with Clarissa's suicide; Septimus, who was not part of her early thinking about the novel, grew out of the initial conception of Clarissa, taking from her many of her traits, including her decision to kill herself. Septimus can be thought of as a death-obsessed version of Clarissa in whom the yearning for annihilation triumphs over a very real commitment to life. Insulated by class and connections from the full weight of Septimus's despair, Clarissa succeeds in keeping her psychic balance precariously tipped in favor of living. Ostensibly sane, she is spared the violation of her soul that Septimus is forced to endure at the hands of Holmes and Bradshaw. Nevertheless she instinctively realizes the horror of men like Bradshaw (she doesn't seem to know Holmes), and her severe distrust of them—'they make life intolerable' (203)—connects her not only to Septimus but to Woolf as well, for whom such men are the embodiment of evil. Woolf's animus towards Bradshaw—felt in every sentence she writes about him—is not gratuitous: its roots lie in Woolf's own encounters with physicians during the intermittent attacks of illness she suffered throughout her life. Leonard Woolf's description of the pathetically inadequate treatment extended to his wife correspond perfectly with Bradshaw's advice to Septimus: hobbies, rest, milk, not thinking too much about the self. The quality of Septimus's madness and his relationship with those who seek to remedy it, like Holmes and Bradshaw, are clearly imaginative recreations of experiences in which Woolf was herself intimately involved.

But it is not the therapeutic failures of Bradshaw that enrage Woolf so much as his insidious lust for power over other human beings. Offering help but seeking only to control, Bradshaw turns his patients into victims, crushing them with his will into accepting his singular version of health and proportion. A callous manipulator of other men's souls, Sir William represents all that Woolf in particular and Bloomsbury in general detested. The portrait of Bradshaw, in fact, provides by contrast a splendid summary of what Bloomsbury was about. For it is clear that Woolf is excoriating in Sir William not simply a grossly insensitive nerve specialist but a whole world view, a view which abhors diversity and can only be content with subduing people to its own restricted premises.

The Proportion that Bradshaw imposes on his victims has an even less pleasant sister who is endlessly engaged, Woolf tells us (111),

> in the heat and sands of India, the mud and swamp of Africa, the purlieus of London . . . in dashing down shrines, smashing idols, and setting up in their own place her own stern countenance. Conversion is her name and she feasts on the wills of the weakly, loving to impress, to impose, adoring her own features stamped on the face of the populace.

Whether in the service of a moral, political, or religious cause, the will to convert was anathema to Bloomsbury, involving as it does the oppression of the individual. Sir William stands as the arch bully; it is his mentality which lies behind wars, quests for empires, and other forms of trespass upon the sovereignty of individuals or entire nations. *Mrs. Dalloway* is Woolf's strongest protest against the use of power in human affairs. The violence practiced by Bradshaw on Septimus is echoed on a larger scale by the First World War, which lurks in the background not only of *Mrs. Dalloway* but *Jacob's Room* and *To the Lighthouse* as well. The 'Goddess whose lust is to override opposition, to stamp indelibly in the sanctuaries of others the image of herself' (113), takes many forms, and Bloomsbury vehemently repudiated all of them.

Although the human exploitation of wars and empire building has largely been the special privilege of the masculine world, the example of Miss Kilman shows that the Goddess Conversion is not a deity worshipped only by men. Perpetually swathed in her green mackintosh, Doris Kilman flaunts her poverty as proudly as the more fortunate might their elegance. The shapeless mackintosh successfully keeps the prying eyes of the world from glimpsing her body, and symbolizes the completeness with which Miss Kilman has closed herself off from life. But the renunciation of worldly pleasures has not kept her from desiring another kind of triumph: outwardly grateful to the Dalloways for the employment they have given her as tutor to their daughter, Miss Kilman seethes inwardly with the need to humiliate the gracious and lovely Clarissa. Having turned to the church some two years before as a refuge for her loneliness, Kilman wields her faith as a weapon to combat Clarissa's charm. Her spiritual certitude enables her to see Clarissa's beauty as a sign of her triviality and her own plainness as clear evidence of a moral ascendency. Clarissa may indeed be able to give successful parties and wear attractive clothes, but what need has she for such frivolities when her soul is so much grander? The splendor of Kilman's belief permits her to pity Clarissa instead of envying her, but even pitying her is not sufficient. She must subjugate her altogether, and in God's name, not her own (138):

> But it was not the body; it was the soul and its mockery that she wished to subdue; make her feel her mastery. If only she could make her weep; could ruin her; humiliate her; bring her to her knees crying, You are right! But this was God's will, not Miss Kilman's. It was to be a religious victory.

Although her motivation and personality are totally different from Bradshaw's, Miss Kilman is nevertheless a converter, one of those 'dominators and tyrants' (15) just like Sir William. In fact, Septimus thinks about Sir William in almost precisely the same terms as Clarissa responds to Miss Kilman. Clarissa, of course, is far less vulnerable than Septimus, and Miss Kilman's efforts to overcome her are channeled into an attempt to possess the soul of her daughter, Elizabeth. Elizabeth becomes the battleground on which the two women fight—Clarissa to keep her affection and Miss Kilman to lure her into the ways of communion, prayer books, and God. The struggle is unresolved: Elizabeth does go to Clarissa's party (which Kilman, on principle, refuses to attend), but Clarissa also knows that Kilman's spiritual assaults on her daughter will continue. And it is these she can neither understand nor forgive, for human beings must not be tampered with: 'Had she ever tried to convert anyone herself? Did she not wish everybody merely to be themselves?' (139).

Clarissa's passionate defence of the privacy of the human soul leads her to distrust all solutions to the problems of loneliness or unhappiness which in any way involve compromising that privacy. Miss Kilman's religion is clearly one such unacceptable response to the difficulties of living, and Peter Walsh's love is another. Continually brandishing his pocket knife (the symbolism of which is too obvious for comment), Peter embodies a masculine, sexual threat to Clarissa's psychic autonomy which she cannot endure. More strongly attracted to Peter than she had ever been to Richard, Clarissa simply could not meet the kinds of demands that Peter made on their relationship. The total involvement that Peter aggressively insists upon contrasts sharply with Richard's passivity, his willingness to honor the gulf between people that is so dear to Clarissa. Sleeping in separate rooms and asking almost nothing of one another, Richard and Clarissa live a life almost unsullied by passion or exhaustive commitments.

Having opted for the security of a relationship that requires very little, Clarissa can never entirely suppress the gnawing doubts that she has somehow failed Peter—as well as herself—in choosing Richard. Peter's return awakens in her the sort of giddy ecstasies—'If I had married him, this gaiety would have been mine all day' (52)—that only he is capable of producing. But her regrets at the lost pleasures that might have been hers are more than compensated for by the emotional freedom Richard has given her (10):

> For in marriage a little licence, a little independence that must be between people living together day in and day out in the same house; which Richard gave her, and she him . . . . But with Peter everything had to be shared; everything gone into.

Clarissa's obsessive concern for the privacy of the soul is a complicated feature of her character, at once her genius and, to a degree, her failure. Philosophically, her recognition of the uniqueness of each human spirit and her refusal to sanction any coercion of that spirit partake of the highest good for Woolf. Clarissa's understanding of the old lady whom she sees twice through the window performing her lonely domestic chores—'that's the miracle, that's the mystery; that old lady' (140)—epitomizes for Woolf the ultimate human awareness. For the old lady going about her mundane tasks is the unadorned human soul engaged in the quintessential, solitary act of living, and

97

Clarissa's simple acceptance of that soul, without trying to possess it, convert it, or impose upon it the general panaceas of religion and love, represents the kind of profound intelligence which Woolf most esteems. Mired in the social milieu of luncheons and tea parties and surrounded by manipulators and dominators of various sorts, Clarissa never permits the privacy of the individual soul to be entirely obscured from her view.

But if Clarissa's views on privacy are admirable philosophically, psychologically they are rather more ambiguous. Although Peter's accusations against her must always be understood in the context of his own anger and frustration over losing her to Richard, it is at the same time true that the charges of 'coldness,' 'hardness,' and 'woodenness' he brings against her at various points in the novel do speak to something very real in her character. There is in Clarissa, particularly in her relationship with men, an instinctive shying away from experience, a fear of intimate contact with another. It is a fact about herself which she is quick to admit (36):

> She could see what she lacked. It was not beauty; it was not mind. It was something central which permeated; something warm which broke up surfaces and rippled the cold contact of man and woman, or of women together. For *that* she could dimly perceive. She resented it, had a scruple picked up Heaven knows where, or, as she felt, sent by Nature . . . .

In part, then, Clarissa's insistence that the privacy of the soul be respected serves as the theoretical justification for her own inability to accept being touched. She maintains an inviolable chastity about her which successfully rebuffs all attempts at passionate entanglement. Her choice of Richard over Peter, of course, symbolizes her commitment to emotional and sexual virginity. For loving and protecting her as he does, Richard would never think of intruding on that considerable stretch of privacy Clarissa has staked out around her. And although grateful for such tact—which Peter, with his aggressiveness, could never display—Clarissa is correspondingly unmoved by her relationship with Richard. Clarissa herself is not unaware of what she has given up in preferring Richard's gentleness to Peter's demands.

In fact, it is neither Richard nor Peter who entirely absorbs Clarissa's imagination but Sally Seton, or more accurately, the memory of her relationship with Sally Seton. If Clarissa can ever be said to have been in love it was with Sally, while they were growing up, and one of the fine achievements of the novel is the evocation of the depth and delicacy of Clarissa's feelings for her friend. Smoking cigars, running naked down the hall, bicycling around the parapet on the terrace, Sally exerted an irresistible fascination over Clarissa, a fascination totally different from anything she ever felt for a man: 'The strange thing, on looking back, was the purity, the integrity, of her feeling for Sally. It was not like one's feeling for a man. It was completely disinterested, and besides, it had a quality which could only exist between women, between women just grown up' (40). Married to Richard, attracted to Peter, and treasuring as the 'most exquisite moment of her whole life' a kiss Sally bestowed on her lips, Clarissa indicates how complex the emotional life of adults can be. Transcending any simple definition of social or sexual roles, the range of Clarissa's feelings attests to Woolf's conviction about the flexibility and fluidity of the human psyche.

All of Clarissa's relationships converge at the party which she gives at the end of the day and at the end of the novel. It is here that she meets the Bradshaws and hears of Septimus's death; that she encounters Sally again after many years and realizes that the magic and potential of her youth have deserted her, now that she is Lady Rosseter, married to a Manchester mill owner and the mother of five sons; that we find Peter struggling with his own sense of failure, his contempt for the trivial social creatures fluttering around him, and his overwhelming adoration, in spite of everything, for Clarissa; that we see Clarissa herself, playing the role of 'the perfect hostess' which Peter has always detested, at once part of the polite, perfunctory world of the Whit-breads, Lady Bruton, and the others, and at the same time totally removed from them, communing, in the depths of her soul unimagin-ed by those on the surface, with the old lady across the street and with the young man who committed suicide.

Clarissa's parties are an essential feature of her character which Peter only partly understands. He interprets them as belonging totally to that conventional side of Clarissa which selected the respectable, proper Richard over his own more jagged, iconoclastic self. Life with Richard involves the social graces in a way that life with him would not, and Peter's decription of Clarissa as 'the perfect hostess' contains all of his censure for her having chosen such a sterile form of existence. Much of Peter's criticism, of course, is justified. Clarissa, as Richard's wife, is very much a social being, and her elegant and somewhat trivial parties do represent the consequences of a deliberately chosen way of life. But what Peter cannot understand is that her parties are much more than merely social affairs. They are, as she herself says, offerings, attempts made to withstand life's entropy by bringing people together, to establish enclaves of order and communication against the silence and indifference separating everybody (134–5):

> Here was So-and-so in South Kensington; some one up in Bayswater; and somebody else, say, in Mayfair. And she felt quite continuously a sense of their existence; and she felt what a waste; and she felt what a pity; and she felt if only they could be brought together; so she did it. And it was an offering; to combine, to create; but to whom?
>
> An offering for the sake of offering, perhaps. Anyhow, it was her gift.

In giving her parties, Clarissa functions in the same way Mrs Ramsay does in *To the Lighthouse*, and with the same purpose: to affirm life, to manufacture moments of order in the face of chaos. Although Clarissa perhaps lacks the substance of Mrs Ramsay (Woolf herself thought her 'tinselly'), she shares the same commitment to the struggle against disorder and death. Thinking of her party as an effort 'to kindle and illuminate' (7), Clarissa reminds us of Mrs Ramsay's identifying herself with the beam of the lighthouse, which breaks through the darkness, or with the warmth and light of Mrs Ramsay's own dinner party, in which for a moment, around the candle-lit dinner table inside the room, 'seemed to be order and dry land; there, outside, a reflection in which things wavered and vanished, waterily' (*To the Lighthouse*, 151).

Regarded simply as a social event, Clarissa's party is neither more nor less successful than most parties. Always the lovely hostess (a role she admits is strained and rather unreal for her), Clarissa presides over the normal gossip and boring pleasantries. People do not come together in meaningful ways, and no one has any notion that the party represents anything other than the usual polite gathering of the usual polite faces. But the success or failure of the party is not important. What matters is that for Clarissa the party is a kind of ritual celebration of life, a gesture full of meaning for her which Woolf wholeheartedly affirms. Clarissa's party, in fact, is the logical extension and expression of that same rapturous attitude towards living which was Woolf's own. For Clarissa, from the very first page of the novel, is in love with life, and her ecstatic awareness of being alive, dimmed, but never completely obscured by her understanding of the anguish and terror also involved, is precisely that of her creator. Whatever her defects—her minor snobberies, coldness, prudery, and timidity—they are rendered insignificant by her extraordinary ability to respond to everything happening around her (6):

> For Heaven only knows why one loves it so, how one sees it so, making it so, building it round one, tumbling it, creating it every moment afresh; but the veriest frumps, the most dejected of miseries sitting on doorsteps (drink their downfall) do the same; can't be dealt with, she felt positive, by Acts of Parliament for that very reason: they love life. In people's eyes, in the swing, tramp, and trudge; in the bellow and the uproar; the carriages, motor cars, omnibuses, vans, sandwich men shuffling and swinging; brass bands; barrel organs; in the triumph and the jingle and the strange high singing of some aeroplane overhead was what she loved; life; London; this moment of June.

In spite of her limitations, 'What she liked was simply life' (134), and it is this fact which makes even Peter see that his own reservations about her are finally mere quibbles. The rare gift she possesses—'to be; to exist; to sum it all up in the moment as she passed' (191)—distinguishes her from everyone else in the novel, and commands not only the reader's admiration but Peter's as well. Struggling with his own unhappiness and uncertainty, Peter marvels at the way Clarissa, despite her own frustrations, is able to give herself over to the act of living. Above all else, it is this dimension of Clarissa which the novel extolls. The last line of *Mrs. Dalloway*—'For there she was' (213)—echoes Peter's earlier description of Clarissa—'Not that she was striking; not beautiful at all; there was nothing picturesque about her; she never said anything especially clever; there she was, however; there she was' (85), and suggests the full metaphoric weight of Clarissa's presence throughout the novel. Totally absorbed in life (to the point where she can understand the importance of, and even be tempted by, death), Clarissa can finally no more be judged than can life itself. About them both, Woolf makes clear that we can say, 'There they are,' but not much more that matters.

The final words of the novel help define our response not only to Clarissa herself but to the entire novel, for *Mrs. Dalloway* demands the kind of acceptance that we give to the woman who dominates it. It embodies the experience of living the same way Clarissa does; it too 'is there' the same way she is, eliciting our intuitive, emotional assent to the quality of life it conveys. As an early attempt by Woolf to net her vision, *Mrs. Dalloway* succeeds in ordering the randomness of life into a coherent form which captures, as *Jacob's Room* does not, the nature of being alive. Exploring both the sunlit surface of a June day in London as well as the murky, private interiors of the people who move through that day, Woolf brilliantly manages to document what Peter Walsh calls (177)

> the truth about our soul . . . our self, who fish-like inhabits deep seas and plies among obscurities, threading her way between the boles of giant weeds, over sun-flickered spaces and on and on into gloom, cold, deep, inscrutable; suddenly she shoots to the surface and sports on the wind-wrinkled waves; that is, has a positive need to brush, scrape, kindle herself, gossiping.

8

To the Lighthouse

Woolf's own estimate of *To the Lighthouse*, written during the final throes of the novel's revision in 1926—'My present opinion is that it is easily the best of my books' (*A Writer's Diary*, 102)—is certainly accurate; it would be equally as accurate if the statement had been made in 1941, for *To the Lighthouse* remains Woolf's finest achievement. In the wind-swept island in the Hebrides presided over by Mrs Ramsay, Woolf creates an affecting image of the human condition which not only succeeds, as she says, in 'dredging up more feelings and characters' (*A Writer's Diary*, 101) than she had managed in the past, but which also weaves them together to produce for the reader an almost tactile sense of felt experience. *To the Lighthouse* captures Woolf's vision on paper just as, at the end of the book, the painter Lily Briscoe captures hers on canvas. Lily's final words (and the final words of the novel) do not speak simply to her own efforts, but to Woolf's as well: 'Yes, she thought, laying down her brush in extreme fatigue, I have had my vision' (320).

Part of the impulse behind *To the Lighthouse* was autobiographical, as a 1925 entry in her diary indicates: 'This is going to be fairly short; to have father's character done complete in it; and mother's; and St Ives; and childhood . . . .' (*A Writer's Diary*, 76). But however much Mr Ramsay owes to Virginia's actual experience of Sir Leslie Stephen, or Mrs Ramsay to Julia Duckworth Stephen (and it is interesting to note that Vanessa thought the book 'an extraordinarily fine and moving portrait' (*A Writer's Diary*, 107) of their mother), it is clear that the final characterization of the Ramsays is not in any limiting way topical or narrowly personal. Both transcend the models on which they are based. Both, in fact, transcend at times even their own selves in the novel, transformed, as Lily Briscoe points out, by (114–15) the meaning which, for no reason at all . . . descends on people, making them symbolical, making them representative . . . and made them in the dusk standing, looking, the symbols of marriage, husband and wife. Then, after an instant, the symbolical outline which transcended the real figures sank down again, and they became, as they met them, Mr and Mrs. Ramsay watching the children throwing catches.

The Ramsay relationship, then, cannot be taken as any simple paradigm of what life was like in the Stephen household. Although it is certainly true that Mrs Ramsay, radiating love, strength, and under-standing, constitutes an eloquent tribute to Woolf's sense of her mother, it is also true that Mrs Ramsay is, at the same time, a totally self-contained character, one of the great independent presences in modern fiction. Similarly, Mr Ramsay's strict rationalism and inces-sant self-pitying, though surely owing much to austere Sir Leslie's own posturings, finally belong to the father of the eight Ramsay children, not to Virginia's father.

Mrs Ramsay, of course, is the center of the family just as she is the center of the novel. Always catering to the needs of her children, her husband, and their friends, she is the seemingly limitless source of energy and life from which all the other characters draw their susten-ance. She helps hold together Mr Ramsay's precarious ego with the same deftness she uses to protect James's feelings from the insensitive assaults of his father. Feeling at times that she is 'nothing but a sponge sopped full of human emotions' (54), Mrs Ramsay manages to put those emotions at the service of those around her. Despite Woolf's feminist interests, Mrs Ramsay, it is important to realize, has rather a counter-revolutionary stature, conceived as she is in almost arche-typally traditional feminine terms. Fiercely committed to home and to children—'She would have liked always to have had a baby. She was happiest carrying one in her arms' (94)—Mrs Ramsay embodies all the conventional maternal virtues. Intuitive, compassionate, non-intellectual, protective, she represents the wisdom of the heart which professes to know nothing of the complicated workings of the head. Rooted in a far deeper reality than her husband, with his philosophical investigations, is ever able to achieve, she looks upon his intellectual endeavors with a kind of bemused respect. Her infinite patience with Ramsay's work and the great delicacy with which she assures him of its importance do not disguise her feeling that 'this admirable fabric of

104

the masculine intelligence' (164) which she cannot hope to fathom is, when compared to her profound understanding of things, concerned with the silliest sorts of trivialities. 'The influence of something upon somebody' (24) is her superb assessment of what philosophy is about, and in her heart she must admit that 'she liked the boobies best. They did not bother one with their dissertations. How much they missed, after all, these very clever men!' (155)

Immersed in a world of feelings and giving constantly to whoever needs her, Mrs Ramsay has neither time nor inclination for the cerebral amusements of her husband and his colleagues. Her interests are at once simpler and deeper than theirs. Lily complains throughout the novel about Mrs Ramsay's obsession with people getting married, and it is true that she can understand no other possible form of existence. Marriage—with its promise of love, security, and children—is the only kind of fulfillment she can imagine for people, and it is not without satisfaction that Lily, who has always felt herself censured for being unmarried, notes the failure of the marriage between Paul and Minta which Mrs Ramsay had passionately desired: 'She would feel a little triumphant, telling Mrs Ramsay that the marriage had not been a success' (269). A number of times in *To the Lighthouse* Mrs Ramsay is described as being 'short-sighted,' and although in each instance the term refers to her actual perceptual difficulties, it also applies—more importantly, in fact—to her moral and spiritual vision as well. Mrs Ramsay's short-sightedness is not a deficiency to be rectified. She is short-sighted in the way any natural force can be thought to be short-sighted. Totally involved in the process of generating love and order and life, she cannot see beyond her own creative instincts—nor does she have any need to. Her limited horizons which seem to encompass nothing less than life itself, are perhaps best defined by Lily: 'It was her instinct to go, an instinct like the swallows for the south, the artichokes for the sun, turning her infallibly to the human race, making her nest in its heart' (301). It is typical of Mrs Ramsay's genius that although she is totally indifferent to Lily's painting—feeling it a sterile waste of energy—she nevertheless 'returns' in the last section of the novel, years after her death, to enable Lily to complete her canvas. 'It was part of her perfect goodness to Lily' (14), as it is part of her general concern for everybody.

This is not to say that Mrs Ramsay is in any way intended as a paragon of human excellence. There are numerous reservations about her character voiced not only by those who love her but even by herself: her tendency to coerce or manipulate in the interests of her marital vision, as in the case with Paul and Minta; her occasional willfulness; her inability to acknowledge that Lily's solitary way of life can be as authentic as her own; her refusal to admit the claims of reason if they conflict with her own impulses, such as when she persists in maintaining that James will be able to make the trip to the lighthouse in the face of Mr Ramsay's sober assessment of the bad weather conditions. And her own doubts about the degree to which her ego satisfactions may be secretly involved in giving to others—'was it that she wished so instinctively to help . . . that people might say of her, "O Mrs. Ramsay!" . . . and need her and send for her and admire her?' (68–9)—are supported, in part, by Lily's feeling that at times her judgments (or misjudgments) 'arise from some need of her own rather than of other people's' (132). Mr Bankes is not at all pitiable, Lily insists; it is simply Mrs Ramsay's compulsion to make him so.

'Presiding with immutable calm over destinies which she completely failed to understand' (81), Mrs Ramsay is at once a creative force as well as a complex woman guilty of all the inadequacies and imperfections of being human. In her complexity and richness, Lily feels, 'One wanted fifty pairs of eyes to see with' (303), and even 'Fifty pairs of eyes were not enough' (303) to embrace fully the spiritual immensity of Mrs Ramsay. Although the novel cannot quite satisfy this demand, it does provide the eyes of Bankes, Tansley, Carmichael, the Ramsay children and their father, Paul, Minta, Lily, and most important, Mrs Ramsay herself to enable us to experience, from a variety of angles, aspects of the mystery which is Mrs Ramsay. This is the way we apprehend not simply Mrs Ramsay but the others as well, for the novel insists that the truth of human character cannot be given whole but can only be known in the context of its relationships and through a series of partial, individual, and inconsistent views. Woolf is fascinated by the way the mind perceives itself and those things and people around it, and *To the Lighthouse* deals not with stable notions of character but with the actual dynamics of interaction between people, with the fluctuations and uncertainties that constitute human relationships. Mrs Ramsay's feelings about Bankes and his complex and at times contradictory feelings about her comprise one minute portion of the truth about them both. Bankes's attitude towards Mrs Ramsay may have nothing at all in common with Carmichael's or Mr Ramsay's, or even Mrs Ramsay's own, but all of them, taken in their

106

complication together, suggest something real about Mrs Ramsay and the rather murky, haphazard process by which we experience people in general. As a result, the novel does not permit us the luxury of any easy assessment of character. All such judgments, Lily makes clear, distort the delicate tissue of feelings which connect us to others. Having been able momentarily fo find Bankes superior to Mr Ramsay, Lily is suddenly overcome by a sense of Bankes's limitations and realizes the futility of seeking neat emotional preferences (42–3):

> How then did it work out, all this ? How did one add up this and that and conclude that it was liking one felt, or disliking? And to those words, what meaning attached, after all? Standing now, apparently transfixed, by the pear tree, impressions poured in upon her of those two men, and to follow her thought was like following a voice which speaks too quickly to be taken down by one's pencil, and the voice was her own voice saying without prompting undeniable, everlasting, contradcitory things. . . .

The various eyes surrounding Mrs Ramsay, then, present us with different appraisals of her public self which interacts in social situations with other human beings, supporting, manipulating, and loving them. But there is another part of Mrs Ramsay which the eyes cannot see, a part only she can understand. For beneath the self concerned always with the needs of others lurk the cherished, private depths of Mrs Ramsay into which she must plunge from time to time to escape the endless twitter of human demands. She renews herself by fading away from the surface and taking refuge in 'a wedge-shaped core of darkness, something invisible to others' (99), where she is able to experience her essential self without the interruptions of everyday life. It is as this shaped darkness that Mrs Ramsay, the mother of eight, communes with the most precious part of herself and with the deepest current of reality (100):

> There was freedom, there was peace, there was, most welcome of all, a summoning together, a resting on a platform of stability. Not as oneself did one find rest ever, in her experience . . . but as a wedge of darkness. Losing personality, one lost the fret, the hurry, the stir; and there rose to her lips always some exclamation of triumph over life when things came together in this peace, this rest, this eternity.

Living a life devoted to the care of others, Mrs Ramsay nevertheless maintains the capacity to descend in delicious solitude to the still center of things where she can revel in feelings for which her normal activities leave her little time. For Woolf, Mrs Ramsay's ability to do both testifies to her greatness.

Of Mrs Ramsay's many considerable talents, none is more important than her skill in creating, from the flux and chaos around her, moments of order, in which for a fleeting time life is made to take on a coherence and permanence it does not otherwise possess. She alone has the power to fashion out of the evanescent stream of experience things that endure. The Boeuf en Daube dinner at the end of the first part of the novel is one such moment of creation. Bringing people together by force of her love, she instills in them the sense that 'they were all conscious of making a party together in a hollow on an island; had their common cause against that fluidity out there' (151–2). Although she uses neither words nor colors, Mrs Ramsay is as much an artist as Woolf, Mr Carmichael and Lily Briscoe are. If her artifacts are not as tangible as books and paintings, they nevertheless achieve a permanence in people's minds which belies their insubstantiality. Mrs Ramsay's own instincts about her dinner—'Of such moments, she thought, the thing is made that remains for ever after. This would remain' (163)—are confirmed, ten years later, in the last section of the novel when Lily Briscoe draws from Mrs Ramsay and her dinner inspiration to complete her own vision. Lily, in fact, makes explicit the particular kind of creative genius which is Mrs Ramsay's (295–6):

> There might be lovers whose gift it was to choose out the
> elements of things and place them together and so, giving them a
> wholeness not theirs in life, make of some scene, or meeting of
> people (all now gone and separate), one of those globed
> compacted things over which thought lingers and love plays.

Surviving the ravages of ten years' time, Mrs Ramsay's creation—the globed, compacted thing she has wrought out of formless life—is as authentically a work of art as any sculpture or painting.

'Making of the moment something permanent (as in another sphere Lily herself tried to make of the moment something permanent)' (249), Mrs Ramsay wrestles to achieve her vision with an adversary every bit as intractable as that which Lily—or Woolf herself, for that matter—must subdue in order to gain hers. For the blank canvas and empty page which constantly mock the creative powers of Lily and Woolf are certainly no more formidable than Mrs Ramsay's 'old antagonist, life' (124). Threatening to undermine through suffering, death, or the simple erosion of time the structures of order and love she attempts to establish, life, Mrs Ramsay feels, is always trying to get the better of her, and she is forced to labor unceasingly in the interests of her craft to prevent it—'terrible, hostile, and quick to pounce on you if you gave it a chance' (96)—from winning. An artist who works in a difficult medium, Mrs Ramsay triumphs over the obstacles in the way of her vision just as Lily finally manages to solve the formal problem of how to connect the two masses which have prevented her from finishing her painting. For both, success is of a purely subjective sort. Her painting, Lily knows, will be hung in dusty attics, ignored, and in the end destroyed, and Mrs Ramsay's creation, existing solely in the minds of those who witnessed it, is meaningful primarily for herself alone. And yet for both, the ephemerality of their creations does not detract from their grandeur or importance. For Woolf, the completed vision is all, and at the end of *To the Lighthouse* the three artists—Mrs Ramsay, Lily Briscoe, and Woolf herself—all rest secure in having achieved theirs.

If Mrs Ramsay spends much of her time giving to others, Mr Ramsay spends most of his taking from them, particularly from his wife. A man with impeccable intellectual credentials, he is completely dependent emotionally on Mrs Ramsay, demanding from her at every turn encouragement to sustain him through his chronic seizures of self doubt and self-pity. Neither his important books nor the accolades of his students nor the lectures he is asked to deliver can obviate his need for endless reassurance, and it is only Mrs Ramsay who is willing to satisfy that need. While Lily retreats in the face of his assault on her sympathy, and James steadfastly ignores and resents him, Mrs Ramsay somehow manages, however exhausting the effort, to find the strength to respond to his mute but plaintive beseeching. Again and again the creative female is equal to the task of nourishing the insatiable demands made upon her by the frail masculine ego (61–2):

> Mrs. Ramsay, who had been sitting loosely, folding her son in her arm, braced herself, and, half turning, seemed to raise herself with an effort, and at once to pour erect into the air a rain of energy, a column of spray, looking at the same time animated and alive . . . and into this delicious fecundity, this fountain and spray of life, the fatal sterility of the male plunged itself, like a

beak of brass, barren and bare.

Mr Ramsay is what Sara Monday, the great lady of Joyce Cary's first trilogy, would call 'a poor manny.' Eminently successful in his philosophical work, he seems almost helpless otherwise, requiring the constant nurture of Mrs Ramsay to keep him in touch with himself and with life. She must provide him with that sense of being involved in the vital processes of living which he is unable to generate for himself (62):

> It was sympathy he wanted, to be assured of his genius, first of all, and then to be taken within the circle of life, warmed and soothed, to have his senses restored to him, his barrenness made fertile, and all the rooms of the house made full of life—the drawing-room; behind the drawing-room the kitchen; above the kitchen the bedrooms; and beyond them the nurseries; they must be furnished, they must be filled with life. . . .
> He must be assured that he too lived in the heart of life; was needed; not here only, but all over the world.

Burdening others with his emotional vulnerability, Mr Ramsay is nevertheless capable of maintaining an independent, fiercely rigorous philosophical view of the universe that co-exists with his dependency of spirit. Both courage as well as weakness are embodied in his strict linear categorization of human achievement (56–7):

> For if thought is like the keyboard of a piano, divided into so many notes, or like the alphabet is ranged in twenty-six letters all in order, then his splendid mind had no sort of difficulty in running over those letters one by one, firmly and accurately, until it had reached, say, the letter Q. He reached Q. Very few people in the whole of England ever reach Q . . . . But after Q? What comes next? After Q there are a number of letters the last of which is scarcely visible to mortal eyes, but glimmers red in the distance. Z is only reached once by one man in a generation. Still, if he could reach R it would be something. Here at least was Q. He dug his heels in at Q. Q he was sure of.

Foolishly sterile in one way, his finely graded sense of accomplishment also has something heroic about it. Ramsay's desire to go beyond himself, to push his limits one step further, speaks to what is indomitable—and compelling—about him. While he artificially

110

creates his own standards of failure for himself—'He would never reach R' (57)—he at the same time reveals an honesty as well as an aspiration for permanence and achievement that are thoroughly admirable. Although he finally lacks the strength to do anything about it, his willingness to confront, if only momentarily, 'the dark of human ignorance' (72), to accept without the solace of comforting illusion the fact that 'we know nothing and the sea eats away the ground we stand on' (72), represents a genuine kind of courage which earns the profound respect not only of Mrs Ramsay but of Bankes, Tansley, and Lily as well. For in spite of his weakness, his self-pity, his greedy feasting off the emotional resources of those around him, Ramsay is by no means an unimpressive man. If his commitment to the truth seems to involve, as in the case of James's desire to go to the lighthouse, indifference to human feelings, it is still an authentic commitment which cannot be lightly dismissed. Ramsay's principles are as life-giving in their own way as Mrs Ramsay's instincts are in quite another. His insistence that people honor the facts clashes with her maternal desire to protect everybody from them, and although Mrs Ramsay's view is obviously more comfortable, Woolf sees both as crucial. However much James objects to his father's intrusive masculine presence at the beginning of the novel, Mr Ramsay's refusal to grant praise except for actual achievement—praise which his son finally pries loose from him at the end of the novel when he successfully steers the boat to the lighthouse –is as important for James's growth into maturity as the love Mrs Ramsay freely bestows on him simply for being her son. James's discovery, as he nears the lighthouse, that what had seemed in his youth 'a silvery, misty-looking tower with a yellow eye that opened . . . softly in the evening' (286), was from up close 'stark and straight; he could see that it was barred with black and white' (286), suggests, among other things, his coming to terms with his father's masculine understanding, his realization that reality is not only what Mrs Ramsay made it out to be. The trip to the lighthouse at once earns for James the praise he has always sought from his father and confirms Mr Ramsay (and the masculine view he represents) in James's eyes.

The image conjured up in Lily's mind by Mr Ramsay's work—a scrubbed kitchen table—provides an appropriate metaphor for assessing the tenor of his whole character as well. For if kitchen tables are not notable for their warmth, charm, or flexibility, they certainly possess the kind of enduring stolidity and integrity which Ramsay

111

embodies. Although the bare table is peculiar to Lily's view of Ramsay, it nevertheless helps to explain part of Mrs Ramsay's complex response to her venerable yet ridiculous husband. Outraged by his insensitivity to others, Mrs Ramsay at the same time genuinely esteems the principled goodness which is also his. Oscillating between the poles of resentment and affection, Mrs Ramsay's feelings are exquisitely detailed in all their contradictoriness. In her ability to adore Ramsay one minute and despise him the next, Mrs Ramsay exemplifies perfectly the truth about the fluidity of human feelings which is so crucial to the novel's meaning. Within the pleasant but uneventful trivialities that absorb the Ramsays and their guests from late afternoon through the evening, Woolf has captured the subtle rhythms running through all personal relationships. The innocuous action is merely the vehicle for the drama of human consciousness flickering below the surface. Mrs Ramsay's shifting feelings for her husband not only serve to illuminate one particular relationship, they seem to speak to human interaction in general.

Moving in and out of individual minds, Woolf weaves from fragments of thoughts, fantasies, and impressions, a tapestry of consciousness which presents us with one coherent image (the possibilities are obviously infinite) of how people experience each other and themselves. Through its fidelity to the mundane, *To the Lighthouse* manages to achieve in its pages that very sense of what it is to be alive which Lily hopes her own tenacious scrutiny of reality will produce on canvas (319–20):

> One must keep on looking without for a second relaxing the intensity of emotion, the determination not to be put off, not to be bamboozled. One must hold the scene—so—in a vice and let nothing come in and spoil it. One wanted, she thought, dipping her brush deliberately, to be on a level with ordinary experience, to feel simply that's a chair, that's a table, and yet at the same time, it's a miracle, it's an ecstasy.

The miracle of the ordinary is a fine way of describing what Woolf's novels achieve. It is not surprising that Lily's description of her efforts should so closely parallel Woolf's own, for Lily is the first of those artists in Woolf's fiction—Orlando, Bernard, and Miss La Trobe follow—whose aesthetic vision clearly represents some fundamental part of their creator's. This is not to imply that Lily is in any sense a surrogate Virginia Woolf. As a character she owes nothing at all to

Woolf, though as an artist working with color and shape she struggles
with the same kind of problems—formal, psychological, and otherwise—Woolf was forced to solve when confronting the blank page.
Lily's non-representational canvas suggests a metaphoric version of
Woolf's non-realistic fiction. Both attempt to fix the precise nature of
reality through the creation of unique forms that do not depend on
conventional narrative or representational technique.

Living totally outside of the dense network of personal relationships
swirling around Mrs Ramsay, Lily Briscoe is in many ways her direct
opposite. Solitary where Mrs Ramsay is somehow plural, reluctant to
impose herself on a reality which Mrs Ramsay unabashedly manipu-
lates from the start, Lily has none of that fecund, female energy which
always seems available to the friend she so admires. In the presence of
Mrs Ramsay's rich abundance Lily is made to feel her own 'poverty of
spirit' (157), her own distance from the center of things where Mrs
Ramsay instinctively resides. What unites the two of them, despite
their vast personal differences, however, is their mutual reverence for
life and their desire to make something ordered and whole out of the
flux around them. For both, the creative act is essentially an act of love.
Rooted in the midst of her family, Mrs Ramsay seeks to make the
moment of oneness round the Boeuf en Daube permanent. 'Life
stands still here,' she commands, hoping to establish a structure of love
that will withstand the chaos outside of the dining room and the
erosion of time. And although Lily herself does not share any compar-
ably nourishing emotional life, her painting is in part at least a celebration of Mrs Ramsay and the life impulse she embodies. Standing
outside the house and watching Mrs Ramsay reading to James, Lily is
sufficiently moved by the scene of mother and son to include them in
her composition as color and mass (85):

> But the picture was not of them, she said. Or, not in his [Mr
> Bankes's] sense. There were other senses, too, in which one
> might reverence them. By a shadow here and a light there, for
> instance. Her tribute took that form, if, as she vaguely supposed,
> a picture must be a tribute.

Affirming the possibility of human coherence in a random world, art
in all of its manifestations constitutes for Woolf a very real tribute
to life, mankind's most eloquent form of protest against its own
mortality.

Shaped from the living people surrounding her, Mrs Ramsay's

creation can be more immediately achieved than Lily's, freed, as it is from the formal burdens involved in successfully finishing a canvas or, for that matter, a novel. The moment of order Mrs Ramsay forges out of her own strength and love in the course of an evening cannot be so neatly managed by the painter or novelist. In Lily's case, ten years pass between the inception and completion of her picture. The problems confronting her, and by extension, all artists, are both strictly aesthetic and broadly human. The aesthetic, which are clearly tied to the resolution of the latter, involve Lily in the question of 'how to connect this mass on the right hand with that on the left. She might do it by bringing the line of the branch across so; or break the vacancy in the foreground by an object (James perhaps) so. But the danger was that by doing that the unity of the whole might be broken' (86). A unified composition is not possible without a unified vision, and it is this, rather than any technical organization of mass or color, that Lily struggles with throughout the novel. If the formal difficulty seems to be one of joining masses without violating the balance of the painting, the substantive difficulty (of which the formal is but a reflection) concerns Lily's effort to embrace in one harmonious view all the varied elements that make up the Ramsay household. Specifically, it is Mr Ramsay with his aggressive intellectualism and unyielding demands for pity whom Lily is unable to integrate, either emotionally or imaginatively, into her life. Everything about him oppresses Lily; his mere presence on the beach is enough to make her fold up her easel to prevent him seeing what she is doing. Unlike Mrs Ramsay, Lily has neither the compulsion nor the capacity to cater to the needs of all those who come into contact with her. Whereas Mrs Ramsay can always find something, even at the cost of dissembling, to extend to her husband, Lily only wants to avoid both him and his debilitating demands for reassurance. In her refusal to incorporate Ramsay into the field of her sympathy, to see him not as a dissonant element, but as an authentic part of the whole, Lily struggles with an incomplete view of reality which makes creation difficult (229):

> But with Mr. Ramsay bearing down on her, she could do nothing. Every time he approached—he was walking up and down the terrace—ruin approached, chaos approached. She could not paint. She stooped, she turned; she took up this rag; she squeezed that tube. But all she did was to ward him off a moment. He made it impossible for her to do anything.

As long as Lily girds herself against Ramsay he retains the power to disrupt her painting (231):

> Let him be fifty feet away, let him not even speak to you, let him not even see you, he permeated, he prevailed, he imposed himself. He changed everything. She could not see the colour; she could not see the lines; even with his back turned to her, she could only think, 'But he'll be down on me in a moment, demanding'—something she felt she could not give him.

What she must learn to do is precisely what Cam and James must learn to do on the sail to the lighthouse with their father: to cease to 'resist tyranny to the death' (252) and learn to understand Ramsay with the same kind of loving compassion demonstrated by Mrs Ramsay. A sensibility irritated by grievance and dislike is not conducive to the creation of art, as Woolf makes clear in *A Room of One's Own*. The completion of Lily's canvas coincides with her ability to think with genuine human warmth about Ramsay. Initially responding to his beseeching for support which 'poured and spread itself in pools at her feet' by drawing 'her skirts a little closer around her ankles, lest she should get wet' (236), Lily moves during the last section of the novel to a state of active acceptance of Ramsay and all that he stands for. In doing so, the 'discomfort of the sympathy which she held undischarged' (250) is assuaged, permitting her access to that incandescent imaginative state which had previously eluded her.

Lily's ability to reconcile herself to Ramsay's needs—a considerable human achievement that seems to free her sufficiently from inner chaos to enable her to render her vision on canvas—owes much to Mrs Ramsay. Unsettled by her partial view of things, Lily totally lacks her friend's mysterious grace which 'resolved everything into simplicity; made these angers, irritations fall off like old rags' (248). Finding the Ramsay house to be 'full of unrelated passions' (230) after Mrs Ramsay's death, Lily is unable to pull things together as Mrs Ramsay had always managed to do, a fact which clearly bears upon the difficulty she experiences in trying to shape her painting. For Woolf, an ordered vision of the whole is crucial for any successful creation. The antipathies which prevent Lily from including Ramsay in her world ensure that all her efforts at solving the organizational problems of her canvas will be futile until she can deal with her own lack of harmony. Her impetus for doing this comes from Mrs Ramsay, whose sudden, silent reappearance before Lily points the way to Lily's own enhanced humanity (310):

> 'Mrs. Ramsay! Mrs. Ramsay!' she cried, feeling the old horror come back—to want and want and not to have. Could she inflict that still? And then, quietly, as if she refrained, that too became part of ordinary experience, was on a level with the chair, with the table. Mrs. Ramsay—it was part of her perfect goodness to Lily—sat there quite simply, in the chair, flicked her needles to and fro, knitted her reddish-brown stocking, cast her shadow on the step. There she sat.

Lily's immediate response to this vision makes clear that she has understood what Mrs Ramsay was saying to her: she sets out to find Mr Ramsay (310):

> And as if she had something she must share, yet could hardly leave her easel, so full her mind was of what she was thinking, of what she was seeing, Lily went past Mr. Carmichael holding her brush to the edge of the lawn. Where was the boat now? Mr. Ramsay? She wanted him.

Having at last managed (in her own mind only, Mr Ramsay at this point being in the process of landing on the lighthouse island) to give him 'whatever she had wanted to give him, when he left her that morning' (319), Lily is now able to perceive precisely what it is her canvas needs. With the tension 'between two opposite forces; Mr Ramsay and the picture' (296), entirely dissipated, the solution to the formal problems of the painting presents itself with luminous clarity (52):

> She looked at the steps; they were empty; she looked at her canvas; it was blurred. With a sudden intensity; as if she saw it clear for a second, she drew a line there, in the centre. It was done; it was finished.

As an artist, Lily is able to transcend some of the personal limitations within which she generally functions. The diffidence which makes personal relations uneasy for her does not carry over into her creative life. If in comparing herself to Paul she sees him 'bound for adventure; she, moored to the shore' (158), her painting takes her well away from the shore where few venture: 'Out and out one went, further and further, until at last one seemed to be on a narrow plank, perfectly

116

alone, over the sea' (265). A solitary, placid spectator in the realm of everyday living, she risks everything in the throes of her creative work. To the outside world, of course, which knows nothing of the perils and anguish involved in imaginative labor, Lily is always the same slightly desiccated woman whom life has passed by: 'No one had seen her step off her strip of board into the waters of annihilation. She remained a skimpy old maid, holding a paint-brush on the lawn' (278).

Lily's creative raptures, so different in intensity from the rather decorous life she otherwise leads, associate her firmly with both Mrs Ramsay as well as Woolf. Her total absorption in the act of painting in which, losing all dimensions of a social self, she is instead 'drawn out of gossip, out of living, out of community with people into the presence of this formidable ancient enemy of hers—this other thing, this truth, this reality' (244–5), is similar to Mrs Ramsay's experience of plunging away from the surface of things into that private solitude of darkness where, divested of the trappings of personality, she can renew herself. Lily's ancient enemy which goads her on to try to wrench a coherent vision out of the muddle is a close relative of that 'old antagonist, life,' over whom Mrs Ramsay is always struggling to triumph. In their capacity for sudden escape from the trivialities of the present, both partake of Woolf's own ability to immerse herself, while creating or in some way apprehending the 'reality' around her, in a deeper consciousness than she normally is in touch with. Lily's gradual loss of any awareness of 'outer things, and her name and her personality and her appearance' (246) as she enters the labyrinth of her canvas is echoed, in her diary, by Woolf's comment that when she writes she must become 'very, very concentrated, all at one point, not having to draw upon the scattered parts of one's character, living in the brain. Sydney comes and I'm Virginia; when I write I'm merely a sensibility' (*A Writer's Diary*, 48).

Despite their important similarities—and allowing for the obvious difference in media—Lily's creative struggle as a painter is distinct from Woolf's as a novelist in one fundamental way: organizing her canvas with subtle combinations of color, mass, and line, Lily fashions her depiction of reality without any need to grapple with the human experience of time which is so crucial to Woolf's whole artistic concern. The technical problems confronting Lily as she contemplates the blank surface of the canvas do not include finding some compelling form through which to embody her vision of the nature of time. Lily is

117

freed by the flatness of her canvas from any such preoccupation. But time plays an essential role in *To the Lighthouse*, providing a consciously felt framework in which Lily, Mr and Mrs Ramsay and the others conduct their lives. Much of the novel's power, in fact, comes from Woolf's imaginative treatment of the flow of time.

Although the novel covers a chronological span of ten years, it is divided into three sections of strikingly unequal length, which effectively describe the course of a single day. Beginning in late afternoon, the first section closes with the onset of night. The second part, entitled 'Time Passes' moves from the 'immense darkness' (195) of formless night to the early morning of a late September day in which Lily wakes up once again in the Ramsay house from which she had been absent for ten years. And the last, beginning with Lily seated at the breakfast table slightly before eight in the morning, culminates in the afternoon with Ramsay's arrival at the lighthouse and Lily's completion of her painting. Although the passage of ten years from opening section to last seems to mock young James's anticipation, stated on the very first page of the novel, that the trip to the lighthouse was at last 'after a night's darkness and a day's sail, within touch' (11), we can see that metaphorically at least, the structure of the novel affirms James's hopes. The lighthouse is indeed only a night's darkness and a day's sail away, even if it takes ten years to negotiate that darkness.

Following Woolf's careful dissection of the filaments of the present in the first section, the compression of ten years' time into thirty pages in the next comes as an enormous shock to the reader. Some critics have been sufficiently traumatized by the abrupt shift in tone and point of view to suggest that the 'Time Passes' section belongs to a different novel altogether. But of course the radical difference between the two is intentional, and vital to the conception of the book as a whole. Devoting 190 pages to unraveling the personal interaction of a few hours and then juxtaposing that to the thirty-page treatment of the succeeding ten years makes us experience both the stillness and the flow which are central to Woolf's conception of time. The sustained moment of the first part, presided over by Mrs Ramsay and dense with human significance, gives way to the shapeless 'flood, the profusion of darkness' (196) against which, in fact, Mrs Ramsay has been fighting. Where human consciousness is everything in the first and third sections, in the second it is completely absent, overwhelmed by the impersonal forces of time and nature. Dominated by the natural imagery of wind and rain and seasons, 'Time Passes' embodies that formless reality, indifferent to human aspiration, out of which all the characters carve their various kinds of order. Among other things, it makes us appreciate the full magnitude of Mrs Ramsay's achievement in saying 'Life stand still here,' in 'making of the moment something permanent' (249).

The wholeness—perfect if ephemeral—that Mrs Ramsay had willed means nothing to those impersonal powers which take possession of the house once the Ramsays and the others leave. The delicate human order is engulfed by the ravages of time and the destructive powers of the night so that almost nothing remains. In the firm grip of the non-human, boundaries collapse into shapelessness, making it impossible 'that we should ever compose from their fragments a perfect whole or read in the littered pieces the clear words of truth' (199). The impulse to create ordered structures, which the novel ultimately celebrates, is mocked by the reign of chaos (199):

> Should any sleeper fancying that he might find on the beach an
> answer to his doubts, a sharer of his solitude, throw off his
> bedclothes and go down by himself to walk on the sand, no
> image with semblance of serving and divine promptitude comes
> readily to hand bringing the night to order and making the world
> reflect the compass of the soul.

Linking the two sections of distinctly human achievement—Mrs Ramsay's creation of her evening and the successful completion of Lily's painting and Mr Ramsay's trip to the lighthouse—with what Woolf called 'this impersonal thing . . . the flight of time' (*A Writer's Diary*, 80), is a brilliant device which invests both sections with a weight of meaning they would otherwise not have. Technically, it was a daring experiment, for 'Time Passes' had to be written without the anchor of any human point of view whatever. Having moved deftly from human consciousness to human consciousness in the first part, Woolf dramatizes the flow of ten years by exploring its effect on the deserted Ramsay summer house. For Woolf, it was 'the most difficult abstract piece of writing—I have to give an empty house, no people's characters, the passage of time, all eyeless and featureless with nothing to cling to' (*A Writer's Diary*, 89). Sensuously tracing 'those sliding lights, those fumbling airs' as they wander through the house, 'nosing, rubbing . . . descending' (197), she documents their confrontation with the bare house in such a way that we can feel it

119

fading under the siege of the agents of dissolution. Seen from the vantage point of these natural forces, human life is a paltry affair indeed, an afterthought not to be taken seriously. The painstaking attention lavished on every nuance of personal feeling and relationship in the first part of *To the Lighthouse* thus appears ridiculous when placed in the context of the larger rhythms of life of the second. Woolf underscores the insignificance of the human enterprise when looked at from without by enclosing in brackets—suggesting the intrusion of something of secondary importance—all mention of the experiences that befall the Ramsays and their friends. Thus we learn through brackets about Mr Carmichael's fame as a poet, Prue's marriage, her death because of complications following childbirth, and the senseless destruction of Andrew Ramsay in the First World War, blown apart by a shell. Most extraordinary of all is the way Woolf dispatches Mrs Ramsay (199–200):

> [Mr. Ramsay stumbling along a passage stretched his arms out
> one dark morning, but Mrs. Ramsay having died rather
> suddenly the night before he stretched his arms out. They
> remained empty.]

The startlingly matter-of-fact tone makes clear precisely how much a human life means to the universe at large—and precisely why each individual life is so precious. Against 'that fluidity out there' (152) which is nothing to us, as Mrs Ramsay knows, we have only ourselves and others for support. While the first section of the novel addresses the threat of that fluidity from the safety of dry land, the second places us squarely in the middle of the flux itself as it engulfs everything in its way. The bracketed accounts of the Ramsay deaths, surrounded by that impersonal sea 'in which things wavered and vanished, waterily' (151), makes the indifference of the world to all that is human something we not only feel but actually see on the page. Rarely has a typographical device been used to such powerful effect.

Stripped by the absence of its occupants of any animating intelligence or will, the Ramsay house itself teeters on the brink of dissolution. Left on its own, the repository of the Ramsay spirit has few defences against the relentless assault of time and the elements. The aimless fertility of nature seems intent on subduing this alien human structure which has prevailed for so long (212–13):

> The long night seemed to have set in; the trifling airs, nibbling,
> the clammy breaths, fumbling, seemed to have triumphed . . . . A

120

thistle thrust itself between the tiles in the larder. The swallows nested in the drawing room: the floor was strewn with straw: the plaster fell in shovelfuls; rafters were laid bare; rats carried off this and that to gnaw behind the wainscots.

But the human spirit is not without its own instinct for survival. For just as the house is about to capitulate—'One feather, and the house, sinking, falling, would have turned and pitched downwards to the depths of darkness' (214)—a countervailing force, slow-moving but irresistible gradually lumbers into action. In the persons of two aged cleaning ladies, Mrs McNab and Mrs Bast, Woolf embodies that primitive human capacity to endure which doggedly resists the destructive forays from outside. There is nothing exalted or heroic about such a power: 'But there was a force working; something not highly conscious; something that leered, something that lurched; something not inspired to go about its work with dignified ritual or solemn chanting' (215). Acting under orders from the children to make the house habitable again, the two crones commence their efforts against the decay (215):

> Slowly and painfully, with broom and pail, mopping, scouring, Mrs McNab, Mrs Bast stayed the corruption and the rot; rescued from the pool of Time that was fast closing over them now a basin, now a cupboard; fetched up from oblivion all the Waverley novels and a tea-set one morning.

With the cleaning, dusting, digging, and cutting finally completed, the house is ready for use, and late in a September evening, ten years after Mrs Ramsay's triumphant Boeuf en Daube dinner, it is once again filled with people. It is not, of course, the same house that existed ten years previously. The deaths of Prue, Andrew, and particularly Mrs Ramsay guarantee that although the physical structure is essentially unchanged, its character is totally different. Returning after her long absence, Lily finds it fragmented and alien, without the coherence it possessed when Mrs Ramsay was holding things together. She feels herself a stranger, cut off from all those connections which nourished her ten years before: 'How aimless it was, how chaotic, how unreal it was, she thought' (227). Deprived of the comforting presence of Mrs Ramsay, Lily is unable to make sense of the confusion of feelings sweeping over her as to what the business of living is all about. She cannot even define the problem to herself, for words are far too imprecise to carry the burden of articulating those ultimate but essentially ineffable questions about existence which plague her (274):

> And she wanted to say not one thing, but everything. Little words that broke up the thought and dismembered it said nothing. 'About life, about death; about Mrs. Ramsay'—no, she thought, one could say nothing to nobody. The urgency of the moment always missed its mark. Words fluttered sideways and struck the object inches too low. Then one gave it up . . . . For how could one express in words those emotions of the body?

The closest she can come to posing the question is through the formulaic—and thoroughly inadequate—'What does it mean then, what can it all mean' (225), which opens the third section and dominates her consciousness to the end. The answer, of course, can never be expressed verbally, nor does it have any general applicability outside of Lily's own subjective vision. Lily's answer is uniquely her own, too deep for words, and found on her canvas when she finally succeeds in uniting the different masses with the final stroke in the center. In Woolf's universe, individuals must work out for themselves the particular significance of the revelation that 'In the midst of chaos there was shape' (249). While Lily's understanding, finally embodied in her painting, may never be communicated to anyone else (as Lily knows, it will no doubt be hung in an attic or destroyed), it is nevertheless with supreme satisfaction that she is enabled to put down her brush at last, complete in the realization of having arrived at the truth she had been pursuing for so long.

Lily is by no means the only one to feel dislocated and alone as the morning breaks over the island at the beginning of the third part of the novel. Stumbling about full of self-pity and pain, Mr Ramsay desperately misses that vital emotional support he could always count on from his wife. Despite his virtuoso display of groans and posturings, he is unable to conjure into being the current of sympathy that has helped keep him afloat throughout his years of marriage. Lily resents his intrusions and egregious demands, while Cam and James, feeling coerced by his will, join together in a silent pact of resistance. With no Mrs Ramsay available to cater to his needs or offset the hostility he generates, he is forced, in a sense for the first time, to confront his children and himself without the possibility of refuge. It is difficult, not only for the great metaphysician himself but for the two children as well, who have also used the maternal security of Mrs Ramsay to avoid coming to terms with their father. But however difficult, such confrontations are the stuff of growth, permitting contact and understanding which could never have taken place as long as Mrs Ramsay was protecting everybody from everybody else. Awkward and unpleasant at the start, the relationship between Ramsay and his children ends, at the lighthouse island, on a note of shared respect and love. The unspoken oath shared by Cam and James to oppose Mr Ramsay's 'tyranny to the death' (255), yields to an equally unspoken acceptance of him, and his integrity and courage, while Ramsay, praising James for his mastery in steering the boat, finally gives his son the paternal affirmation he has been lacking all these years.

Beginning in disarray, then, the third section closes in a state of wholeness and resolution: Lily's painting is completed, the lighthouse has been reached, the relationship between the Ramsays breaks through its previous unhappy restraints. Although the isolation of both Lily and Ramsay is caused by the physical absence of Mrs Ramsay, their movement out of emotional chaos into what is at least a fleeting harmony depends in large part on their ability to sustain contact with the woman who has been dead ten years. The most dramatic example of Mrs Ramsay's capacity to endure, of course, is her sudden appearance to Lily—'There she sat' (310)—which inspires her to break through the obstacles preventing her from finishing her painting. But Mrs Ramsay's explicit return to Lily does not begin to exhaust her presence in the last part of the novel. The entire trip to the lighthouse, insisted upon by Mr Ramsay over the opposition of Cam and James, is in itself a tribute to Mrs Ramsay, representing as it does the completion of the expedition she had so fervently wanted for James ten years before. Mr Ramsay's impatience to go, which is not based on any easily comprehensible need, can only be understood in the context of the past, in Mrs Ramsay's concern that six-year-old James, with his passion for the lighthouse, should manage to get there.

In fact, though long since gone, Mrs Ramsay is very much present throughout the third section, living on in the minds of Lily, Ramsay, and his children. Mrs Ramsay's ability to endure the passage of ten years' time confirms her crucial understanding that 'there is a coherence in things, a stability; something, she meant, is immune from change, and shines out . . . in the face of the flowing, the fleeting, the spectral. . . .' (163) Mrs Ramsay's persistence makes clear that, however powerful the flux, transient moments of human order partake of

123

a kind of permanence every bit as real as the volume of poetry or the completed canvas. At the same time, her survival is part of the larger fabric of the past which weaves itself into the present action taking place in the third section. Woolf has carefully fashioned the novel so that what we perceive happening in the present during the first part of the book returns as the destiny of the past in the third. Reading the last section of *To the Lighthouse*, we constantly find ourselves re-experiencing aspects of the afternoon and early evening we initially encountered in the first part of the novel. The dynamics of the present are always informed by the burdens of the past. By having Lily, Ramsay, and the others think back on interactions and feelings that involved them ten years earlier, Woolf brings past and present together in a way which underlines the wholeness the last section achieves and the entire novel celebrates.

While Mrs Ramsay plays a large role in Mr Ramsay's obsession to go to the lighthouse, she is at the same time strongly identified with the lighthouse itself. As a symbol, of course, the lighthouse cannot be reduced to any conclusive set of meanings. Rich symbolic complexes go well beyond any effort to assign significance to them, and the lighthouse is sufficiently various in its functions and guises to elude simplistic explanations. Austerely phallic and yet appearing from a distance soft and misty, it presides inflexibly over the chaos of the sea while illuminating the darkness with its predictable stroke of light, at once stern and beautiful. To apply labels to it as critics occasionally do—God, eternity, a phallus, and ingenious others—is to engage in an altogether futile exercise. It is sufficient that the rugged and delicate lighthouse, a permanent source of order and light cutting across the watery flux, is very much there, the object of a quest that holds the novel together over a passage of ten years' time.

This is not to deny that there are contexts of meaning that surround the lighthouse and in which the lighthouse clearly participates. Without question, Mrs Ramsay is one of the most important of these. Herself a source of order and light, she instinctively embraces the third stroke of the lighthouse, 'the last of the three, which was her stroke, for watching them in this mood always at this hour one could not help attaching oneself to one thing especially of the things one saw; and this thing, the long steady stroke, was her stroke' (100). Pure, unhurried, immune from the uncertain shiftings of the waves, the steady beam of light embodies the strength and serenity which Mrs Ramsay herself radiates (101):

124

She looked up over her knitting and met the third stroke and it seemed to her like her own eyes meeting her own eyes, searching as she alone could search into her mind and her heart, purifying out of existence . . . any lie. She praised herself in praising the light, without vanity.

What Mrs Ramsay finds in the lighthouse, then—a comforting permanence that somehow bestrides time, very much as she does—is essentially what we find in it as well. The object and the person reinforce one another, and we share Mrs Ramsay's sense that one occasionally felt about inanimate things (in this case the lighthouse) that 'they expressed one; felt they became one; felt they knew one, in a sense were one; felt an irrational tenderness thus (she looked at that long steady light) as for oneself' (101).

But Mrs Ramsay's perceptions by no means encompass the totality of the lighthouse. There is much about it that has very little to do with her understanding, though this fact does not nullify the significance of her view. For as James realizes when he approaches the island, 'nothing was simply one thing' (286). The lighthouse is both what Mrs Ramsay makes it out to be from across the water and what James sees it to be up close: 'stark and straight' with windows and even laundry scattered on the rocks to dry. Totally different from the blurry tower of his youth, the lighthouse James visits is large enough to include coherently in itself all the disparate meanings attached to it by various people.

While Mrs Ramsay always discovers peace and nourishment in the security of the beam, James finds that the bare, exposed tower, stripped of any comforting fantasies, speaks to an altogether different sense of reality (312):

It satisfied him. It confirmed some obscure feeling of his about his own character . . . . Old Mrs. Beckwith, for example, was always saying how nice it was and how sweet it was and how they ought to be so proud and they ought to be so happy, but as a matter of fact James thought, looking at the Lighthouse stood there on its rock, it's like that. He looked at his father reading fiercely with his legs curled tight. They shared that knowledge.

Seen in this way, the lighthouse seems to embody that kind of unadorned factuality which Ramsay has always emphasized at the

125

expense of all human feeling: 'He was incapable of untruth; never tampered with a fact; never altered a disagreeable word to suit the pleasure or convenience of any mortal being, least of all his own children' (13). It is for this, indeed, that James hates him, resenting him not only for shattering his illusions but also ridiculing Mrs Ramsay's efforts to maintain them. Insisting at the start of the novel that the weather would not permit a trip to the lighthouse the next day, Ramsay earns the fierce emnity which persists throughout the intervening ten years, so that as the sailboat makes it way across the bay with its two unwilling passengers, the impulse to strike Mr Ramsay through the heart is as real as ever to James. And though Cam's hostility is far less violent than her brother's, she too seethes with anger at his selfish tyrannies.

For Mr Ramsay, it is the act of sailing to the island rather than any features or functions of the physical lighthouse which is important. Although relatively innocuous in itself, the trip comes to represent a self-justifying achievement of the highest order. His impatience to start suggests the significance he himself senses in the expedition. Completing Mrs Ramsay's wishes of ten years before, the sail enables him to resolve the antipathies nurtured by his children and earn from them, particularly James, a sympathetic appreciation of his point of view which they had never exhibited before. The trip to the lighthouse marks an enormous personal breakthrough for Ramsay. If his arrival at the island does not necessarily take him, in his intellectual calculus, past the letter Q at which he feels himself stuck, it permits him to transcend, at least temporarily, the self-imposed restrictions of such categories. Praising James for having steered them successfully, Ramsay manages to leave his alphabet behind altogether, gaining instead the respect of his children. Cam knows that praise from his father is what James has been waiting for, not just for this trip but for his whole life, and her pleasure in hearing it given is every bit as great as James's in receiving it. Just as Lily, on the far shore, finally reaches out to Ramsay, eager to give him the sympathy she had previously withheld, so the children end their sail in a similarly supportive way: 'What do you want? they both wanted to ask. They both wanted to say, Ask us anything and we will give it you' (318). Fiercely alone and totally involved in his own thoughts, Ramsay says nothing. The last description of him, however, suggests the heroic but still human stature his honesty and essential goodness have achieved for him in his children's eyes (318):

126

He rose and stood in the bow of the boat, very straight and tall, for all the world, James thought, as if he were saying, 'There is no God,' and Cam thought, as if he were leaping into space, and they both rose to follow him as he sprang, lightly like a young man, holding his parcel, on to the rock.

Ramsay's arrival at the lighthouse coincides almost exactly with Lily's finishing of her painting. Both the painting and the landing speak to some completed sense of things which cannot be translated into a series of propositions. The possibility that Ramsay might be thinking before he jumps off the boat onto land, 'I have reached it. I have found it' (318), is echoed by Lily, peering into the blue haze across the bay and saying, as they land, 'He must have reached it.' And it obviously corresponds to the same kind of ultimate recognition expressed by Lily's 'I have had my vision' which concludes the novel. Each represents an intensely personal triumph of understanding and achievement which manages, however briefly, to make sense out of the whole chaotic business of living. For a moment at least there is an experience of order and fulfillment—all that one can hope for in a world which does not offer any guarantees of happiness. The connection between the two is important—in her diary Woolf mentions her wrestling with the problem of 'how to bring Lily and Mr R. together and make a combination of interest at the end' (*A Writer's Diary*, 99)—for it establishes a final context of order larger than that of two individual visions. Mr Ramsay's voyage to the lighthouse and Lily's struggle with her canvas are both absorbed into a final symmetry which sees the two acts as different versions of the same human aspiration. If the final celebration of order needs to be sanctified by some deity, that service is provided by Mr Carmichael, the poet, who from the beginning of the novel has had about him an almost mythic aura of self-contained wisdom. As Christian deities do not preside over Woolf novels, he appears 'now like an old pagan God, shaggy, with weeds in his hair' (319), to extend his benediction over the scene (319):

He stood there spreading his hands over all the weakness and suffering of mankind; she thought he was surveying, tolerantly, compassionately, their final destiny.

9

Orlando

Orlando is as marvelously different in tone from the rest of Woolf's work as *The Secret Agent* is from everything else Conrad ever wrote. An exuberant, richly satiric book containing what is probably the single most implausible event in all of prose fiction, *Orlando* flies giddily along on the wings of fantasy, impelled by a comic inventiveness which will never again appear in Woolf's writing. Conceived in part as 'an escapade after those serious poetic experimental books whose form is so closely considered' (*A Writer's Diary*, 105), it blends into a unique amalgam two early ideas for books she was considering after *To the Lighthouse* was finished. The first, a fantasy called *The Jessamy Brides*, which would contain satire, sapphism, and mock everything, including her own lyric style; and the second, an 'amusing book. . . . Truthful but fantastic' (*A Writer's Diary*, 114) about the lives of some of her friends, involving among others, a portrait of Vita Sackville-West as Orlando, a young nobleman. The result is a 'biography' of Orlando—a whimsical, loving treatment of Vita and her exotic gypsy and Sackville-West ancestry—which runs from the middle of the sixteenth century, when Orlando is an aspiring poet of sixteen, through a rather unexpected change of sex from male to female experienced somewhere early in the eighteenth century at the age of thirty, to 11 October 1928, when she is a celebrated writer of thirty-six.

Like the theme, the texture of the book is wild and free, filled with bold, exaggerated strokes that succeed, as *The Jessamy Brides* intended, in mocking everything, especially its own pretensions as a biography. Above all—and there is no other word for it, however out of place it may seem in a discussion of Woolf—the book was meant to be 'fun' as nothing else she ever wrote was. Throughout her diary she mentions it always as something half-laughing, a joke, a writer's holiday, and the enormous pleasure she took in writing it communicates itself to us on every page as we read it. Woolf herself recognized that it was off the main path of her formal explorations—'I never got down to my depths and made shapes square up, as I did in the *Lighthouse*' (*A Writer's Diary*, 136), but *Orlando* is none the less successful for comprising a gay interlude in that solemn quest of artistic discovery in which she was endlessly engaged during her creative lifetime.

In fact, although the fun, fantasy, and looseness of structure provide Woolf with a respite from her central preoccupation with form, *Orlando* is by no means a trivial entertainment designed solely to amuse. If its form is not in itself of compelling interest to Woolf, its concern with the creative imagination, the experience of time and selfhood, the fact of sexual inequality very definitely are; far from being a precious oddity, *Orlando* is a substantial work of art whose lighthearted treatment of serious subjects does not belie their importance. It is without question a significant part of Woolf's total achievement.

The book's happy irreverence appears on the very title page itself, officially declaring *Orlando* to be a biography. The sacred obligation of the biographer, 'to plod, without looking to right or left, in the indelible footprints of truth' (62), is invoked at crucial points to justify the most outrageous events the narrator is forced to relate. The week-long sleeps, the great frost, the sex change—all are faithfully recounted, in spite of their seemingly improbable nature, because of the biographer's unswerving commitment to the truth. Dutifully following Orlando through three and a half centuries of romantic adventures and literary dabblings, the biography seeks only to honor the facts, whatever they might be. Woolf heartily enjoys playing on every page with the nature of historical and biographical truth and the earnest efforts of those who seek to unravel the past. *Orlando*'s method, of course, is to rely on historical documents whenever possible, though sometimes Woolf admits, when sources are destroyed as in the case of the records dealing with Orlando's tenure as ambassador to Turkey, other measures must be employed (110):

> Just when we thought to elucidate a secret that has puzzled
> historians for a hundred years, there was a hole in the manuscript
> big enough to put your finger through. We have done our best to
> piece out a meagre summary from the charred fragments that
> remain; but often it has been necessary to speculate, to surmise,
> and even to use the imagination.

The pleasure Woolf takes in spoofing the august responsibilities of the biographer is part of the explicit self-consciousness about the act of writing the book which is ironically present throughout *Orlando*. If Woolf's authorial self is completely absent from the tightly wrought forms of all her experimental novels, here it is conspicuously before us everywhere, scrutinizing and commenting on her own sentences even as she composes them. The reader's attention is constantly drawn to the process of creating *Orlando* going on before him: 'Nature, who has so much to answer for besides the perhaps unwieldy length of this sentence' (73), Woolf writes, for example, directing us away from the content to consider the shape of the prose itself. Or, 'This method of writing biography, though it has its merits, is a little bare, perhaps, and the reader, if we go on with it, may complain that he could recite the calendar for himself and so save his pocket whatever sum the Hogarth Press may think proper to charge for this book' (240). A blank space on the page which the reader must think to be 'filled to repletion' (228), and a footnote explaining that Alexander Pope's witticisms are omitted from the text because they are too well known to be worth the bother and in any case can be found in his published works are other of the numerous instances of the self-mocking spirit that animates the whole. Woolf's muse in this playful treatment of her own fictional enterprise is Lawrence Sterne, whose *Tristram Shandy*, deeply admired by Woolf, obviously provided a model for the comically self-aware narrative voice in *Orlando*. Sterne is one of the many people Woolf acknowledges in her preface as having helped her with the book, along with almost every Bloomsbury friend she had at the time, in addition to her two nephews, Julian and Quentin.

In broad outline, as well as in specific details and allusions providing many private laughs for the informed reader, Orlando's life is based not only on Vita's personal experiences but on the composite experience of her whole family—both the Sackville-Wests on her father's side and the Spanish gypsy dancer, Pepita, on her mother's. Although it is certainly possible to enjoy *Orlando* without realizing the extent to which it faithfully, albeit fantastically, renders the facts of Vita's own life and those of her ancestral past, a minimal familiarity with at least some of them can help us to appreciate the humor and imaginative elegance of Woolf's accomplishment.

The family history Woolf weaves into *Orlando* is dealt with somewhat more directly by Vita herself in *Pepita*, the intriguing story of Vita's exotic grandmother. Known professionally as 'the Star of

Andalusia,' Pepita danced her way through Europe and into the arms of Lionel Sackville-West, Vita's grandfather and a direct descendant of Thomas Sackville (1536–1608), cousin to Queen Elizabeth I, poet, politician, and ultimately Lord High Treasurer of England. English nobility and Spanish peasant blood produced five illegitimate children over the course of nineteen years, one of whom, Vita's mother, eventually married yet another Sackville-West, her younger cousin, Lionel. From this union Vita was born in 1892, making it perfectly appropriate that Orlando, having endured some 350 years of English history, be exactly thirty-six years old when the novel concludes in 1928. Briefly, then, to the aristocratic Sackvilles Orlando owes the affection of Queen Elizabeth I and his appointment as her Treasurer, his career as statesman, and most important, the 365-bedroom estate with its fifty-two staircases which remains a fixed point of affection for Orlando throughout all the changes both she and England experience in the book. For Vita, the Knole in which she grew up represented the ideal form of graciousness and civilization she cherished above all else. More than simply a place, it became for her a lasting center of value. Orlando's intense love of her ancestral home accurately reflects the emotional bond which always existed, even after she moved away, between Vita and Knole.

To Vita's dancing grandmother Orlando owes a shapely pair of legs, admired by queens of England and sea captains alike, his marriage, while still a male, to one Rosina Pepita, 'a dancer, father unknown, but reputed a gipsy' (122), and her sustained interlude, following the sex change, with the gypsies in Turkey. And from the illicit relationship itself of the grandparents comes the legal suit which took Vita's mother considerably less time to settle than the century during which it occupies Orlando's energies. The actual suit involved elements of farce worthy of Woolf's own comic imagination here. As the illegitimacy of old Lionel's children meant that Knole went to a cousin (eventually Vita's father), an attempt was made by Lionel's oldest son (Vita's uncle) to prove that Pepita and Lionel had actually married, so that he would be entitled to Knole. To support this claim, he had initially to show that Pepita had divorced her first husband with whom she had stayed a few months before running off to Europe, a complicated process which involved forged documents of various sorts in small Spanish towns, tampering with different registers, and all manner of high intrigue. Although the job was botched, sufficient bogus evidence was manufactured to institute the case. Vita's mother, who had only come into possession of Knole through her marriage, thus found herself in the socially curious position of having to argue for her own illegitimacy, and that of her brothers and sisters as well, in order to defend her right to the estate. After much publicity and expense, Vita's mother succeeded in irrevocably proving all of them bastards, thereby assuring her tenure at Knole. Orlando's satisfaction at having the children of his marriage to Pepita officially certified as illegitimate—'so they don't inherit, which is all to the good' (229)—is a mild version of the relief Vita's mother felt at being guaranteed an uncontested lifetime at her stately home.

→ Orlando's literary life draws on Vita's own in several ways. The fluency with which Vita started writing at an early age—beginning her first novel when she was fourteen and then moving on to plays in French, verse dramas and other novels and assorted forms—clearly accounts for Orlando's prolific outpouring: 'Thus had been written, before he was turned twenty-five, some forty-seven plays, histories, romances, poems; some in prose. Some in verse; some in French, some in Italian; all romantic and all long' (72). And Orlando's prize winning poem, 'The Oak Tree', which causes Sir Nicholas Greene, after having scoffed at it three hundred years earlier, to compare her with Milton, is Vita's 'The Land,' recipient of the Hawthornden Prize in 1927.

As interesting as some of the specific correspondences between Orlando and Vita are, biographical fidelity is not the point of the book. Although in its own wry way *Orlando* constitutes a sensitive treatment of Vita, the portrait of the artist which emerges transcends its real life model to embody views of art and the creative process central to Virginia Woolf, not Vita Sackville-West. The three hundred-year gestation period of 'The Oak Tree,' paralleling Orlando's own growth as an artist, provides Woolf with a rich opportunity to explore the development of the literary imagination.

Afflicted from the start with the dread writing disease, a shameful ailment for anybody but particularly for a nobleman, Orlando in his early efforts shows the influence largely of his own immaturity, producing tedious works dealing with the personal crisis of some mythological luminary, such as The Death of Hippolytus, The Birth of Pyramus, Iphigenia in Aulis. Following Sasha's cruel betrayal of his love, he decides explicitly to channel his despair into the quest for poetic immortality. The distinction conferred upon him through the written word will more than compensate for the human solitude which must now necessarily be his forever. He seeks the literary advice of the well-known poet and critic, Nicholas Greene, who in between his denunciations of Elizabethan literature—'the art of poetry was dead in England' (82)—counsels Orlando always to pursue 'La Gloire (he pronounced it Glawr, so that Orlando did not at first catch his meaning)' (83). But Greene does not really answer the questions besetting Orlando of what poetry is, or truth, or love, or even (and most important) Orlando himself. And when Greene responds to Orlando's gracious hospitality by pillorying his person, habits, and bombastic literary creations in the fiercely satiric 'Visit to a Nobleman in the Country', Orlando in a fit of anger burns everything he ever wrote except 'The Oak Tree,' an unassuming, slim poem altogether different in style and theme from those mightily ambitious works designed to bring him his fame. It is too personal and innocent to destroy, constituting the first version of Orlando's simple but intense love of the English countryside and the rhythms of nature. Hardly the stuff out of which literary reputations are forged.

But his renunciation of 'Glawr' and vow to write only to please himself are not sufficient to complete the poem. Scratching out more lines than he writes in, Orlando at times seems on the verge of eliminating altogether the poem he is trying to finish. For the artist must first discover himself before he can create his art, and Orlando has a sex change and three hundred years of experience to absorb in the process of making that discovery. Kept close to Orlando's bosom for the next three centuries, the manuscript encounters everything she does; like Orlando, it is 'sea-stained, blood-stained, travel-stained' (213). Orlando's growth also marks the growth of her poetic vision, and when she actively returns to the poem at the end of the nineteenth century, she suddenly begins to realize that it represents something enduring about her own self and values that had managed to survive the changes of mood, sex, and centuries she had witnessed: 'Yet through all these changes she had remained, she reflected, funda-mentally the same. She had the same brooding meditative temper, the same love of animals and nature, the same passion for the country and the seasons' (214). She is impelled to complete the poem because of her own urgent need to articulate that vision of things she now under-stands has been a vital part of her for nearly three hundred years.

Certain about what it is she wants to express, she picks up her pen—and is horrified by the insipid slop that pours forth. There yet remains one last enormous obstacle between Orlando and successful creation: the unyielding demands of what Woolf calls 'the spirit of the age.' Having sympathetically partaken, in turn, of the Restoration and eighteenth-century spirit, Orlando finds herself an alien in nineteenth-century culture which insists on a respectable marital state for all its citizens. Fight it as she might, Orlando cannot rise above the acute discomfort and creative blockage caused by the absence of a thin gold band on the appropriate finger of her left hand (219):

> For it would seem—her case proved it—that we write, not with the fingers, but with the whole person. The nerve which controls the pen winds itself about every fibre of our being, threads the heart, pierces the liver. Though the seat of her trouble seemed to be the left hand, she could feel herself poisoned through and through, and was forced at length to consider the most desperate of remedies, which was to yield completely and submissively to the spirit of the age, and take a husband.

Although Woolf is having fun here with notions of the *zeitgeist* and its formidable powers, the necessity of the artist to reach at least a minimal accommodation with his age in the interests of his own creative wellbeing is something she strongly believes at this point in her career. As the isolated, anguished figure of Miss La Trobe in *Between the Acts* indicates, Woolf later comes to see a state of estrangement as viable for the artist; now, however, Orlando finds her adverse position in society to be inimical to the completion of her poem. A solution to Orlando's problem fortunately presents itself in the person of Marmaduke Bonthrop Shelmerdine, who not only marries her but then immediately thereafter returns to his voyages around Cape Horn, leaving her at once happily married and happily alone. Having made her peace with the age while at the same time remaining true to her own solitary identity, Orlando is at last free to do her work (239–40):

> And she heaved a deep sigh of relief, as indeed, well she might, for the transaction between a writer and the spirit of the age is one of infinite delicacy, and upon a nice arrangement between the two the whole fortune of his work depends. Orlando had so ordered it that she was in an extremely happy position; she need neither fight her age, nor submit to it; she was of it, yet remained herself. Now, therefore, she could write, and write she did. She wrote. She wrote. She wrote.

And what she writes she wants to have published, not in the cause of the 'Glawr' that obsessed her 330 years before, but because of her recognition that the poem itself needs an audience in order fully to realize its own nature as a work of art (245):

> The manuscript which reposed above her heart began shuffling
> and beating as if it were a living thing, and . . . Orlando, by
> inclining her head, could make out what it was that it was saying.
> It wanted to be read. It must be read. It would die in her bosom
> if it were not read.

The seven editions the poem immediately goes through, the 'Burdett Coutts' Memorial Prize, and the admiration of Sir Nicholas Greene earn for Orlando all the fame she ever sought, but which she now sees as totally irrelevant to the act of writing poetry. Having weathered the illusions, delusions, and superficial attractions of the literary life, Orlando comes finally to understand that poetry is at heart 'a secret transaction, a voice answering a voice' (292), and that all the rest is nonsense. Orlando's assessment of her own poem is Woolf's way of paying eloquent tribute to Vita's voice in 'The Land' (292):

> What could have been more secret, she thought, more slow, and
> like the intercourse of lovers, than the stammering answer she
> had made all these years to the old crooning song of the woods,
> and the farms and the brown horses standing at the gate, neck to
> neck, and the smithy and the kitchen and the fields, so
> laboriously bearing wheat, turnips, grass, and the garden blowing
> irises and fritillaries.

As Vita and Virginia are very different kinds of writers, part of *Orlando*'s success is its ability to honor Vita and her achievement in 'The Land' while at the same time using that achievement as a vehicle for illustrating Woolf's own views on the nature of the creative imagination.

The central event in Orlando's growth both as a person and a poet, of course, is her transformation from male to female at the age of thirty while serving as ambassador to Turkey. Most poets, like most people, do not ordinarily experience a sudden sex change during the course of their lives, and Vita was certainly no exception. As Vita was born and unquestionably remained female throughout her life, Orlando's rather startling development cannot be attributed to the oddness of her model, or to the biographer's sacred dedication to the truth. Instead, it is an imaginative way of focusing on the nature of sexual identity and the problems of women. Although Woolf certainly enjoys (and exploits) the comic possibilities of the shift, at the same time it is employed in the service of ideas not in the least comic.

Woolf's concern for women's rights and the necessity to avoid simplistic—and destructive—stereotyping is directly addressed in two non-fictional works, *A Room of One's Own* (1929) and *Three Guineas* (1938). While *Orlando*'s treatment of these problems is altogether different in tone from her two sustained essays, it is no less telling. Whimsy and humor help *Orlando* manage the difficult task of dealing with serious issues in a properly lighthearted vein which does not violate the spirit of the work.

Although Orlando's is the only instance of actual sexual transformation in the novel, the sexual identity of a number of characters is frequently difficult to ascertain with any certainty. Orlando's first glimpse of Sasha, for example, leaves him wondering whether it is a man or woman he is looking at. The Archduchess Harriet Griselda of Finster-Aarhorn, whose fulsome advances finally drive Orlando to flee to Turkey, turns out to be Archduke Harry who had fallen helplessly in love with a portrait of the young Orlando and had donned his female disguise in order better to approach him. And if Marmaduke Bonthrop Shelmerdine, Esquire, is the male he seems to be, the most intense moment of his relationship with Orlando occurs when each recognizes the presence of the opposite sex in the other (227):

> 'You're a woman, Shel!' she cried.
> 'You're a man, Orlando!' he cried.

The ambiguities of gender and the incidents of deliberate sexual disguise, such as when Orlando, after her change, wanders through London dressed as a boy, derive in some degree at least from Vita's own life. Vita's lesbianism, which did not prevent her from spending her life married to Harold Nicholson and bearing two children, obviously provided the inspiration for the theme of uncertain sexual identity running throughout the novel. And more specifically, at one point in her life she actually enjoyed putting on male garb and masquerading for several days at a time as a young man. Beyond the merely personal, however, these motifs are part of Woolf's assault on all rigidly categorized notions of adult identity. If the two sexes remain happily distinct for Woolf, there nevertheless exists no firm demarcation between proper male or female behavior. The complex adult should be capable of responses and perceptions all too frequently attributed exclusively to one sex or the other: 'Different though the sexes are, they intermix. In every human being a vacillation from one to the other takes place' (172). And what is true of people in general is (or should be) especially true of the artist. As she goes on to argue in *A Room of One's Own*, the artist in particular must transcend the traditional polarities of sexual classification which insist that the male be aggressive, rational, tough-minded, the female passive, intuitive, sympathetic. The complete human being, like the receptive writer, should embrace within a flexible self all manner of so-called male and female impulses. A woman who lived the first thirty years of her life as a man, Orlando knows the mind and feelings of each, and clearly epitomizes the personality that has escaped from the limited, stereo-typed notions of selfhood perpetuated by society. Out of the considerable psychic muddle of Vita's own life, Woolf creates in the person of Orlando a healthy, mature personality unthreatened by its own diversity.

In addition to illustrating in rather stunning fashion Woolf's commitment to an adult sexual identity which actively recognizes both male and female components, Orlando's transformation produces the ideal point of view from which to record the difficulties of women in a distinctly unliberated world. For who is better qualified to document the abuses of a sexist society than a woman who spent the first part of her life gaily perpetuating those abuses as a thoughtless male? Considering herself still to be the same human being as she was before the change, Orlando is appalled by the unfairness of a society which no longer permits her the freedom of expression, movement, and thought that was hers when she was wearing trousers instead of skirts. Her new costume, Orlando fears as she nears the cliffs of England on her voyage from Turkey, perhaps 'meant conventionality, meant slavery, meant deceit, meant denying her love, fettering her limbs, pursing her lips, and restraining her tongue' (149), and her actual experience as a woman proves that she is not far wrong. From the moment she arrives in England in the middle of the eighteenth century she encounters all those debilitating prejudices about the nature and capability of women against which Woolf struggled all her life. Modifying her behavior so as not to offend, Orlando soon realizes how life-denying are the expectations men formulate for women—and to which women are foolish enough to adhere. The chastity, sobriety, and decorousnesss she eschewed as a man are now

137

necessarily hers with the advent of her femininity. The very notion of pursuing a career as a writer, of course, is antithetical to proper canons of female conduct (242):

> Surely, since she is a woman, and a beautiful woman, and a woman in the prime of life, she will soon give over this pretense of writing and thinking and begin at least to think of a gamekeeper (and as long as she thinks of a man nobody objects to a woman thinking). And then she will write him a little note (and as long as she writes little notes, nobody objects to a woman writing either).

Orlando mocks all the anti-feminist canards Woolf loathed: the inability of a woman to write, think, enjoy another's company, or want anything more out of life than the love signified by the respectable marriage. While very much a celebration of Orlando's (and Vita's) personal and artistic triumph, the book at the same time exposes—and protests against—the sexist prejudices of society.

Orlando's exuberance in treating social issues is a direct result of its non-experimental nature. Unburdened by those formal preoccupations central to Woolf's exploratory novels, *Orlando* enjoys the freedom to play with ideas shared by none of her 'serious prose' books. Although the condition of women and the vagaries of sexual identity are perhaps the most important and pervasive themes, *Orlando*'s sharp wit also embraces the sacred institution of marriage, the fascinations of high society and the nature and practice of the literary life, to name only a few. The fatuous Nick Greene who in the course of 350 years moves from scruffy, ill-paid poet to successful establishment critic provides Woolf with a delightful instrument to excoriate the business of letters. He marvelously embodies the time-tested technique of making a reputation as an eminent critic by invoking the glories of the past to dismiss the debased state of whatever is current. When Orlando first meets Nick in the sixteenth century, he is already railing against 'the precious conceits and wild experiments' (83) of the Elizabethans, finding nothing of value in Shakespeare, Jonson, Marlowe, Browne, Donne, and others. The last great age of literature, he dismally announces, ended with the Greeks. Three centuries of unremitting literary despair finally produce the desired result: when Orlando again bumps into him in the latter part of the nineteenth century, he is now Sir Nicholas, the most influential critic of the time. Well-fed, well-clothed, cleanshaven, and altogether respectable, he nevertheless remains true to his critical principles: the degeneracy of the period is now illustrated by the likes of Carlyle, Browning, and Tennyson, whose work is 'marked by precious conceits and wild experiments' (250) the Elizabethans would not have tolerated for a moment. The days of Jonson and Shakespeare, Dryden and Pope are over forever.

Verging on seventy when Orlando meets him in the nineteenth century, Nick has grown old far more precipitously in three centuries than has Orlando. Both, of course, weather the passage of hundreds of years rather well. Like Orlando's change of sex, the inordinately long lifetimes of Nick and Orlando are not simply a purely fantastic invention that allows Woolf the perspective (in this case, historical) necessary for much of her satire. Whatever the satiric possibilities it opens, the fact of Orlando's ageing twenty years in 350 is part of Woolf's serious concern with the perception of time found, in one way or another, in all of her books. External, linear chronologies have little to do with the inner experience of time which can be complicated, parodoxical, and totally at variance with how things appear on the surface. The theory behind Orlando's extraordinary life span is explicitly stated near the end of the novel (274–5):

> And, indeed, it cannot be denied that the most successful practitioners of the art of life, often unknown people by the way, somehow contrive to synchronise the sixty or seventy different times which beat simultaneously in every normal human system so that when eleven strikes, all the rest chime in unison, and the present is neither a violent disruption nor completely forgotten in the past. Of them we can justly say that they live precisely the sixty-eight or seventy-two years allotted them on the tombstone. Of the rest some we know to be dead though they walk among us; some are not yet born though they go through the forms of life; others are hundreds of years old though they call themselves thirty-six. The true length of a person's life, whatever the *Dictionary of National Biography* may say, is always a matter of dispute.

The manner in which people experience the variety of times at work within as well as outside of themselves is crucially related to the way in which they experience their own selves. For Woolf, every attempt at self-definition necessarily involves, whether consciously or not, some sort of accommodation to inner and outer flux: 'For if there are (at a venture) seventy-six different times all ticking in the mind at once, how many different people are there not—Heaven help us—all having lodgment at one time or other in the human spirit? Some say two thousand and fifty-two' (277). Trying to pull a viable identity together out of the welter of the past, Orlando is faced with a particularly bewildering array of different temporal selves. A life covering three centuries and a miraculous sexual transformation does not make selection easy. What is she? Is she the young nobleman, the Turkish Ambassador, the gipsy, the Patroness of Letters?

Orlando's attempt at the end of the novel to summon one unified self out of the myriad available seems destined to fail when she is suddenly seized by the image of a wild goose flying out to sea, symbolizing the elusive reality the Woolfian artist is committed to pursue. She understands that throughout everything she has been and done, it has always been this quest for the goose in which she has essentially been engaged (282):

> But the goose flies too fast. I've seen it, here—there—England, Persia, Italy. Always it flies fast out to sea and always I fling after it words like nets (here she flung her hand out) which shrivel as I've seen nets shrivel drawn on deck with only sea-weed in them; and sometimes there's an inch of silver—six words—in the bottom of the net. But never the great fish who lives in the coral groves.

The importance of this search to Woolf herself, not primarily Vita, is suggested by a comment Woolf makes in her dairy upon finishing *The Waves*, when she refers to having finally 'netted that fin in the waste of water' (169) which appeared to her as she was working on *To the Lighthouse*.

Absorbed by her role as an artist and no longer earnestly striving to fashion a complete self, Orlando immediately achieves precisely that. Without the interference of her will, she comes into contact with that same 'wedge-shaped core of darkness' at the center of her being that Mrs Ramsay reaches when she is left alone (282):

> The whole of her darkened and settled, as when some foil whose addition makes the round and solidity of a surface is added to it, and the shallow becomes deep and the near distant; and all is contained as water is contained by the sides of a well. So she was now darkened, stilled, and become, with the addition of this Orlando, what is called, rightly or wrongly, a single self, a real self. And she fell silent.

Orlando's discovery of her essential artistic self marks the appropriate conclusion for a book which is finally less concerned with Vita Sackville-West than with depicting Woolf's own sense of the workings of the creative imagination. Like *To the Lighthouse*, *Between the Acts*, and *The Waves*, *Orlando* closes with an affirmation of art. The writer here not only finds herself a best-selling author, but more importantly comes to understand who she is and what her craft is all about. Feeling herself 'one and entire' for the first time, Orlando pays tribute to the land which nurtured her for so long and which made possible that 'secret transaction, a voice answering a voice' (292), which is 'The Oak Tree.' The novel, however, does not stop with honoring what Orlando has already achieved but instead celebrates the ongoing nature of the creative process itself. Orlando's final words—'"It is the goose!" Orlando cried. "The wild goose,"' (295)—point the way to the necessarily unfinished task of the artist in the pursuit of reality. Embedding that pursuit firmly in the heart of the present, the last sentence of the novel—'And the twelfth stroke of midnight sounded; the twelfth stroke of midnight, Thursday, the eleventh of October, Nineteen hundred and twenty eight' (295)—testifies to the importance of the creative enterprise for Woolf. The strains of parody, biography and satire fall away and Woolf is left, as always, endorsing the life-giving energies of art.

10

The Waves

The Waves is unquestionably the most difficult of Virginia Woolf's novels. 'An abstract mystical eyeless book: a playpoem' (*A Writer's Diary*, 137), as she herself calls an early version of it, its form poses problems for even the most experienced Woolf reader. Her own testimony in the diary confirms the difficulty: no book resisted its conception or execution more doggedly than did *The Waves*. Certainly none was more exhausting to complete. 'Never have I screwed my brain so tight over a book,' she writes (*A Writer's Diary*, 167), and the exultation she experienced on Saturday 7 February 1931, when she finished at last was perhaps more intense than at any other point in her creative life.

The struggle, as always, was to shape her intuitions about reality into a form which would at once be different from anything she had done before while at the same time conveying her vision coherently to the world. In this case, the form was the most ambitious and demanding she had yet attempted, and her anxiety, when the novel was finished, was that no one would understand what it all meant: 'What I want to be told is that this is solid and means something. What it means I myself shan't know till I write another book' (*A Writer's Diary*, 174).

The diary records Woolf's tentative gropings towards what was to be the novel's final form. As early as 1926 she notes that she is haunted by the notion of a novel about the life of a woman in which all shall 'be told on one occasion; and time shall be obliterated . . . . My theory being that the actual event practically does not exist—nor time either' (*A Writer's Diary*, 102). Originally to be called *The Moths*, her 'completely new attempt' (*A Writer's Diary*, 133) gradually begins to acquire those fragments of theme and method out of which *The Waves* will painstakingly emerge. To the idea that neither time nor actual

142

events really exists, Woolf blends her intention to give 'the moment whole; whatever it includes. Say that the moment is a combination of thought; sensation; the voice of the sea' (*A Writer's Diary*, 139). Whatever else it includes, the moment has nothing to do with the reality Woolf finds conventionally embodied in novels. Woolf's moment is saturated, intense, and altogether more abstract than anything found in her contemporaries' work. 'I am not trying to tell a story' (*A Writer's Diary*, 143), she emphasizes, though she acknowledges that:

> perhaps it might be done that way. A mind thinking. They might be islands of light—islands in the stream that I am trying to convey; life itself going on . . . . I shall have the two different currents—the moths flying along; the flower upright in the centre; a perpetual crumbling and renewing of the plant. But who is she? I am very anxious that she should have no name. I don't want a Lavinia or a Penelope: I want 'she.' But that becomes arty, Liberty greenery yallery somehow: symbolic in loose robes.

As the novel develops, the question of narrative consciousness becomes more and more central to the design: who is thinking the novel, and what relationship does Woolf have to the thinker? From the nameless single women, Woolf moves to what she herself calls 'a series of dramatic soliloquies' (*A Writer's Diary*, 159)—six separate voices expressing themselves in a formalized, highly artificial language that is altogether different from the way people either think or speak. And the voice of the sea, which Woolf wants to sound throughout the novel, appears in the nine densely imagistic interludes which trace the movement of the sun across the sky, thus framing the voices within the context of a single day.

Woolf's 'mystical eyeless book,' then, finally resolves itself into two formal components: the italicized, poetic interludes, beginning always with the position of the sun in the sky and including the interaction of light, shadow, wind, wave and bird; and the six voices speaking in their oddly impersonal way of all that is human. Or, to use the language of Bernard, the artist who attempts to summarize the human experience of the novel, *The Waves* consists of Woolf's rendering of what people are and 'of what is outside us, of what we are not' (197). It is in the relationship between them that Woolf hopes to catch the reality of what life itself is like. To borrow Bernard's phrase again, 'to fix the moment in one effort of supreme endeavour' (28), to tell 'the true story' (135).

Woolf's story, like Bernard's, does not involve any kind of traditional narrative technique. As she suggested in her diary, actual events practically do not exist here, nor does the passage of time make itself felt in any psychologically plausible way. More unsettling, the voices—all of which are attached to what appear to be specific human identities, namely Bernard, Susan, Rhoda, Neville, Jinny, and Louis—share a highly stylized, undifferentiated language which is the discourse neither of conversation nor of human consciousness scrutinizing itself. The six speakers inhabit a self-contained verbal universe in which the usual signposts of time and space have very little relevance. Although their language is indeed referential, speaking about recognizable human experiences and feeling such as school, jealousy, love, business, marriage, death, and the like, the voices were not intended to be fictional characters participating in any kind of felt social or psychological world. Woolf has taken pains to seal them into a richly textured verbal environment away from the contamination of quotidian reality. It is only through 'great freedom from "reality,"' (*A Writer's Diary*, 144), as Woolf maintained throughout her career, that one is capable of getting to 'the "real" life.' The ritualistic use of 'said' (Bernard said, Rhoda said, Neville said) to introduce every single speaker in the novel makes it difficult to mistake the soliloquies for any simple rendering of a person's thought processes. Even more significant is the fact that although the different speakers all have different points of view and preoccupations, they use the same kind of sentence rhythms and employ similar kinds of image patterns. If the substantive concerns of each speaker vary—Louis involved with his isolation and, later, his business enterprises, Rhoda with her agony, Jinny her body, Bernard his phrases—the texture of their language does not. Together the six separate speakers constitute one common voice.

One effect of having disparate sensibilities embracing one undifferentiated mode of expression is to make us see them all as part of a single unity. However isolated they feel, however unique their individual perceptions, all are intimately connected, well below the level of their own conscious understanding, with everyone else. The fact of isolation and union, of course, is a basic Woolf tenet insisted upon in every novel. People are at once separate and at the same time plural. Bernard, who like every Woolf artist is gifted with particularly telling insight, makes this clear as he analyzes the experiences of himself and his friends (197):

> It is not one life that I look back upon; I am not one person; I am many people; I do not know altogether who I am—Jinny, Susan, Neville, Rhoda, or Louis: or how to distinguish my life from theirs.

Achieving the fusion of isolation and oneness through the texture of the language itself is perhaps the most daring imaginative foray Woolf was ever to attempt.

Participating in a totally verbal universe of their own creation, the voices were never intended by Woolf to be thought of as fictional 'characters' such as those who inhabit *To the Lighthouse*, *Between the Acts*, or any other of her novels. She comments with some amusement that it is 'Odd, that they [*The Times*] should praise my characters when I meant to have none' (*A Writer's Diary*, 175). Although all have been involved with each other since infancy and refer to interactions that have indeed occurred between them, no real contact—or conversation—actually takes place during the course of the novel. Speaker follows speaker in hermetically sealed succession, each expressing images, ideas, and feelings which are not in any strict sense spoken or thought—or communicated to anyone else. Perhaps the best way to describe the relationship of language to the voices is to say that the soliloquies are *attached* to the speakers, revealing views which exist almost independent of human volition. Even when they speak of their bodies, as Jinny, Neville, and Susan frequently do, we are not meant to invest the voices with any tangible physical selfhood. They remain always abstractions, designed to illuminate the truth of human experience without themselves being part of it. It is only through such distancing that Woolf felt she could in fact get at the truth.

At the same time that Woolf did not conceive of these voices as adding up in any way to literary 'characters,' it is not possible to create a distinctly human voice meditating on the experience of living without having it take on some of the lineaments of human character. It is a necessary impurity that neither Woolf nor the reader can avoid altogether. Although Woolf was obviously seeking to escape the confines of character drawing, *The Times* was not totally obtuse: as she noted in her diary of 1930, 'What I now think (about *The Waves*) is that I can give in a very few strokes the essentials of a person's character' (*A Writer's Diary*, 157). And just as Woolf could not manufacture a human voice which did not to some degree take on the blemish of human character, so, too, the critic, in spite of his best efforts, finds himself investing these voices with the trappings of character. It is not, however, a serious flaw or contradiction; as long as we recognize the difficulty, the inevitable imprecision of Woolf's categories and our own descriptive abilities need not bother us.

Woven out of a common verbal fabric, the six voices together attempt to fix the nature of experience. Woolf orchestrates from their separate voices a coherent, wholly internalized universe which seeks to give meaning and shape to the fragmented, transitory act of living. While they constitute the realm of all that is distinctively human in the novel, the nine interludes comprise the voice of all that is outside man and vastly indifferent to human aspirations and values—the workings of time and nature. The careers of the six unfold in the context of the implacable passage of the sun across the sky and the beating of the waves against the shore. Richly metaphoric and suggestive, the interludes establish that impersonal realm of 'what we are not.' The reality Woolf is trying to convey in her novels always consists of an understanding of both realms as well as the relationship between the two. Such a relationship cannot be talked about in explicit propositions but only demonstrated imaginatively, and *The Waves* is Woolf's most brilliant effort to present their interaction.

Just as the six voices share one language, so, too, the interludes have their own. The two languages are altogether different, a difference emphasized by the italics of the interludes, so that effectively the realms of the human and non-human are each characterized by a separate kind of discourse. The poetic elaboration of the passage of the sun, the effect of light and shadow on the sand and grass, the behavior of the birds, the appearance of flowers, and the rhythm of the waves provide the novel with a tone and texture of images which (with some significant exceptions) cannot be found in the soliloquies. In place of the human 'I' there is only the neutral descriptive voice recording the sensory details of color, movement, and sound (147):

> The sun was sinking. The hard stone of the day was cracked and light poured through its splinters. Red and gold shot through the waves, in rapid running arrows, feathered with darkness. Erratically rays of light flashed and wandered, like signals from sunken islands, or darts shot through laurel groves by shameless, laughing boys. But the waves, as they neared the shore, were

robbed of light, and fell in one large concussion, like a wall
falling, a wall of grey stone, unpierced by any chink of light.

Simply through the language itself, then, Woolf succeeds in creating
two separate realms—the human and the non-human—and distinguishing one from the other. The sharp demarcation between them
suggests, of course, the sharp isolation of man from the universe at
large in which Woolf so strongly believed. It is precisely for this
reason that creative effort is essential for all of Woolf's characters, as
Bernard comes to understand at the end of *The Waves*. But while the
two distinct verbal universes of the novel embody in themselves the
fact of man's isolation from what is outside himself, isolation does
not represent the total condition. There are always, in Woolf,
moments of communion as well, not just between people who are
generally insulated from one another, but also between man and the
impersonal universe without. And these mergings, too, are drama-
tized in the language, for as the two realms of discourse move
through the novel, images of one occasionally—and emphatically—
appear in the other. Thus the 'turbaned warriors . . . with poisoned
assegais' (54), which describes in several interludes the movement of
the waves, suddenly shows up in one of Rhoda's soliloquies as 'the
drumming of naked men with assegais' (100). Or consider a passage,
for example, from Bernard, in which the imagery of sun and water
and, in particular, the mention of the sea-holly is pure interlude in
character (207):

Day rises; the girl lifts the watery fire-hearted jewels to her brow;
the sun levels his beams straight at the sleeping house; the waves
deepen their bars; they fling themselves on shore; back blows the
spray; sweeping their waters they surround the boat and the
sea-holly. The birds sing in chorus; deep tunnels run between the
stalks of flowers . . .

Crossing from one linguistic context to the other, these images create
the moments of contact that Woolf never ceased to feel were fleetingly possible between what we are and what we are not. In both
instances, then, the texture of the language itself enacts the condition
of isolation and union which Woolf found basic to the human enterprise.

But the interludes do much more than allow an alien verbal context to be juxtaposed to that of the different soliloquies. More important, they set the human scene firmly in the grip of passing time, so that we are always aware, as the speakers go about responding to various events in their lives, of the movement of the sun across the heavens, marking out the progress of the day. The rhythm of the day closely parallels the different stages in the experience of the speakers so that it rises during their childhood, reaches its zenith (and thus begins its decline) at the moment when everyone is informed of Percival's death, a death which marks the end of their youth and hope, and sets when Bernard begins his final summary of all that has happened. The steady, inexorable passage of the sun contrasts with the typical human perception of time as consisting of fragmented, unevenly weighted moments of varying significance. For Bernard, for example, the synthesizing intelligence of the group, 'Time tapers to a point. As a drop falls from a glass heavy with some sediment, time falls. These are the true cycles, these are the true events' (131). The tendency to divide time into distinct, specific stages is, of course, central to the human mind and no less legitimate than the recognition that it exists as a continuous, uninterrupted flux. Rooting the discrete moments which are examined in the soliloquies within the smooth, unbroken flow embodied in the interludes, Woolf manages simultaneously to present both perceptions of time. Both are central to that one true story she, like Bernard, is striving to tell.

The sustained moments around which the soliloquies cluster as the sun moves to its height run from early childhood to boarding school to university, culminating at a meeting in a French restaurant where all gather to say good-bye to Percival, the hero they adore, as he leaves for India. Then follows one section in which several speakers respond to news of Percival's accidental death in India; two in which the nature of their maturity and realization of lost youth and diminished options gradually descend upon everybody; a final meeting of the six at Hampton Court; and the concluding summary and evaluation by Bernard. Each episode reveals the different speakers in the painful—and never-ending—process of trying to forge viable identities in the face of their own terrors and the treacheries of experience. The task of achieving coherent selfhood is an anguished one for Woolf, involving the negotiation of perils both within and without, but there is no human undertaking of greater urgency. Although the six sensibilities are all different, the quest to make sense out of oneself and the world outside is the same for all of them, constituting, in fact, variations on a

148

single theme. Exploring the different strains of isolation that plague each of them, their vulnerabilities, their fantasies, their perceptions of themselves and others, the six can actually be thought of as comprising a single, multifaceted sensibility in search of reality. In Bernard's terms, as long as Percival lives, 'a single flower . . . a seven-sided flower, many-petalled . . . a whole flower to which every eye brings its own contribution' (91). And after Percival's death (162),

> A six-sided flower; made of six lives . . . . 'Marriage, death, travel, friendship,' said Bernard; 'town and country, children and all that; a many-sided substance cut out of this dark . . . . Let us stop for a moment; let us behold what we have made. Let it blaze against the yew trees. One life. There. It is over. Gone out.'

Woolf introduces the encounter of self with the world by investing each voice with a simple, unadorned sense perception, a metaphoric rendering of a child's unsophisticated response to reality (6):

> 'I see a ring,' said Bernard, 'hanging above me. It quivers and hangs in a loop of light.'
> 'I see a slab of pure yellow,' said Susan, 'spreading away until it meets a purple light.'
> 'I hear a sound,' said Rhoda, 'cheep, chirp; cheep, chirp; going up and down.'
> 'I see a globe,' said Neville, 'hanging down in a drop against the enormous flanks of some hill.'
> 'I see a crimson tassel,' said Jinny, 'twisted with gold threads.'
> 'I hear something stamping', said Louis. 'A great beast's foot is chained. It stamps, and stamps, and stamps.'

As the sun climbs during the day, illuminating additional details of the land, so the speakers' awarenesses rapidly grow complex, moving from their initial, rather primitive sense impressions to lengthier, more inclusive formulations about themselves and reality. Intensely conscious of each other's behavior and intensely sensitive to their own needs, the six set about the process of experiencing the world which is to occupy them for the whole course of the novel. With the exception of Bernard, who is to grow significantly by the end, the 'characters' (such as they are) of the other five remain relatively fixed from the start. Although they make their first appearance as children, their sensibilities are already fully formed, and they respond in adulthood

149

precisely as they do before they even leave for school. The passage from childhood to maturity, that is, does not record any development of sensibility but instead provides a series of different contexts which stimulate the essentially unvarying points of view to reflect on what is happening to them. While the contexts change, the nature of the voices does not. Thus Rhoda's torment, the fear that she is faceless and alone, is as true at the outset of the novel as it is right before she commits suicide many years later. Similarly, Neville, with his passion for order and precision, and his physical frailty, feeling condemned always to inspire revulsion in those he desires; Jinny, living freely in the body and seeing things 'with the body's imagination' (125), engaged in an endless stream of affairs with different men; Louis, the social misfit and successful man of business, ashamed of his Australian origins and determined to belong, to gain access to the 'grained oak door' which has resisted him; and Susan, hearing nothing else than rustic music, 'glutted with natural happiness' (125), and understanding only 'cries of love, hate, rage, and pain' (94) as she raises her children—all move through the successive phases of their lives with a basic consistency, true at every stage to their initial definition. What is of interest is not any one voice responding to the facts of loneliness, love, friendship, and death as they present themselves to each, but the way the six together (including Bernard) manage to speak to the common experience of living.

Beginning with the opening flow of sensory observations, Woolf immediately entangles the voices, through the alternation of static soliloquies, in a network of common childhood experience. From the first moment in the garden, each speaker expresses those defining characteristics of self which are essentially to endure unchanged throughout the novel. Although thoroughly insignificant, the interaction in the garden, such as it is, embodies all that is to follow. Obsessed by the separateness conferred on him by his Australian accent, Louis stands alone, feeling that deep connection with the earth and history that is peculiarly his: 'My roots go down to the depths of the world, through earth dry with brick, and damp earth, through veins of lead and silver. I am all fibre' (8). Watching the others playing together catching butterflies, he stands hiding behind the hedge. Suddenly he is kissed by Jinny, who functions easily and sensually in the present in a way that Susan and Rhoda do not. Lighter and gayer than her two friends, she is at once less searching and less burdened with agonies than they are (30):

I cannot follow any thought from present to past. I do not stand lost, like Susan, with tears in my eyes remembering home; or lie, like Rhoda, crumpled among the ferns, staining my pink cotton green, while I dream of plants that flower under the sea, and rocks through which the fish swim slowly. I do not dream.

Witnessing the kiss and feeling herself frustrated and alone, Susan wraps 'my agony inside my pocket-handkerchief' (9). While Jinny glitters on the surface, Susan seeks deeper, more private satisfactions: 'I do not want as Jinny wants, to be admired. I do not want people, when I come in, to look up with admiration. I want to give, to be given, and solitude in which to unfold my possessions' (39). Her emotional life, more primitive than Jinny's or Rhoda's, involves the two poles of love and hate.

As Susan walks away, crying with unhappiness, she is seen by Bernard, who is already at work shaping his phrases and looking for the true story of things. While Susan feels herself limited to solitary words, Bernard is from the start finding ways to link individual words into larger units of meaning. For him (at least at the start of the novel) language is everything (11):

'But when we sit together, close,' said Bernard, 'we melt into each other with phrases. We are edges with mist. We make an unsubstantial territory.'
'I see the beetle,' said Susan. 'It is black, I see; it is green, I see; I am tied down with single words. But you wander off; you slip away; you rise up higher, with words and words in phrases.'

Bernard's tendency to distance himself from experience through the buffer of language is altogether different from the terrible isolation of Rhoda, who feels herself totally cut off, without a face or body, from the human community: 'The world is entire, and I am outside of it crying, "Oh, save me, from being blown forever outside the loop of time!"' (15) Unable to exist fully within the confines of current reality, Rhoda endlessly sends her imagination out on voyages through dangerous seas. The petals in her basin become ships braving fierce waves (13):

Some will founder. Some will dash themselves against the cliffs. One sails alone. That is my ship. It sails into icy caverns where the sea-bear barks and stalactites swing green chains. The waves rise; their crests curl . . . . They have scattered, they have

151

foundered, all except my ship which mounts the wave and sweeps before the gale and reaches the islands where the parrots chatter and the creepers . . . .

And as Rhoda dreams of adventure and fulfillment, Neville, an almost palpably felt Lytton Strachey-like creature, insists on imposing his need for precision on a world which proceeds sloppily at best: 'I hate dangling things; I hate dampish things. I hate wandering and mixing things together;' (14). While Bernard follows people wherever they go, trying to weave all their disparate stories into one, Neville strives always for clarity and order; '"Each tense," said Neville, "means differently. There is an order in this world; there are distinctions, there are differences in this world, upon whose verge I step"' (15). An admirer of the 'exactitude of the Latin language, with its well-laid sentences' (22), Neville is particularly fond of Catullus, whose passion is 'never obscure or formless' (22).

Existing 'not only separately but in undifferentiated blobs of matter' (174) as well, the six pass from childhood to maturity as a group, each aware, within the highly rigid restraints of the form, of each other. Although they move through the novel at the same pace, encountering the various events of their lives simultaneously, Woolf was faced with the problem of organizing the novel in such a way that, without violating its texture, the speakers would have an opportunity to come together physically at several points. The solution—he is, of course, far more than merely a structural device—is Percival, the schoolboy friend worshipped as a hero by all of them. Gathering to wish him farewell as he sets off for India, the six assemble in a restaurant, united not only in space but also by the common object of their concern.

In his mundane, corporeal self, Percival is one of those easy, effortless 'bloods,' the bane of every awkward or diffident British public school child. Spontaneous, graceful, and marvelously unreflective, he has clearly never suffered the torments of self-consciousness. Living in untroubled physical splendor, he seems wholly integrated, at home in a world in which winning at cricket is all that matters: 'He sees nothing; he hears nothing. He is remote from us all in a pagan universe' (25–6). What matter that he is in fact extraordinarily limited, that he is almost entirely lacking in subtlety and substance? The fact remains that the merest flick of 'his hand to the back of his neck' (26), is a gesture for which 'one falls hopelessly in love for a lifetime.' With no

152

discernible sign of intellect and living totally at one with nature—'Not a thread, not a sheet of paper lies between him and the sun, between him and the rain' (35)—Percival is a close relation to those natural, pagan characters who inhabit E. M. Forster's novels, like Stephen Wonham of *The Longest Journey* or Gino of *Where Angels Fear To Tread*. Unable to read it, they are nevertheless, like Percival, capable of inspiring poetry. Beyond even the mythic stature with which he is invested by his admirers, Percival exists as pure symbol, embodying the youthful affirmation and optimism of a corporate innocence as yet untempered by experience. He is, in a sense, a projection of the finest aspirations harbored by each speaker, a repository of unlimited potential. His going off to India to encounter unknown adventures heralds the similar journeys on which they all feel they are about to embark. Percival's moment is clearly their own; with his appearance, 'The reign of chaos is over' (88), the separate selves becoming fused into the 'seven-sided flower.' Like Mrs Ramsay's dinner, Percival's presence creates a coherent moment out of time, temporarily investing life with a richness and permanence which cannot be maintained. Each speaker well understands the significance of the moment, filtering it through the lens of his own needs. Desperately anxious that nothing should change as Percival leaves, Louis employs the same image of unity—the globe—that plays such an important role in *To the Lighthouse* (104):

Do not move, do not let the swing-door cut to pieces the thing that we have made, that globes itself here, among these lights, these peelings, this litter of bread crumbs and people passing. Do not move, do not go. Hold it for ever.

For Jinny, too, the globe best expresses the wholeness Percival seems to have wrought out of their separate lives. Always conscious of the body as she is, she particularly finds youth and beauty contained in his creation (104):

'Let us hold it for one moment,' said Jinny; 'love, hatred, by whatever name we call it, this globe whose walls are made of Percival, of youth and beauty, and something so deep sunk within us that we shall perhaps never make this moment out of one man again.'

Rhoda finds in the moment the promise of solitary adventure well beyond the alien confines of human society (104):

'Forests and far countries on the other side of the world,' said Rhoda, 'are in it; seas and jungles; the howlings of jackals and moonlight falling upon some high peak where the eagle soars.'

Neville's vision is far more subdued than Rhoda's, speaking to the cultured leisure which is at the heart of his sensibility (104):

'Happiness is in it,' said Neville, 'and the quiet of ordinary things. A table, a chair, a book with a paper-knife stuck between the pages. And the petal falling from the rose . . . as we sit silent, or, perhaps, bethinking us of some trifle, suddenly speak.'

Susan finds in Percival's moment those natural rhythms of life she wishes to live by (104):

'Weekdays are in it,' said Susan, 'Monday, Tuesday, Wednesday; the horses going up to the fields, and the horses returning; the rooks rising and falling, and catching the elm-trees in their net, whether it is April, whether it is November.'

And Bernard, always trying to link things together into larger wholes—to tell, that is, coherent stories—is inspired to speculate how this moment connects to those which are to follow (104):

'What is to come is in it,' said Bernard. 'That is the last drop and the brightest that we let fall like some supernal quicksilver into the swelling and splendid moment created for us from Percival. What is to come? I ask . . . what is outside? We have proved, sitting eating, sitting talking, that we can add to the treasury of moments.'

Besides serving to bring the speakers together in a single location so they can all see and comment on one another, the celebration for Percival marks a celebration of their own lives. With the sun at its height, their futures beckon to them uncertainly but attractively, and they view themselves and their options with an unsullied freshness: 'sitting together now we love each other and believe in our own endurance.' But such moments are always fleeting in Woolf. Just as Mrs Ramsay, looking over her shoulder at the end of the evening, realizes the precarious order she fashioned around her Boeuf en Daube dinner is already a thing of the past, so Percival's departure from the restaurant signifies the shattering of the globe that had existed so briefly; '"Now the cab comes; now Percival goes . . . . Now Percival is gone"' (105).

Percival's exit is final. Following the next interlude, Neville's first sentence indicates how permanent the dissolution of the moment is (107):

'He is dead,' said Neville. 'He fell. His horse tripped. He was thrown. The sails of the world have swung round and caught me on the head. All is over. The lights of the world have gone out.'

In its needless absurdity, Percival's death introduces the speakers to the unavoidable reality of the universe they never had to deal with seriously before. Outside of the contexts of their own image-making powers there lurk facts that will not disappear. Death is one such fact. For Neville, death has the same concrete reality as the apple tree which he recognized in his youth existed, solid and incontrovertible, beyond the reality of his desires or fantasies. However fluid and far-ranging the human sensibility, there is a 'stricture and rigidity' (18) we cannot affect. But Percival's awareness, in childhood, that 'we are doomed, all of us by the apple trees, by the immitigable apple tree which we cannot pass' (191), has not been effectively borne out by experience until now.' Ravaged by the death of the man he loves, Neville experiences the full emotional impact forced upon him by the presence of 'the tree which I cannot pass' (107).

Although the speakers scatter over their individual existences after Percival leaves the restaurant, his death—and the passing of that levity he temporarily called into being—affords another opportunity for a survey of different responses. Appropriately enough, there is a common view of the catastrophe. As Neville is the most passionately absorbed in Percival, he experiences a desolation the others cannot know. For him, all seems over, though as Rhoda correctly—and maliciously—intuits, he will be quick, perhaps too quick, to transfer his affections elsewhere. Bernard cannot enjoy the total grief in which Neville immerses himself, his sorrow at Percival's death necessarily matched by the joy he feels at the birth of his son. In addition, the artist in him requires that he not falsify experience, and though he finds emptiness, he also finds a kind of triumph, feeling that if taking Percival from them is the worst the world can do, they have little to fear for life still goes on, still has value: 'I am not going to lie down and weep away a life of care. (An entry to be made in my pocket book; contempt for those who inflict meaningless death)' (110).

For Rhoda, always the tormented solitary, Percival's death represents a triumph of a different sort: it confirms her in her sense that

155

human life is ugly and meaningless; the pain she feels at his loss provides the conclusive evidence which she has been seeking for her conviction that 'I am alone in a hostile world. The human face is hideous. This is to my liking . . . . Percival, by his death, has made me this present, has revealed this terror, has left me to undergo this humiliation' (114). Spurred on by the encouragement Percival's death lends to her contempt for human life, she goes on brilliantly to parody what she imagines the responses of her friends to be (114–15):

> Consider the friends with whom we sit and eat. I think of Louis, reading the sporting column of an evening newspaper, afraid of ridicule; a snob. He says, looking at the people passing, he will shepherd us if we will follow. If we submit he will reduce us to order. Thus he will smooth out the death of Percival to his satisfaction, looking fixedly over the cruet, past the houses at the sky. Bernard, meanwhile, flops red-eyed into some arm-chair. He will have out his notebook; under D, he will enter 'Phrases to be used on the deaths of friends.' Jinny, pirouetting across the room, will perch on the arm of his chair and ask, 'Did he love me?' 'More than he loved Susan?' Susan, engaged to her farmer in the country, will stand for a second with the telegram before her, holding a plate; and then, with a kick of her heel, slam to the oven door. Neville, after staring at the window through his tears, will see through his tears, and ask, 'Who passes the window?'—'What lovely boy?' This is my tribute to Percival; withered violets, blackened violets.

Although neither Jinny nor Susan makes any comment, Rhoda is not far wrong about Louis. Well-established as an important businessman, Louis is too busy etching his commercial empire across the map to dwell for long on Percival's death. It is simply one of many things he must deal with as he forges ahead, 'from chaos making order' (119), while in the process trying to extinguish all traces of his banker father and his accent which haunted him throughout his childhood. Percival's death, that is, does not differ substantially from the fact that 'Susan has children; Neville mounts rapidly to the conspicuous heights. Life passes. The clouds change perpetually over our house' (121). What matters to Louis is not any single discreet human event but the larger, impersonal task of business success into which he has poured his various selves. Finding relief from his personal anguish in the notion that it is 'by dint of our united exertions we send ships to the remotest parts of the globe; replete with lavatories and gymnasiums. The weight of the world is on our shoulders. This is life' (120), Louis cannot permit himself the luxury of indulging other features of himself. It is the schedule of 'Mr. Prentice at four; Mr. Eyres at four-thirty' (120), that holds him together, gives him the illusion that he is an integrated, valuable being doing something significant in the world.

Percival's death, occurring at the height of the day, marks the beginning of the descent into the evening of middle age's responsibilities, rigidities, and narrowed options. Rapidly finding themselves fixed in well-defined personal and professional roles, and feeling the press of time previously unknown to them, the voices continue to meditate on the enigmas of their own selves and the elusiveness of others'. The realization that they are no longer young, that 'Change is no longer possible' (151), underscores the urgency to make sense of it all. Certainly no answers are to be found in the specific shape each has managed to achieve. Indeed, that out of the many selves each possesses should have emerged the recognizable shapes of businessman (Louis), mother (Susan), father and artist (Bernard), and man of letters (Neville) only contributes to the oddness each feels about the nature of reality. Rummaging through images of the past—the kiss Jinny inflicted in the garden, the sensations generated by Mrs Constable's warm sponge—to see what significance lurks there, and intensely conscious of what their friends have made of their lives, the six strive to wrench some coherent meaning out of the flux around them.

They meet together one final time at Hampton Court, on this occasion without the unifying presence, provided at their dinner years before, of Percival. They come not to celebrate, confident in their youth, but to assess, to see how each has managed his life (150):

> Being now all of us middle-aged, loads are on us. Let us put down our loads. What have you made of life, we ask, and I? You, Bernard; you, Susan; you, Jinny; and Rhoda and Louis?

Vulnerable and partial, each speakers looks around with anxiety, fearful that a dazzling vision of someone's wholeness will bring home his own sense of imperfection and failure. Thus Neville clings to the credentials in his pocket which prove his superiority, feeling threatened by Susan's natural life and the maternal satisfactions she has experienced; while Susan, aware of all that her life has omitted, immerses herself in the healthy color of her hands, in the hard, clean feeling of a body well used, to rebuke Neville, 'whom I discredit in order to be myself' (152).

Seeing himself 'wrapped round with phrases, like damp straw' (154), with which he has never been able to tell the one true story he seeks, Bernard feels thoroughly undermined (154):

> And what are phrases? They have left me very little to lay on the table beside Susan's hand; to take from my pocket, with Neville's credentials. I am not an authority on law, or medicine, or finance.

While Bernard waits for the true story to present itself so that he can fashion his isolated phrases into one coherent whole, he admires the certitude and energy of Louis, who 'has formed unalterable conclusions upon the true nature of what is to be known' (155). But Louis's ordered life, the business empire he runs with ruthlessness and efficiency, as we know, serves only to hide from the world 'my shivering, my tender, and infinitely young and unprotected soul' (155). Still smarting from his childhood humiliations, Louis has none of the easy confidence Bernard blithely attributes to him. Kept afloat by his appointments and the network he commands, Louis is also a solitary, loving broken windows and chimney pots every bit as much as the gold and purple vestments of his public life.

Unlike Louis, Jinny conceals nothing. Following her own impulses wherever they lead her, she moves from one relationship to the next, seeing only 'what is before me' (156). Unhindered by dreams, she lives fully in the body (157):

> The torments, the divisions of your lives have been solved for me night after night, sometimes only by the touch of a finger under the tablecloth as we sat dining—so fluid has my body become, forming even at the touch of a finger into one full drop, which fills itself, which quivers, which flashes, which falls in ecstasy.

The satisfactions Jinny is able to glean are not shared by Rhoda, for whom everything human is torment. Pleased that she is able to walk up to her friends directly, rather than 'circling round to avoid the shock of sensation as I used' (157), she knows that it is simply a trick she has taught herself, that inwardly everything is as it always was (158):

> I fear, I hate, I love, I envy and despise you, but I never join you happily . . . . I perceived, from your coats and umbrellas, even at a

distance, how you stand embedded in a substance made of
repeated moments run together; are committed, have an attitude,
with children, authority, fame, love, society; where I have
nothing. I have no face.

Encased in their separate selves into which no one else is permitted
to intrude, the six sit down to their meal, acutely aware of the discrete
beings of their friends ranged around the table. As the dinner progresses, however, the anxiety and the uneasy comparisons begin to sub-
side, replaced by a slowly developing feeling of oneness which transcends the boundaries erected by each individual personality. Rhoda is
the first to sense the possibilities of this kind of union (159):

> Yet there are moments when the walls of the mind grow thin;
> when nothing is unabsorbed, and I could fancy that we might
> blow so vast a bubble that the sun might set and rise in it and we
> might take the blue of midday and the black of midnight and be
> cast off and escape from here and now.

Taking a walk after dinner, the six continue to melt into one, so that
Bernard recognizes that the seven-sided flower summoned into existence by Percival has now reconstituted itself as a 'six-sided flower;
made of six lives' (162). Leaving the confines of self temporarily
behind, they are all drawn together out of consciousness, out of the
'insanity of personal existence' (165), to forge a moment of union
which is timeless, perfect, and free from all taint of mortality: '"All
seems alive," said Louis, "I cannot hear death anywhere tonight.
Stupidity, on that man's face, age, on that woman's, would be strong
enough, one would think, to resist the incantation, and bring in death.
But where is death tonight?"' (163–4) (It is interesting to remember
that in the Percival episode earlier Louis had a distinct premonition of
death being present.)

Going back over this incident in his concluding evaluation, Bernard
invests it with the full significance that is not articulated by anybody—indeed, could not be—as it actually occurs (197):

> And who were we? We were extinguished for a moment, went
> out like sparks in burnt paper and the blackness roared. Past time,
> past history we went . . . . Against the gateway, against some
> cedar tree I saw blaze bright, Neville, Jinny, Rhoda, Louis, Susan
> and myself, our life, our identity . . . . But we—against the brick,
> against the branches, we six, out of how many million millions,

159

for one moment out of what measureless abundance of past time and time to come, burnt there triumphant. The moment was all; the moment was enough.

Partaking of what can only be thought of as profound mystical illumination, such moments are essentially ineffable and brief. No insight can be brought back from them, only the unspoken acknowledgment that some ultimate kind of understanding has been achieved. Watching Susan, Bernard, Neville, and Jinny walk back, having gone past him, Louis charts the moment's passing, the recommencing of all the mundane activities that normally occupy them (165):

Illusion returns as they approach down the avenue. Rippling and questioning begin. What do I think of you—what do you think of me? Who are you? Who am I?—that quivers again its easy air over us.

As the intensity of the moment subsides, the speakers, aware of what they have lost, at the same time welcome the relief of a return to the 'illusory' rhythms of life which generally sustain us. Louis understands that the 'insanity of personal existence' is necessary if life is to be endured by all—a vital point which Bernard emphasizes (166):

There is a sound like the knocking of railway tracks in a siding. That is the happy concatenation of one event following another in our lives. Knock, knock, knock, Must, must, must. Must go, sleep, must wake, must get up—sober, merciful word which we pretend to revile, which we press tight to our hearts, without which we should be undone. How we worship that sound like the knocking together of trucks in a siding.

Celebrating those instants of mystical perception which lift us out of ourselves, Woolf at the same time does not turn her back on the salutary nature of all those routines and obligations which serve to hold us together through life. Like Bernard, she recognizes the importance of both.

With the end of the episode in Hampton Court, the voices of Louis, Neville, Jinny, Susan, and Rhoda are no longer heard. Their disappearance is not marked by any dramatic expostulations, or articulation of general truths. Having experienced their temporary merging, they pass back into their separate selves and re-enter the flux quietly and without self-consciousness. Life goes on and they are part of it—that is the only conclusion Woolf grants them. But there is still a final summing up to be done, and appropriately it is to the artist, Bernard, that Woolf entrusts this task. The last section—the largest in the novel—belongs to him alone, the struggling writer who has all along been trying to find the right phrases to fashion his experience, and those of the others, into one consecutive story.

A compulsive storyteller and phrase-maker, Bernard is afflicted with a chronic inability to endure his own solitude. Drenched with sensation as a child from the water pouring off Mrs Constable's sponge, he hunts greedily from the very beginning for stimulation from sources outside of himself. He strictly avoids the terror of confrontation with his own self, following people wherever they go in order to record their stories. His imagination demands the presence of others if it is to generate images (95):

> I cannot bear the pressure of solitude. When I cannot see words curling like rings of smoke round me I am in darkness—I am nothing. When I am alone I fall into lethargy . . . . I only come into existence when the plumber, or the horse-dealers, or whoever it may be, says something which sets me alight. Then how lovely the smoke of my phrase is, rising and falling, flaunting and falling, upon red lobsters and yellow fruit . . . . Thus my character is in part made of the stimulus which other people provide and is not mine . . . .

Admiring the fierce solitude of Louis and Rhoda, he laments the fact that he 'cannot contract into the firm fist which those clench who do not depend upon stimulus . . . . I shall never succeed, even in talk, in making a perfect phrase . . . . Because there is something that comes from outside and not from within I shall be forgotten' (96).

Paradoxically, then, it is Bernard's very attachment to the external world that prevents him from creating his true story about it. Pursuing every human scent that crosses his path, gathering in his notebook all the phrases suggested to him by experience, he effectively cuts himself off from the free play of his uncompromised imagination—the only source, for Woolf, of any true story. Serving reality as faithfully as he does, he is doomed never to catch it. If it is too simplistic to see in Bernard's dilemma Woolf's repudiation of the realist method in fiction, it is clear that through Bernard she is treating the larger question of the artist's proper relation to the experience he is trying to render.

Bernard is not without his understanding of the problem (50):

The fact is I have little aptitude for reflection. I require the concrete in everything. It is only so that I lay hands upon the world. A good phrase, however, seems to me to have an independent existence. Yet I think it likely that the best are made in solitude. They require some final refrigeration which I cannot give them dabbling always in warm soluble words.

Nevertheless, he cannot break away from what is essentially his passive desire to find the 'perfect phrase that fits this very moment exactly.' Looking always outside of himself for the neatly patterned sequences that can slip smoothly into a phrase extracted from his notebook, Bernard remains blind to the intractable, discontinuous, haphazard stuff of reality which is all around him. Woolf plays with this ironically throughout the novel. Listing some 'useful' phrases in his notebook, Bernard suddenly recognizes his tendency to become distracted 'by a hair like twisted candy, by Celia's Prayer Book, ivory covered' (26); but without being aware that the process of the inter-ruption—and the fresh image it generates—reveals far more about reality than could ever be found in his methodically alphabetized phrases, he continues with his listing: '"The lake of my mind, unbroken by oars, heaves placidly and soon sinks into an oily somnol-ence." That will be useful' (26). Or again, boarding a train while engaged in the search for his perfect phrase, he resents the interruption posed by the request that he show his ticket, oblivious to the fact that it is precisely this uneven, jagged process of living, not the contours of a well-wrought expression, which he as an artist should be after.

Fleeing from the spectre of solitude, seeking to embrace experience while at the same time remaining safely insulated from it through the swaddling of his phrases, Bernard ensures his artistic failure. His commitment to the perfect phrase and the hope of finding a means of linking a number of them together in harmonious sequences with beginnings, middles, and ends, keep him firmly nailed to the surface of experience, unable to penetrate to the core, either in his writing or in his own life. Aware of his own debilitating passivity—'Thus waiting, thus speculating, making this note and then another I do not cling to life. I shall be brushed like a bee from a sunflower' (154)—he appears to lack the strength to change.

Bernard's weaknesses do not prevent him from being a formidably astute commentator on the human scene. His appraisals of others are generally accurate and he understands the notion of unity and multiplicity of personality, which is so important to the novel, in greater depth than his companions do. Throughout *The Waves* his voice speaks with the force and authenticity Woolf tends to grant her artist-characters. He is even capable of articulating, long before his final conversion when he actually is able to embody it in his own experience, the insight—Woolf calls it the theme—that 'effort, effort, dominates: not the waves; and personality: and defiance' (*A Writer's Diary*, 162). Summarizing the impact of the meeting with Percival, he points out the significance of the active striving contained in the moment (104–5):

> We are not slaves bound to suffer incessantly unrecorded petty
> blows on our bent backs. We are not sheep either, following a
> master. We are creators. We too have made something that will
> join the innumerable congregations of past time. We too, as we
> put on our hats and push open the door, stride not into chaos,
> but into a world that our own force can subjugate . . . .

But it is not until his last soliloquy that we see Bernard shedding the trappings of his old self and emerging reborn, a different kind of man and a different kind of artist. Bernard's summary of his life—and the lives of his friends which his own, in a sense, embraces—is a rich and dense meditation, bringing together all those thematic concerns with the shifting nature of human identity and varied experience of time which appear throughout the novel. With the sun now sunk so that 'sky and sea were indistinguishable' (167), as they were at the start of the book, Bernard sets out to explain the meaning of his life to an unnamed stranger sharing a table with him in a London restaurant. His initial impulse, of course, is to tell him all the innumerable stories of which his life consists. But even as he starts this process, he expresses really for the first time his displeasure with the notion of ordered sequences and neat phrases, his sense of how little they reveal of life (169):

> How tired I am of stories, how tired I am of phrases that come
> down beautifully with all their feet on the ground! Also, how I
> distrust neat designs of life that are drawn upon half sheets of
> notepaper. I begin to long for some little language such as lovers
> use, broken words, inarticulate words, like the shuffling of feet
> on the pavement. I begin to seek some design more in accordance

163

with those moments of humiliation and triumph that come now
and then undeniably . . . . What delights me then is the confusion,
the height, the indifference and the fury.

Although he is not yet ready to act on this insight, which involves a
new conception of himself and his art, he has at least formulated the
goal; his conversion at the end simply involves his ability to take on
fully—emotionally as well as intellectually—all the implications of this
fresh understanding.

In the meantime, however, he must work his way through his fabric
of stories in order to reach that point. Returning to the nursery and
Mrs Constable's sponge, he moves to what 'we call optimistically,
"characters of our friends"' (173), recounting to his dinner companion
the nature of his friends, the experiences they shared. But even as he
progresses smoothly from character to character, from one point in his
life to the next, he is aware of how false any consecutive, ordered
account of life necessarily is (182):

> Faces recur, faces and faces—they press their beauty to the walls
> of my bubble—Neville, Susan, Louis, Jinny, Rhoda and a
> thousand others. How impossible to order them rightly; to
> detach one separately, or to give the effect of the whole—again
> like music. What a symphony, with its concord and its discord
> and its tunes on top and its complicated bass beneath, then grew
> up!

False but not altogether dispensable, for it is also true that life ambles
on straightforwardly, that 'Tuesday follows Monday; then comes
Wednesday' (182). The biographic style, too, has its point: 'one cannot
despise these phrases laid like Roman roads across the tumult of our
lives, since they compel us to walk in step like civilized people. . . .'
(184).

Embedded in his own identity of Bernard the father and husband,
while at the same time aware that 'I am not one person; I am many
people: I do not altogether know who I am' (196), he recounts how
one day the rhythm of life that had previously sustained him, had kept
him moving through Monday, Tuesday, and Wednesday, suddenly
stopped, without any warning. Viewing the incompleteness of his life,
he asks himself how he can continue. Addressing the self that had
always accompanied him through his adventures, Bernard is terrified
to hear no answer (201):

I waited. I listened. Nothing came, nothing. I cried then with a
sudden conviction of complete desertion. Now there is nothing
. . . . Life has destroyed me. No echo comes when I speak, no
varied words.

Stripped in an instant of all sense of meaning or motivation, Bernard
looks around and within and sees nothing (202):

The woods had vanished; the earth was a waste of shadow. No
sound broke the silence of the wintry landscape. No cock
crowed; no smoke rose; no train moved. A man without a self, I
said. A heavy body leaning on a gate. A dead man. With
dispassionate despair, with entire disillusionment I surveyed the
dust dance . . . .

What Woolf is rendering here is the abrupt, mystical dying away of
the old self which must precede any new growth. Finding his life to be
without any value, simply a clutter of sterile phrases recording, he
now realizes, only shadows and illusions, Bernard is forced to experience the sheer nullity of his existence. The descent into such darkness
is as sudden and inexplicable as the return to the light. Having confronted the abyss, he finds himself again on the surface, walking along
a landscape restored to its living color. But if the landscape is the same
as it was before his symbolic death, the man is clearly different (203):

From me had dropped the old cloak, the old response; the
hallowed hand that beats back sounds. Thin, as a ghost, leaving
no trace where I trod, perceiving merely, I walked alone in a new
world, never trodden; brushing new flowers, unable to speak
save in a child's words of one syllable; without shelter from
phrases—I who have made so many; unattended, I who have
always gone with my mind; solitary, I who have always had
some one to share the empty grate, or the cupboard with its
hanging loop of gold.

The Bernard who emerges no longer needs the props of people and
phrases on which he formerly depended. Possessing now a depth and
serenity he never before understood, he feels capable of enjoying the
resources of his own imagination for the first time (206):

Immeasurably receptive, holding everything, trembling with
fullness, yet clear, contained—so my being seems, now that desire
urges it no more out and away; now that curiosity no longer

dyes it a thousand colours. It lies deep, tideless, immune, now
that he is dead, the man I called 'Bernard,' the man who kept a
book in his pocket in which he made notes—phrases for the
moon, notes of features; how people looked, turned, dropped
their cigarette ends; under B butterfly powder, under D, ways of
naming death.

But the new self-contained powers of the imagination he has just
discovered cannot be expected to alter radically the nature of the
world. Exulting in his freedom, he suddenly feels skewered by his
companion's glance back into the elderly, slightly puffy middle-aged
man he had for a moment pretended he no longer was. Depression
replaces ecstasy until the next stage of his illumination occurs, and he
comes to understand that life is not totally constraint or freedom but a
highly impure mixture of both, embracing the decaying body as well
as the glowing, transcendent imagination. Angry at his companion for
bringing him precipitously to earth, he is finally grateful for the
unintentional correction he provides: 'I regain the sense of the complexity and the reality and the struggle, for which I thank you' (208–9).

Relishing the solitude he previously abhorred—'Heaven be praised
for solitude' (209), he repeats three times—he is now free to encounter
and shape experience without the shackles of neat phrases or the
demand for smoothly linked sequences. The loss of his phrase book
signifies the discovery of himself as an artist (209):

My book, stuffed with phrases, has dropped to the floor. It lies
under the table to be swept up by the charwoman . . . . What is
the phrase for the moon? And the phrase for love? By what name
are we to call death? I do not know. I need a little language such
as lovers use, words of one syllable such as children speak when
they come into the room and find their mother sewing and pick
up some scrap of bright wool, a feather, or a shred of chintz. I
need a howl; a cry . . . . Nothing neat. Nothing that comes down
with all its feet on the floor. None of those resonances and lovely
echoes that break and chime from nerve to nerve in our breasts
making wild music, false phrases. I have done with phrases.

The novel thus ends with Bernard not only affirming a vision of
reality that is Woolf's own, but also defining what Woolf sees as the
appropriate creative response to that reality. Embracing the discontinuities and jaggedness of living without despair or regret, he

moves out to confront experience both as 'an elderly man who is getting heavy and dislikes exertion' (210), as well as an artist of untrammeled heroic energy, throwing himself against death. Bernard feels himself part of the natural process; the new day dawns—as it does at the end of *The Years*—and Bernard shares the life-giving rhythm of the 'eternal renewal, the incessant rise and fall and fall and rise again' (211). It is in this sense that his battle against death, doomed to fail, can nevertheless be understood as triumphant. As he rides out to meet death, like Percival, with his spear poised and his hair flying, Bernard achieves fulfillment by exultantly accepting his own mortality. Signifying the implacable nature of his foe, the last sentence of the novel—'*The waves broke on the shore*' (211)—also sounds a note of harmony and completion. In conceding the inevitability of defeat, Bernard ends by affirming the rightness of the battle.

11

The Years

Following her sustained immersion in the internalized depths of *The Waves*, Woolf felt a strong pull to return to the external world, to what she called 'the novel of fact' (*A Writer's Diary*, 189), which she had strictly avoided since her not altogether happy encounter with it in *Night and Day*. The notion of a novel dealing with '"real life"' (*A Writer's Diary*, 197) was exhilarating for her—and as daring as anything she had attempted since she left realism behind her in 1919 (*A Writer's Diary*, 189):

> I find myself infinitely delighting in facts for a change, and in possession of quantities beyond counting . . . . This is the true line, I am sure, after *The Waves*—The Pargiters [the early working title]—this is what leads naturally on to the next stage—the essay-novel.

As originally conceived, the 'essay-novel' grew out of Woolf's plan to write 'a sequel to *A Room of One's Own*—about the sexual life of women: to be called Professions for Women perhaps.'[1] Calling the projected essay on 11 October 1932, 'The Pargiters: An Essay based upon a paper read to the London National Society for Women's Service,' Woolf shortly after returned to the manuscript page and changed the title to read 'A Novel-Essay.' The substitution points to the radical conception of form she had in mind at this point: a novel in which a series of fictional extracts, dealing with a variety of significant ideas about feminism, politics, and education would alternate with essays expounding upon ways in which women writers could take their ideas from the real world and effectively embody them in works

[1] My discussion of the origin of *The Years* is indebted to Mitchell A. Leaska's essay, 'Virginia Woolf, the Pargeter: A Reading of *The Years*,' published in *Bulletin of the New York Public Library*, vol. 80 (Winter 1977), 172–210.

of imagination. The combination of extract and essay would constitute the completed novel.

The stimulus of bringing together the didactic and the fictional to
focus on the external world was fruitful for Woolf: within two
months she finished five fictional interludes and six essays—basically
the first draft of chapter 1, or what was to appear in *The Years* as the
1880 portion which opens the book. But the essay-novel conception
did not survive the initial process of revision. Going over the draft for
the first chapter, Woolf rapidly concluded that the analytic commentary could not easily exist with the imaginative part of the novel,
and the essay material as such was either eliminated entirely or else
blended into the texture of the fictional episodes she had already
written.

What we are left with, then, is not an essay-novel of the sort she had
originally intended but a novel firmly rooted in the social and historical fabric of external reality, coming 'with the most powerful and agile
leaps, like a chamois, across precipices from 1880 to here and now' (*A
Writer's Diary*, 189); a novel she wants to teem with 'millions of ideas
but no preaching—history, politics, feminism, art, literature—in short,
a summing up of all I know, feel, laugh at, despise, like, admire, hate,
and so on' (*A Writer's Diary*, 198).

Woolf's desire to embrace that detailed social existence she had so
scrupulously kept out of *The Waves*, to reveal 'the whole of present
society' (*A Writer's Diary*, 197), did not lead her, as a superficial glance
might indicate, to retreat to the conventionally representational form
she had abandoned thirteen years earlier. *The Years* does not mark a
regression to the method of *Night and Day*, but is rather a genuinely
new attempt, as experimental in its own way as *The Waves*, to shape
her own vision out of the intractable facts of the real world. The
challenge the novel poses for her, to use Woolf's own language, is
whether it is possible 'to give ordinary waking Arnold Bennett life the
form of art' (*A Writer's Diary*, 208). Can the mundane facts of social
existence, in other words, be adapted to serve the purposes of an artist
for whom reality and Arnold Bennett have never had anything in
common?

The solution, Woolf saw as early as 1933, would somehow involve
having '*The Waves* going on simultaneously with *Night and Day*' (*A
Writer's Diary*, 197), an intellectually vexing conception which simply
points to her sense that her new book would attempt to combine fact
as well as vision, the inner and the outer. Two years later, absorbed in

169

the endless toils of rewriting, she emphasized the discovery she has made of 'the combination of the external and the internal. I am using both, freely. And my eye has gathered in a good many externals in my time' (*A Writer's Diary*, 237). Although Woolf speaks exclusively of mixtures and combinations of techniques, another way of approaching *The Years* (though perhaps no less vexing) is to think of it as *The Waves* turned inside out. That is, the intensely patterned texture of *The Waves* which tries to express the nature of 'real life' by artificially removing itself from it, turns in *The Years* into another highly patterned texture that strives for the same end by the equally artificial guise of complete verisimilitude. The timeless internality of the one becomes the consciously time-ridden externality of the other, as the absence of any historical chronology in *The Waves* is replaced, in *The Years*, by explicitly dated chapters moving from 1880 to the present. The lack of concern in *The Waves* with social interaction develops, with *The Years*, into the appearance of an all-consuming obsession with it.

The pleasantly accessible surface of *The Years* with its clear linear chronology and its wealth of precise social observation is not to be confused with something Wells, Bennett, or Galsworthy might have given us. Woolf's realism—if such it can be called—notwithstanding, the novel is as abstract and elusive as any she has written. Its meanings do not emerge directly, as our initial expectations tell us they will, from the broad historical coverage of character and event, but rather indirectly—and even ambiguously—from a richly organized fabric compounded of repetition, echo, and allusion. In its jerky progression over fifty years of British history, it manages to be as intensely saturated and stylized in its own way as, for example, *The Waves* is in quite another. Identical images, bits of dialogue, and similar human responses occur again and again throughout the novel, creating a dense network of connections and associations that resonates with significance. That the final words ever spoken by one character in 1907—'I will tie a knot in my handkerchief' (156), should be repeated—'I'll tie a knot in my handkerchief' (355), by someone else thirty years later in the last chapter, sets up reverberations, brings past and present together in ways that suggest exactly how the whole novel establishes its meaning.

The facts of external life that Woolf delights in, then, are finally not at odds with that internal novel of vision that she has been regularly producing. Treating characters conventionally in the framework of real historical time, Woolf at the same time fashions a highly charged symbolic context for them which permits *The Years* to go well beyond the limits of realism in trying to capture that same truth of what human experience is like sought by all her novels. While the initial impulses behind the 'essay-novel,' with its interest in 'millions of ideas' remain a viable part of the the completed work, *The Years* is not in any simple way a novel of ideas. Whatever argumentative force originally attached to some of the issues the novel addresses, in their final form they have been sufficiently assimilated into the larger, impersonal concerns of the novel so as not readily to call attention to themselves. Although Woolf felt strongly enough about the ideas she was dealing with to label the book at one point 'dangerously near propaganda' (*A Writer's Diary*, 245), at the same time she was aware that the large thrust of the novel had no more to do with ideas as such than did *The Waves*. A specific comment in her dairy, in fact, notes the resemblance between the two. While searching for a title for the book, Woolf conjured up the possibility one night of calling it *Here and Now*, a possibility she temporarily favored because, 'It shows what I'm after and doesn't compete with the Herries Saga, the Forsyte Saga, and so on' (*A Writer's Diary*, 211), and is reminded several months later in a letter from G. Lowes Dickinson that '*The Waves* is also here and now—I had forgotten.' (*A Writer's Diary*, 215).

In the case of *The Years*, the means of illuminating the nature of the here and now is not six disembodied voices inhabiting a verbal universe of their own making, but generations of the Pargiter family spanning a solid chunk of British history. The broad range of doctors, lawyers, suffragettes, farmers, spinsters, professors, businessmen, and others the Pargiters and their friends encompass, experiencing together more than fifty years of English life, not only enables Woolf to create the feeling of 'the individual and the sense of things coming over and over again and yet changing' (*A Writer's Diary*, 260)—a rhythm central to the novel's meaning—but also to work out, from a multiplicity of points of view, those ideas about society basic to the original conception of the book. Moving from their Victorian drawing room in 1880 to Delia's concluding party in the present (1937), the Pargiters thus lend themselves to the novel of fact, with the constellation of social and political ideas allied to it, as well as to the novel of vision, both of which Woolf intended for *The Years*.

The facts of English society, as Woolf projects them, here, are not blithely neutral. Coming, as we have seen, out of *A Room of One's Own*

171

and preceding by only a year the publication of *Three Guineas*, the rather more acerbic treatment of the predicament of women, *The Years* looks carefully at some of the institutions and assumptions of a male-dominated world. While it avoids any of the polemical confrontations with these realities found in the other two works, the novel nevertheless is built on a precise recognition of those conditions and their consequence for women—and society as a whole. In this context—although it does not begin to exhaust the novel's richness—*The Years* can be read as the fictional illustration of the arguments in *A Room of One's Own* and *Three Guineas* which frame it. In a not altogether far-fetched way, these three books can be taken as the 'essay-novel' Woolf had originally projected for *The Years* alone.

Of all the institutions that helped sustain the values and priorities of a patriarchal world, the upper-class Victorian family was certainly one of the most potent. Dispensing privileges unequally, exploiting some members for the benefit of others, Victorian families, such as that presided over by Abel Pargiter, guaranteed that male privilege, like the Empire, would rule forever. Indeed, as we know from *Three Guineas*, the two are intimately connected for Woolf, the manipulations within the family only the domesticated form of those same impulses that lie behind a country's control of a substantial portion of the earth. Earned in the Indian Mutiny, Abel's mutilated hand, which fascinates the children, especially Rose, makes the connection between the two realms ruled by force. With his mistress, his club, his memories of foreign service, his subtle oppression of his children, Abel Pargiter is the first representative in the novel of the cluster of largely masculine values Woolf sees as inimical to full human development of men and women alike. Although by no means a villain, he nevertheless stands behind the various images of brutality, coercion, and insensitivity which pervade the novel, symbolically connected to the violence of the First World War, the fascism of a Mussolini, the rigidities of a society suspicious of difference and intent on keeping half its members from the rights freely extended to the other half. Despite the amenities and the decorous façade of life at Abercorn Terrace, it is perfectly understandable that Delia should expostulate, some fifty years later, '"It was Hell!" she exclaimed. "It was Hell!" she repeated' (450), a judgment with which Martin, one of the other seven Pargiter children, essentially concurs.

The hell of Abercorn Terrace is at once a starting point from which society in some ways develops over the course of fifty years, and at the same time a metaphor for certain of the values and assumptions of society that remain constant throughout the novel. Although the world which permits Peggy Pargiter, at the end of the novel, to be a physician is not the same world which never questioned the fact that Eleanor, her aunt, should stay home and take care of her father while her brothers go off to university and careers, the basic institutional and moral character shared by both are essentially the same. The bastions of privilege and power endure unchanged; the intolerance of diversity, whether social or sexual, is as great; the lunacy of war is still as compelling; in a fragmented world without any coherent center, and where the pieces can't even come together, the possibility of shared experience and genuine communication between people is as rare in 1937 as it is in 1880. The cries of 'Justice and Liberty,' which sound throughout the novel, defining the broad aspirations of the culture, serve as ironic counterpoint to the cramped political, social, and psychological conditions in which people actually exist. 'When shall we live adventurously, wholly, not like cripples in a cave?' (320) Eleanor asks herself in 1917, anticipating North's despairing observation in the final section that 'We cannot help each other . . . we are all deformed' (409–10). In its involvement with the external world of real historical time and real social forces, *The Years* represents Woolf's bleakest view of the human condition. The corporate pathologies of society ensure that people will flourish in that society only as stunted, partial souls.

As a novel of fact, with vestiges of those initial 'essay' impulses still animating it, *The Years* provides us with a harsh indictment of society. Woolf sees its values, institutions, and leaders as offering little possibility for full human satisfaction. The history of the Pargiters in such a society is essentially one of exploitation, restricted options, missed opportunities; and the fears Woolf had about the propaganda in the novel are precisely fears about the unrelenting assault she mounts on society's structure and character. The deformity which Eleanor and North complain of—and which afflicts everyone else in the novel as well—is in fact the normal development in a society that isolates and oppresses the way this one does.

But as we have seen, Woolf's dissection of English society, her pleasure at discovering the substantial amount of 'gold—more than I'd thought—in externality' (*A Writer's Diary*, 190), is only part of the large significance of the novel. At the same time that *The Years* is attached to the specific reality of English life from 1880 to 1937, it also

173

deals with those timeless concerns common to all her fiction, with the shape and substance of human experience. Three generations of Pargiters occupying over half a century enable Woolf to show how life changes and remains the same and in what it essentially consists. While the chronological structure of the novel insists upon our recognizing the inevitable differences that occur both in society and individual psyches over a fifty-year period, Woolf works from within the stream of change to isolate those central preoccupations with order and identity that she sees as basic to life wherever it is found. In the midst of the flux, what finally endures is simply the effort—never to be fully realized—to make sense of it all, to grasp, even fleetingly, the pattern. While issues of where one self ends and the other begins, of 'what is this moment, and what are we?' (360) can never neatly be answered, it is the commitment to them that remains the same human pursuit underlying the superficial distinctions wrought by the passing of decades. Eleanor's questions about her own life define the interest explored by the novel as a whole (395):

> Oughtn't a life to be something you could handle and
> produce?—a life of seventy odd years. But I've only the present
> moment, she thought. Here she was alive, now, listening to the
> foxtrot . . . . Millions of things came back to her. Atoms danced
> apart and massed themselves. But how did they compose what
> people called a life?

As I mentioned earlier, the flux and the effort to comprehend it which together make up the 'here and now' are embodied in the dense pattern of repetition and variation that dominates *The Years*. Pattern in this novel is both vision and method, speaking at once to the recognition of meaning in the universe as well as to the fictional technique Woolf employs to reveal that meaning. If Eleanor testifies to the vision (398)—

> She knew exactly what he was going to say . . . . As she thought
> it, he said it. Does everything then come over again a little
> differently? she thought. If so, is there a pattern; a theme,
> recurring, like music; half remembered, half forseen? . . . a
> gigantic pattern, momentarily perceptible? The thought gave her

extreme pleasure; that there was a pattern. But who makes it? Who thinks it?

—there are innumerable instances of the method at work. A simple description of a day in London on the first page of *The Years*, for example, contains the innocuous statement, 'The stream of landaus, victorias, and hansom cabs was incessant' (1). But as we repeatedly encounter the stream of 'omnibuses, hansom cabs, victorias, vans and landaus' (3), of 'Cabs, vans and omnibuses' (119), 'vans, cars, omnibuses' (172), running throughout the novel, we realize that benign, plausible observation has taken on a richly metaphoric burden of suggesting the flow of life itself endlessly moving past all the characters. Indifferent to their needs or aspirations, it continues inexorably on, a concrete embodiment of the passage of years streaming past the inhabitants of the novel.

The sense of life's fluidity, which time and the flow of traffic combine to render symbolically in *The Years*, contrasts with people's efforts to comprehend it, to shape an individual meaning out of the flux. While the many references to the progression of traffic in the streets build symbolically into an image of life's flow, the innumerable questions in the novel constitute the symbolic human response. From Abel's unuttered question at the start—'He had a question to ask; he turned to ask it; but his friends were gone' (3)—to Eleanor's final words on the last page, '"And now?" she asked, holding out her hands to him' (469), *The Years* is pervaded by a variety of questions, put by almost all the characters, which merge finally into an assertion by Woolf concerning the pressing human need to try to understand what life and the self are all about. The myriad questions appearing everywhere—the 'Where am I?' of Mrs Pargiter (23), Delia (25), and Eleanor (44); Sara's and Maggie's 'What's I?' (150); Rose's 'What is one's past? (180); Eleanor's 'And where are we going?' (229); Kitty's 'What am I doing? Where am I going?' (288); Peggy's 'Where does she begin, and where do I end? . . . But what is this moment; and what are we?' (360); North's 'But what do I mean . . . ?' (443) to name a few—create a fabric of meaning that is infinitely richer than the sum of its different interrogative threads. If separately they remain unanswered, together they make clear the degree to which the process itself of asking, the attempt to clarify and comprehend, is a basic human activity in Woolf's fictional universe.

No answers are forthcoming, of course, as *The Years* does not permit anybody the luxury of precise formulations. The Pargiters lurch through the decades without any clear idea of who they are or where they are going. Seeking illumination, they find only darkness, and in place of firm purpose there is either haphazard movement or else the resigned workings of inertia. Although the progression from 1880 to the 'present day' produces certain greater freedoms, it does not provide any more reliable direction. In the concluding section of the novel, the only force promising any kind of moral or cultural coherence is fascism, and if North rejects its malign temptations—'Not halls and reverberating megaphones; not marching in step after leaders, in herds, groups, societies, caparisoned' (442)—it is not evident that he has the ability to achieve his vision of 'a new ripple in human consciousness, be the bubble and the stream, the stream and the bubble—myself and the world together' (443).

Refusing the lure of a corporate allegiance but uncertain what kinds of meaning he can create in its stead, North's dilemma is exacerbated by his total isolation from the people around him. Despite his need to make life-giving contact with other souls, to be at once 'the bubble and the stream,' he remains the circumscribed bubble, cut off from the possibility of forming any kind of genuine relationship with the external world. In this he is typical of all the characters, who are similarly trapped in their insulated selfhoods. Although practically everyone in *The Years* is connected, either directly or indirectly, to the Pargiter family, there is almost a total lack of communication among them. More profoundly than in any other Woolf novel, people here are shut up and alone in their private worlds, unable to break out of their confines to manage any shared existence with those outside of themselves. In a novel which is very little else but talk, it is extraordinary how little actual conversation there is. People are endlessly speaking at and across one another, but rarely is there an instance in which meaningful ideas, feelings or information are exchanged. Dialogue tends to reduce itself to fragments of monologue, each participant pursuing a separate train of thought, subject to interruption and misinterpretation, which guarantees that no mutual understanding will ever be achieved. Individual human interactions in the novel earn their significance largely because, in their inconclusiveness, in their complete failure to bring people together, they serve to define the impossibility of communication in *The Years*. To listen to any talk in the book is to hear the enormous static that characterizes people's relationships. A casual conversation in 1910 between Rose and Maggie makes the point, though the example could come from any place (184):

> It was quite easy to talk, she found. And there was no need to say anything clever; or to talk about one's self. She was talking about the Waterloo Road as she remembered it when Sara came in with the coffee.
> 'What was that about clinging to a fat man in the Campagna?' she asked, setting her tray down.
> 'The Campagna?' said Rose. 'There was nothing about the Campagna.'
> 'Heard through a door,' said Sara, pouring out the coffee, 'talk sounds very odd.' She gave Rose a cup.
> 'I thought you were talking about Italy; about the Campagna, about the moonlight.'
> Rose shook her head. 'We were talking about the Waterloo Road,' she said. But what had she been talking about? Not simply about the Waterloo Road. Perhaps she had been talking nonsense. She had been saying the first thing that came into her head.
> 'All talk would be nonsense, I suppose, if it were written down,' she said, stirring her coffee.
> Maggie stopped the machine for a moment and smiled.
> 'And even if it isn't,' she said.
> 'But it's the only way we have of knowing each other,' Rose protested.

Rose, of course, is right—it is the only way—and the novel works out the debilitating consequences of living in a world in which people either don't reveal what is important (Rose never mentions to anybody, for example, the traumatic incident of a man exposing himself she witnessed as a little girl), or else lie, as in Martin's vision of family life at Abercorn Terrace where 'all those different people had lived, boxed up together, telling lies' (239); or speak to those who lack the ability or interest to hear what is being told them. Peggy's conversation with her deaf Uncle Patrick at Delia's party serves as an effective symbol for the general quality of communication in the novel (379).

> 'How's the man who cut off his toes with the hatchet?' she said . . . .
> 'Hacket? Hacket?' he repeated . . . . 'Hacket? Hacket?' he repeated.

He looked puzzled. Then understanding dawned.
'Oh, the Hackets!' he said. 'Dear old Peter Hacket—yes.'

Deafness, deformity, and fear—of 'each other,' North thinks . . . .
'Of criticism, of laughter, of people who think differently'—ensure
that no common view will ever bridge the isolation in which people
live. A splendid paradigm for the fragmented perceptions of reality
available to the characters in *The Years* is the parlor game Renny and
others play at Delia's party, drawing a composite picture on separate
folds of a single piece of paper. The inevitably grotesque result testifies
with metaphoric eloquence to the lack of wholeness in their lives
(420):

> Each of them had drawn a different part of a picture. On top
> there was a woman's head like Queen Alexandra, with a fuzz of
> little curls; then a bird's neck; the body of a tiger; and stout
> elephant's legs dressed in child's drawers completed the picture.

Living alone, each in his own cave, and without the means of escape
that a shared language might afford, the characters are nevertheless
capable of harboring visions of wholeness that strain against the
isolation of their lives. While not powerful enough in themselves to be
thought of as redemptive, these aspirations at least constitute some
kind of countervailing force against the conditions of fragmented
sterility that dominate the novel. In a scene which Woolf notes as
central to her conception of the book, Eleanor, after a day with her
brother Morris in 1911, picks up a volume of Dante before she goes to
sleep that her sister-in-law left by her bedside. It is the *Purgatorio*; idly
skimming through it, she comes across some lines that catch her
attention—'a hook seemed to scratch the surface of her mind'
(228)—and with her Italian being as rusty as it is, she turns to the
English (228):

> For by so many more there are who say 'ours'
> So much the more of good doth each possess.

For Eleanor, as for the reader, 'the words did not give out their full
meaning, but seemed to hold something furled up in the hard shell of
the archaic Italian' (228). As with everything else in the novel, the full
meaning emerges slowly and indirectly, coming to fruition only in the
context of what surrounds it. Undramatic in themselves, the lines take
on, in the midst of the private hells that individuals inhabit in *The*

Years, a prophetic message. They speak to the value of the shared experience in a world of partial visions, to a coherence and common purpose that are mocked by the figure with the woman's head and the elephant legs. Asserting the value of existence beyond the narrowly egotistic (a condition unknown to the denizens of *The Inferno*), Dante's lines stand behind the various impulses towards wholeness and community that are expressed by the occupants of Woolf's own separate bolgia. Whether it is Nicholas's toasts to a new world, or North's desire to live spontaneously without the barriers of fear and suspicion we erect between people, or Peggy's glimpse of a 'state of being, in which there was real laughter, real happiness, and this fractured world was whole; whole and free' (420), *The Years* manages to define life-giving possibilities within the solitude and despair that otherwise dominate it. Possibilities merely, not certainties of any sort; *Purgatorio*, after all, is an entire volume away from the beatific vision finally allotted Dante, and if the dawn at the end of the novel is by no means the false dawn that some critics claim, it is nothing more than a highly tentative one, holding out hope but making no promises.

In its postulation of a divine realm in which one is increased, not diminished, by sharing, the lines of the fifteenth canto reverberate throughout *The Years* as both inspiration and rebuke. Its harmonious vision emphasizes by contrast the fallen, fragmented world in which the Pargiters struggle. It is particularly appropriate that it is Eleanor who reads the lines, for it is Eleanor, more than any other character, who has given her life to others (to the point, indeed, of exploitation), and she who remains the strongest force of optimism. It is significant that Woolf entrusts to Eleanor the final, open-ended question of the novel. Unanswerable though it is, her concluding, 'And now?' suggests the ongoing commitment to the future that she and the novel both choose to affirm.

If Dante and Eleanor constitute one symbolic cluster which moves through the novel in various ways, then *Antigone* and Edward constitute another, with quite different implications. A translator of *Antigone*, Edward stands in a curious relationship to the play, defined not by the risks Antigone takes in defying Creon in order to bury her brother, but rather by the imagery of imprisonment and suffocation that attends her fate. Having risked something when young in his love for Kitty, and been disappointed, Edward has effectively shut himself up in the tomb of his scholarship for the rest of his life, minimizing all further opportunity for pain. While his distinguished academic work

179

has brought him fame, it has not put him in touch with himself or others. Envying his mastery of the 'past and poetry' (440), North at the same time recognizes his failure (441):

> There it was, he thought, locked up in that fine head . . . . Then why not prise it open? Why not share it? What's wrong with him . . . . Why can't he flow? Why can't he pull the string of the shower bath? Why's it all locked up, refrigerated? Because he's a priest, a mystery monger, he thought; feeling his coldness; this guardian of beautiful words.

Edward's total inability to encounter human reality without the protection of his discipline can be seen in an incident that occurs at Delia's party. Responding to Eleanor's enthusiasm about *Antigone* by uttering a line in Greek from the play, which can be translated, 'I cannot share in hatred but in love,' he declines North's request to explain what it means in English. Given their powerful emotional content, it is clear that Edward must refuse North (447).

> 'Translate it,' he said.
> Edward shook his head. 'It's the language,' he said.
> Then he shut up. It's no go, North thought. He can't say what he wants to say; he's afraid.

Buried alive with his *Antigone*, Edward thus embodies that quality of fearful, isolated living to which Dante's vision is opposed. Taken together, Edward and *Antigone*, and Eleanor and Dante can be thought of as defining the two extremes of the novel—the suffocating facts of social and psychological isolation and the emancipating vision of wholeness and harmony—within whose confines the different Pargiters make their separate ways.

In surviving fifty uncertain, fragmented years, the Pargiters are all forced to function in various ways as 'Pargeters,' which the *Oxford English Dictionary* tells us are plasterers or whitewashers, those who gloss and smooth things over.[1] (It is interesting in this regard that Eleanor, who sacrifices a good deal of her life to the family, and especially to looking after her father, should actually engage in plastering and repairing some of the family property.) Pargeting is clearly the only viable means of getting through a life that offers no sustaining order, and in this way the activities of the Pargiter family are intended

---

[1] The relationship between Pargiter and pargeter is pointed out by Leaska.

by Woolf to have a universality about them. Just 'ordinary people' (363), going about the business of living, as Eleanor understands. Appropriately, one of the many titles Woolf considered for the book was *Ordinary People*. (In addition to the initial working notion of *The Pargiters*, the others, suggesting the kind of impersonal rhythm she was after in the novel, include *Here and Now*, *Music*, *Dawn*, *Sons and Daughters*, *Daughters and Sons*, and *The Caravan*.)

Tracing the Pargiters' movement to the present through specific episodes in 1880, 1891, 1907, 1910, 1911, 1913, 1914, 1917, and 1918, Woolf builds the coherence of the novel out of isolated moments which serve both to reveal her particular sense of the ordinary and how it is experienced over the course of fifty years from a variety of different points of view. Pattern emerges out of separate fragments, and whether it is Eleanor walking to see Morris conduct a trial, or Sara, Rennie, Maggie, and Nicholas enduring an air raid, or Martin being corrosive to Delia, or any of the other myriad events of which the novel consists, the individual scenes, inconclusive in themselves, help shape the contours of Woolf's universe.

All the pieces are intended to come together in the final chapter ('The Present Day'), the longest and most complexly organized section of the entire novel. 'One should be able to feel a wall made out of all the influences,' Woolf writes in her diary, 'and this should in the last chapter close round them in the party so that you feel that while they go on individually it has completed itself' (258). Completion is not to be confused with anything resembling definitive conclusion here. It is, rather, the final orchestration of the ambiguous and uncertain which are characteristic of everything in the novel. Themes and motifs developed earlier recur throughout this section, taking on a richness, if not a resolution, in their last appearance.

The party itself provides the appropriate metaphoric setting for the concluding scene. For the snatches of broken conversation that pass for communication at parties, the transient and not very substantial contact that people have with one another, the tight proximity without any real intimacy which typifies party dynamics describe perfectly the quality of life we find in *The Years*. And of course the dancing that takes place, with its shifting couples, its formal patterns and repetitions, constitutes in microcosm the workings and method of the entire novel. Above all, the party collects in one place for the first time every surviving member of the Pargiters, so that we can see the younger generation of North and Peggy side by side with their various aunts and uncles. Having taken us through the careers of a whole generation of brothers, sisters, and cousins, with their very real anxieties, aspirations, and failures, Woolf now places them under the scrutiny of North and Peggy, for whom they all appear denizens of a distant age, fascinating as one finds all odd specimens in a museum fascinating, their struggles simply part of a quaint past 'beautiful in its unreality' (358). Cynically detached from the proceedings at the start, and ravaged by feelings of loneliness and bitterness, North and Peggy find themselves deeply affected by the life eddying around them, their initial antiquarian interest finally replaced by an intuitive understanding, never precisely articulated, of the extent to which they all share in the common human predicament. The meeting of past and present, defining differences as well as similarities, is crucial to the novel, dramatizing as it does the central questions of what changes and what remains the same, of how we experience the vagaries of our own identities and those of others.

The final section begins not with the actual party but with the arrangements of different people to come to it together, specifically North with Sally and Peggy with Eleanor. As is true throughout the novel, the desultory conversation and casual action of these preparations are part of Woolf's highly conscious symbolic technique for elaborating the book's meaning. Details are everything in a work that is as minutely organized as this one is. Leaving Eleanor in order to pick up Sara and take her to the party, for example, North exchanges polite compliments with her that sound basic themes. '"It's nice to see you," she said. "And you haven't changed,"' referring to his recent return from his farm in Africa. 'He smiled. "And you haven't changed either," he said' (330). Empty and conventional pleasantries in another context, they are highly charged phrases here, speaking to a central concern of *The Years*.

North's confusion in London, as he tries to find his way from Eleanor's to Sally's, similarly suggests far more than the perfectly reasonable difficulties someone might experience who has been away from a large, sprawling city for a long time. Having sold his farm in Africa where he lived a splendidly solitary life, North finds immersion in London unsettling. His geographic dislocation—'"Where the dickens am I now?" he asked, peering at the name on the street corner' (333), underlines the larger uncertainties of his life: what should he do and where should he go? Thinking back on his evening with Eleanor the night before, as he muddles his way towards Sally's room, he recalls bits of conversation which have a pointed significance not only for North alone but for the sense of the whole novel. While the comment, '"Solitary confinement is the greatest torture we inflict"' (333), refers immediately to prison regulations (provoking one woman to call for its abolition), it also touches upon the crippling isolation of the life in society that people do in fact lead in *The Years*. A passing comment on the inhumanity of prisons becomes an accurate assessment of what people are suffering from within the ostensible freedom of English society.

Certainly it applies precisely to the plight of Sally, living by herself in a tawdry boarding house in a decaying part of the city. North, who has not seen her since she mocked him for his proud military bearing on the eve of his departure for the war—'"How many lumps of sugar does a lieutenant in His Majesty's Royal Regiment of Rat-Catchers require?" she had sneered' (337)—is dismayed by the sordid nature of her surroundings. Rootless and alone in a dwelling that typifies the worst of modern urban living, Sally is a lamentably telling example of life under that sentence of solitary confinement which seems to have been passed on all the inhabitants of *The Years*. While North continues to play with the question of 'Was solitude good, was society bad' (333), Sally provides eloquent testimony to the quality of contemporary society. Reciting at one point in his visit the only poem he knows by heart, Marvell's 'The Garden,' he is interrupted by Sara just as he reaches the end of the second verse—'"Society is all but rude—/To this delicious solitude."' Somebody is having a bath next door, Sara declares, 'the Jew,' who leaves hairs and '"a line of grease round the bath"' (365). The evocation of the Jew, tenement house, and decay reverberates with echoes of 'Gerontion,' T. S. Eliot's articulation of the dead end to which history has brought us. Together with her own version of *The Wasteland* Sara goes on to cite—'"Polluted city, unbelieving city, city of dead fish and worn-out frying Pans—"' (366) they constitute a powerfully bleak image of the sterility and isolation of modern life. The pastoral splendors of Marvell contrast with the prophetic urban despair of Eliot to help define the tensions at the heart of *The Years*.

At the same time that Sara's fate appears in some ways symptomatic of the meanness of modern life, she is far more complicated than any mere victim. She is a good friend, for example, of the enigmatic foreigner who calls himself Nicholas Brown (his real name is Pomjalovsky) whose acquaintance North explains he made at

Eleanor's house. Brown, who first appears in the 1917 chapter, during the air raid scene, and who will later also show up at Delia's party, supplies an enticingly vatic presence to the novel. Eleanor comments when she meets him in 1917, 'There was something queer about him . . . medical, priestly?' (313) As a foreigner and homosexual, standing outside not simply the Pargiter family but English society and convention in general, Brown seems to possess the kind of healing wisdom which only the outsider is privileged to have. Talking always, as Sara says, 'about the soul' (348), he appears a lay shaman of sorts, treading the precarious line between prophet and charlatan. Sara, who loves him, also mocks him, but his obsession that we cannot know other people or make 'laws, religions, that fit . . . when we don't know ourselves,' has a visionary power that dominates much of the last portion of the novel. A staunch believer in human possibility, it is Brown who toasts the human race and its coming maturity at the party. Calling for the necessary re-education of the soul, he diagnoses, in a way that picks up the themes of the whole novel, the current difficulties under which people struggle (319):

> 'Whereas now,'—he drew himself together; put his feet together; he looked like an old lady who is afraid of mice—'this is how we live, screwed up into one hard little, tight little—knot? . . . Each in his own little cubicle; each with his own cross or holy book; each with his fire, his wife . . . .'

Affecting Eleanor, North, Sara, and the others who know him with the intensity of his commitment to the new world, Brown offers a redemptive message at odds with the forces of oppression and isolation around him. Obviously sympathetic to Brown's views, Woolf nevertheless is not naively sanguine about them. They are, after all, the views of someone who, as Sara explains in 1917, might well be put in prison because of his homosexuality. And his rousing toast at the party ends with a fine, undercutting irony: 'He brought his glass down with a thump. It broke' (460).

While North talks to Sara, forming those 'little snapshot pictures' (341) of her he knows 'leave much to be desired' (341), Peggy is busy studying Eleanor 'as if to collect another little fact about her to add to her portrait of a Victorian spinster' (359). Touching upon different conceptions of selfhood, freedom, and happiness, the relationship of Eleanor and Peggy embraces most of the major concerns in the novel.

In their attempts to understand one another, their failure to communicate, and the values, explicit and implicit, that determine their behavior, the aging spinster and the disillusioned physician help shape the full roundness of the here and now the novel seeks.

Although, as Peggy comes finally to realize, she shares far more with Eleanor than she first thought, she is at the same time the product of a different age with a different sensibility and point of view. She has, to begin with, experienced freedoms that were unheard of for Eleanor. While Eleanor does her father's housekeeping, Peggy has her own professional life as a physician. In escaping the assumptions of patriarchal authority, Peggy obviously has far more options open to her than Eleanor ever did. But Woolf's vision is sufficiently complex not to equate professional opportunity with personal fulfilment. As we know from *Three Guineas*, access to the professions is no guarantee of happiness. Indeed, it can be used as a substitute for feeling altogether, as Peggy realizes: 'How to deaden, how to cease to feel; that was the cry of the women bearing children; to rest, to cease to be. In the Middle Ages, she thought, it was the cell; the monastery; now it's the laboratory; the professions; not to live; not to feel; to make money, always money . . . .' (382). The quality of the inner life does not answer directly to the amount of responsibility of the outer, and Woolf is acutely aware of the increased psychological risks imposed by freedom. The progression from Eleanor's servitude to Peggy's autonomy is thus in part an ironic one, for it is Eleanor, at seventy-two, who argues that things have changed for the better, that 'We're happier—we're freer' (416), and Peggy, tense and confined, who puzzles over such foreign sentiments: 'What does she mean by "happiness," by "freedom"? Peggy asked herself' (417). As Peggy understands, Eleanor retains the power to believe, a strength no longer readily available to the modern world. Emancipated from a number of Victorian shackles, Peggy nevertheless shares the modern dilemma of having nothing to cling to. Peggy's bitterness most sharply distinguishes her from Eleanor: '"Always reminds me of an advertisement of sanitary napkins," Peggy blurts out on the way to the party at the sight of noble nurse Edith Cavell's statue, causing Eleanor to respond that Cavell's words were "the only fine thing that was said in the war"' (362).

There is something wistful in her appreciation of Eleanor's fierce response to what appears to be a photograph of Mussolini in the newspaper (357):

It was the force that she had put into the words that impressed her, not the words. It was as if she still believed with passion—she, old Eleanor—in the things that man had destroyed.

The contrast in attitude between Eleanor, with her unswerving commitment to life and Peggy, afflicted with a sense of the meaninglessness of it all, is further documented, in Woolf's characteristic method, by the books each reads. While Eleanor is struck by Dante's vision of wholeness, Peggy stumbles upon sentences, in a book chosen at random, that typify her own alienation (413):

'La médiocrité de l'univers m'étonne et me révolte . . . la petitesse de toutes choses m'emplit de dégoût . . . la pauvreté des êtres humains m'anéantit.'

In their anguish and isolation, Peggy and North circulate among the older Pargiters, curious to explore the mysteries of their relatives' lives to see if anything can be gleaned about their own. While no illumination is forthcoming, their questioning presence helps Woolf unify the 'scraps, orts and fragments' of the different relationships we glimpse at the party. The efforts of Peggy and North to locate themselves lead them to notice, among others, not just Eleanor, Sally, and Nicholas, but also Edward, hiding behind the security and sterility of his scholarship; the indomitable, solitary Rose, still looking determined enough to go to jail for her suffragette beliefs; Delia, the fiery radical, admirer of Parnell, now married to the ponderous and conservative Patrick; the grand Lady Lasswade, the former Kitty Malone, revealing that what she had really wanted all along was to be a farmer, a choice she was not permitted to make as a young woman. Sharing the same partial, stunted existence that their relatives lead, the crippling fears that keep them separate not only from other people but from themselves as well, both North and Peggy at the same time share some of the same yearnings to escape the confines of self that are also present in the novel, though most notably in Eleanor and Nicholas.

Under the strain of the party—'Thinking was torment' [so Peggy reflects]; 'why not give up thinking and drift and dream?' (419)—regenerative impulses receive complicated expression. Hearing people discuss North's future, Peggy struggles to articulate her vision of a world in which wholeness is possible. What emerges, however, is not a blithely happy formulation but a sudden virulent attack on North himself (421):

186

'What's the use?' she said, facing him. 'You'll marry. You'll have children. What'll you do then? Make money. Write little books to make money . . . . You'll write one little book, and then another little book,' she said viciously, 'instead of living . . . living differently, differently.'

The meaning of the assault is not altogether lost on North. Although in its personal hostility it distorts her meaning—'She had broken off only a little fragment of what she had meant to say' (421)—North understands the genuine commitment to life which lies behind her unprovoked attack (456):

'What you said was true,' he blurted out, '. . . quite true.' It was what she meant that was true, he corrected himself; her feeling, not her words. He felt her feeling now; it was not about him; it was about other people; about another world, a new world . . . .

Wrenching themselves out of their initial despair to define their own halting aspirations for some different—and better—kind of existence, the younger generation of Pargiters ends by intuitively understanding the hopes of the older. 'There must be another life,' Eleanor thinks, inspired by a vision of unity which she will not relinquish, however unpropitious the circumstances around her. Her desire to make sense of it all remains a vital instinct of the sort ultimately celebrated by all of Woolf's fiction (461–2):

She held her hands hollowed; she felt that she wanted to enclose the present moment; to make it stay; to fill it fuller and fuller, with the past, the present and the future, until it shone, whole, bright, deep with understanding.

As the party draws to its conclusion, the two children of the caretaker suddenly appear, frightened, awkward, mute. Asked to speak, they remain silent, stimulating in Peggy the mean-spirited comment that 'The younger generation . . . don't mean to speak.' But Peggy is wrong. The new generation does indeed have something to say to the Pargiters. Encouraged by Martin's sixpence, the two children burst into song (462):

Etho passo tanno hai
Fai donk to tu do,
Mai to, kai to, lai to see
Toh dom to tuh do—

The sounds go on for nearly three verses before they suddenly break off. The shrillness and cacophony are unsettling; no one, of course, knows what the song means. While the simple explanation of an incomprehensible cockney accent satisfies the guests, Woolf clearly intends the complete unintelligibility to be indeed the message that the future is conveying to the Pargiters. Eleanor's longing, admirable as it is, to have the present, past, and future shine with understanding comes up against the reality of the gibberish and uncertainty looming ahead. If Eleanor's vision is a very real hope in the novel, Woolf nevertheless knows precisely how frail a hope it is. The dissonance of the children's song speaks eloquently to what is just as real. The capacity to embrace life fully requires a recognition of both. Eleanor, who knows so much in the novel, knows this too. Searching for a way to describe the experience of the children's performance, Eleanor realizes it is impossible to find one word for the whole (465).

> 'Beautiful?' she said with a note of interrogation, turning to Maggie.
> 'Extraordinarily,' said Maggie.
> But Eleanor was not sure that they were thinking of the same thing.

The Pargiters disperse as uneventfully as they came together, with nothing at all having been resolved. The pain is as real as ever, the isolation as numbing. In pulling together the different thematic fragments of the novel, the party does not attempt to provide any solace or answers. The dawn carries no promises, the children's song cannot be understood, and the stem of Nicholas's glass, we remember, breaks with the resounding conclusion of his toast. But while there are no guarantees that Eleanor's belief that 'There must be another life, here and now . . . . This one is too short, too broken' (461), will ever be realized, it is not a note of despair but a vision of a shared relationship that concludes *The Years*. And it is Eleanor, the reader of Dante, who has it. Looking out the window, she sees a cab draw up (469):

> A young man had got out; he paid the driver. Then a girl in a tweed travelling suit followed him. He fitted his latch-key to the door. 'There,' Eleanor murmured, as he opened the door and they stood there for a moment on the threshold. 'There!' she repeated, as the door shut with a little thud behind them.

The evident satisfaction she experiences in seeing the couple becomes ours as well. In their intimacy, their youth, the promise that seems implicit in their crossing the threshold together, the man and woman take on a symbolic meaning, representing Eleanor's deepest wishes for a rich and whole existence. They suggest the possibilities and excitement that Eleanor still feels for life. And turning to Morris with her open-ended, 'And now?' Eleanor makes it impossible for us not to look towards the future with a similar pleasure. Whatever the uncertainties and dangers, Woolf's final sentence once again sets them temporarily to rest in its low-keyed affirmation: 'The sun had risen, and the sky above the houses wore an air of extraordinary beauty, simplicity and peace' (469).

12

Between the Acts

'An interesting attempt in a new method,' *Between the Acts* combines poetry, prose, and dialogue in what was to be Woolf's last effort to 'embody the exact shapes my brain holds' (*A Writer's Diary*, 359). It is her most static and in some ways most elusive book. If it is generally true that nothing really happens in a Virginia Woolf novel, it is particularly true here. Occupying several hours on a June afternoon in 1939, the action involves the production of a pageant celebrating England's history. Around its periphery, different glimpses of human relationships are given, but without resolution of any sort. Mired in the mundane details of an English country afternoon, *Between the Acts* is finally every bit as abstract as the internalized, densely poetic world of *The Waves*. That the novel, like the pageant itself, refuses to permit any simple understanding is part of the full meaning of each.

Both novel and play, in fact, are attempts by their respective authors to 'show us up, as we are, here and now' (217). Like Lily Briscoe in *To the Lighthouse* and Woolf herself, Miss La Trobe struggles to achieve her vision. But her struggle is even more precarious than theirs, for she works not with the relative security of canvas or page but the vagaries of actors and audience. If the book and painting are concrete embodiments of the artist's completed vision, Miss La Trobe's pageant has no existence outside the moment of its presentation, and she has no way of judging its success outside of its effect on the audience. Her endless rage against actors and audience indicates her vulnerability (113):

'Curse! Blast! Damn 'em!' Miss La Trobe in her rage stubbed her toe against a root. Here was her downfall; here was the Interval. Writing this skimble-skamble stuff in her cottage, she had agreed to cut the play here; a slave to her audience,—to Mrs. Sands' grumble—about tea; about dinner—she had gashed the scene here.

But despite the fact that the articulation of her vision is not totally under her control, that it is conveyed by actors who forget their lines to an audience which is largely uncomprehending, Miss La Trobe manages that temporary glow of transcendence which is all that any artist can hope for (244):

> The bells had stopped; the audience had gone; also the actors. She could straighten her back. She could open her arms. She could say to the world, You have taken my gift! Glory possessed her—for one moment. But what had she given? A cloud that melted into the other clouds on the horizon. It was in the giving that the triumph was. And the triumph faded. Her gift meant nothing.

The real action of the book, then, is the working of the creative process itself. Fashioning something whole from the chaos around her, Miss La Trobe does in her pageant what Woolf sought to do in her fiction (180):

> Ah, but she was not merely a twitcher of individual strings; she was one who seethes wandering bodies and floating voices in a cauldron, and makes rise from its amorphous mass a recreated world. Her moment was on her—her glory.

Both novel and pageant affirm the power of art to make ordered shapes out of a random universe. Although Miss La Trobe is by no means a simple persona for Woolf, the vision animating her pageant is much the same as that behind Woolf's novels. The sense of the past informing the present, the recognition of the world as being at once fragmented and unified, and the understanding that it is through art that the world can become conscious of itself are common to all. Part of the novel's interest lies in the complex way in which the form and meaning of the pageant contribute to the larger significance of the book as a whole.

In its most primitive form, the organizing power of art is seen in the fact that everybody in the novel is concerned with the pageant, either as an actor, member of the production staff or, equally importantly, member of the audience. The novel is structured around the pageant; in one way or another, all the characters are brought together at the performance, if only temporarily. From Albert the village idiot to the chic Mrs Manresa, every person in the village and even those simply passing through are occupied with the central event of the book. The value of art in fashioning order relates primarily, of course, to the completed artifact itself, but the ability of the spectacle to engage everyone in its brief life is clearly intended to demonstrate the synthesizing powers of illusion. Performing their parts, struggling with costumes, stage sets, and broken gramophones, and finally submitting themselves, however obtusely, to the pageant's meaning, the villagers testify to Miss La Trobe's success in organizing a disparate community of people in the service of her artistic vision. Miss La Trobe knows well the evanescence of such a hard-won order; part of her anguish is precisely the ease with which it slips away: 'Over there behind the tree Miss La Trobe gnashed her teeth. She crushed her manuscript. The actors delayed. Every moment the audience slipped the noose; split up into scraps and fragments' (145). But before the audience does return to the randomness of its original state, Miss La Trobe at least has the satisfaction of having momentarily coerced it into a single body responding to the stimulus of her art.

Beyond the all-embracing nature of the production itself, Miss La Trobe's vision manages to span approximately six centuries of English history and present them, slightly abridged, in a single afternoon. Such an ambitious imaginative feat stresses the extent to which the past remains a vital part of the present—a theme which the novel insists on in a number of ways. The cesspool built over the Roman road, the antiquity of the barn, Lucy Swithin's reading of ancient history, and the portraits of the Olivers' ancestors all point to the varieties of forms in which the past continues to inhere in the present. The intensely personal connection of past and present in *Mrs Dalloway* is generalized in Miss La Trobe's pageant to suggest the sense in which the experience of a June day in 1939 draws upon the full weight of history, the country, its literature and its people, which preceded it. Evoking England's historical and literary past, Miss La Trobe's production defines a common heritage shared by actors and audience alike. However oblivious Bond the cowman or Hilda the carpenter's daughter may be to Chaucer or Victorian imperialism, they are part of that history and irrevocably tied to it—and to the others who share similar roots. When small Phyllis Jones begins the pageant by shrilly piping, '*England am I*' (194), she proclaims a relationship that goes well beyond the particular role she is playing in the performance.

In Woolf's universe things at once change and remain the same. Figgis's guidebook of the area around Pointz Hall, which is as true in 1939 as it was in 1833, suggests more than merely the fact of the
192

unchanging local scenery. As Lucy understands, explaining to Isa about the Victorians: "'I don't believe,' she said with her odd little smile, "that there ever were such people. Only you and me and William dressed differently"' (203). Although it is partly ironic, of course, that Eliza Cooper the tobacconist should play the august Queen Elizabeth, at the same time the part is perfectly appropriate. Much as Leopold Bloom is *Ulysses*, so in a very real sense Eliza and Elizabeth are one. Not only are the humble shop girl and the queen united by their humanity, but by the fact that in performing as Queen, Eliza fulfills a role in the pageant exactly as Elizabeth did throughout her own lifetime. Temporarily breaking down the barriers between past and present, Miss La Trobe succeeds as well in dissolving established notions of selfhood, so that for a few brief hours at least she manages to fabricate out of the 'scraps, orts, and fragments' (220) of the present a transcendent vision of oneness. Lucy, whose unwavering belief in unity sharply conflicts with her brother's rational scepticism, understands this too: "'What a small part I've had to play! But you've made me feel I could have played . . . Cleopatra!'" . . . "'I might have been—Cleopatra," Miss La Trobe repeated. "You've stirred in me my unacted part," she meant' (179). Miss La Trobe's art helps actualize those latent identifications that permit Lucy and Eliza to understand the ways in which they are not simply their own limited selves but also great ladies of history.

The glimpses of England's literary heritage Miss La Trobe weaves into her pageant end with the audience being exposed to its own reflection in bits and pieces of mirrors held by the actors. Confronting the spectators with their own images as a means of defining the present is a bold and unsettling device, causing those who had questioned Miss La Trobe's ability to know anything about themselves to squirm uneasily in their seats. By forcing the individuals in the audience actively to consider their own selves, following the passive, insulated viewing of their ancestry, La Trobe at once succeeds in provoking in each one a sense of the immediacy and meaning of the present while at the same time acknowledging her own artistic limitations in dealing with the intractable nature of the here and now. That the flashing of the mirrors concludes the historical pageant is not only chronologically appropriate but also suggests the degree to which the present can only be grasped in the context of the past. The audience's understanding of what has gone before makes the impact of the mirrors different from what it would have been had Eliza Clark not per-

193

formed as Queen Elizabeth or Budge the publican not presided with his truncheon over Victorian respectability. The fleeting, partial reflections of the mirror take on their full significance only when embedded in the flow of history preceding them.

The celebration of England's past, compelling people in various ways to sense their connection to the country and its tradition, takes on a peculiar urgency given its setting in the summer of 1939 with Germany readying itself to conquer Europe. Woolf wrote the book during 1940 and 1941, when England was not only at war but also expecting an imminent invasion by Germany, and the choice of a June day in 1939, shortly before the torrent of Nazi chaos was released, was clearly not an arbitrary date for her. It makes the fragile unity of Miss La Trobe's vision all the more precarious—and all the more precious for it. To have set the pageant in the midst of war would have lost all the tension that is now generated by placing it on the very edge of the catastrophe. Woolf carefully builds in references to the ominous threats to civilization developing in Germany. Thus we have Giles, impatient with the 'old fogies' (66) who seem oblivious to a Europe, 'bristling with guns, posed with planes,' as well as other brief mention, in scattered conversations, of the Jews, the possibility of invasion, the unpleasantness of fascism.

The effect of all of these calculated allusions to the impending havoc of the Second World War is not to trivialize the efforts of the villagers to put together their amateur pageant but rather to emphasize the capacity of art to give us order and meaning. The rumblings of violence and cruelty heard on the Continent make the intelligible world of Miss La Trobe's pageant not an avoidance of harsh reality but a necessary life-affirming refuge of the human spirit. Art becomes more, not less important as a means of preserving the sanity of a civilization when the barbarians are on the move.

The pageant itself is a marvelously mixed affair: song, dance, poetry, a parody of a Restoration comedy, and finally a gaily cutting portrait of Victorian imperialism, prosperity, respectability, and religious fervor. In the figure of Budge, moralizing and spouting all the nationalistic slogans of the nineteenth century, Woolf distills much of the animus towards the Victorians found in Strachey's *Eminent Victorians*. Celebrating at the same time that it makes fun of English history, the pageant illustrates the artist's ability to bring together out of a welter of material and forms a coherent vision of things.

What exactly that vision is cannot be fixed precisely; certainly that it presents more questions than it answers is part of Miss La Trobe's intentions. Several interpretative voices speak out at the end of the production to amplify its meaning. The first, anonymously presented but presumably that of Miss La Trobe, harangues the audience through the loudspeaker after some of them had been sufficiently disconcerted by the use of the mirrors to start leaving. The voice demands that the spectators consider themselves honestly, recognizing the baseness of human behavior as well as the small decencies of which it is capable. The evocation of the horror comes first (218):

> The poor are as bad as the rich are. Perhaps worse. Don't hide among rags. Or let our cloth protect us. Or for the matter of that book learning; or skilful practice on pianos . . . . Or presume there's innocency in childhood . . . . Or virtue in those who have grown white hairs. Consider the gun slayers, bomb droppers here or there. They do openly what we do slyly.

But the affirmation argues that there is something other, that we are not merely 'scraps, orts, and fragments' acting solely on separate egotistical impulses. Significantly, the possibility of harmony is not insisted upon syllogistically; it is embodied in the sublime unity of a piece of music (220–1):

> Like quicksilver sliding, filings magnetized, the distracted united. The tune began; the first note meant a second; the second a third. Then down beneath a force was born in opposition; then another. On different levels they diverged. On different levels ourselves went forward; flower gathering some on the surface; others descending to wrestle with the meaning; but all comprehending; all enlisted. The whole population of the mind's immeasurable profundity came flocking; from the unprotected, the unskinned; and dawn rose; and azure; from chaos and cacophony measure . . . . Compelled from the ends of the horizon; recalled from the edge of appalling crevasses; they crashed; solved; united. And some relaxed their fingers; and others uncrossed their legs.
> Was that voice ourselves? Scraps, orts and fragments, are we, also, that?

In Woolf's universe, as we have seen, people are most emphatically both. Trapped in their own isolation and anguish, like Isa or Miss La Trobe, they are at the same time part of something larger than themselves which they are at moments capable of recognizing. Such moments of perception, reconciling disparities and endowing life with a wholeness and meaning not ordinarily felt, are the transcendent values in Woolf's fiction. From the anonymous narrator in 'Unwritten Novel' through all of her work, the experience of these moments is what redeems all the rest.

As the music fades away, the Reverend G. W. Streatfield mounts a soapbox to assess for his flock the meaning of the pageant. Institutions of any sort, particularly religious ones, were viewed with great suspicion by Bloomsbury, and Woolf was certainly no exception. She treats purveyors of spiritual wisdom with the same contempt she lavishes on Holmes and Bradshaw, those pillars of the medical establishment excoriated in *Mrs. Dalloway*. So it is no surprise that Streatfield, about to offer his interpretation, is seen as 'a butt, a clod, laughed at by looking-glasses; ignored by the cows, condemned by the clouds which continued their majestic rearrangement of the celestial landscape; an irrelevant forked stake in the flow and majesty of the summer silent world' (222). But whether it is the tobacco-stained forefinger, indicating that Streatfield has human needs not fulfilled by the church or simply the ironic pleasure Woolf takes in undercutting our expectations, his sense of the play is remarkably accurate. Oversimplifying a good deal and clearly interested in slipping a secular vision into a sacred framework, Streatfield comprehends more than a Bloomsbury-depicted clergyman has any right to (223–4):

> We were shown, unless I mistake, the effort renewed . . . . But again, were we not given to understand—am I too presumptuous? . . . To me at least was indicated that we are members of one another. Each is part of the whole . . . . We act different parts; but are the same . . . . Then again, as the play or pageant proceeded, my attention was distracted. Perhaps that too was part of the producer's intention? I thought I perceived that nature takes her part. Dare we, I asked myself, limit life to ourselves? May we not hold that there is a spirit that inspires, pervades . . . .

If Streatfield stresses the harmony at the expense of the chaos and cupidity, he nevertheless, admitting his own shortcomings as literary critic, helps provide a focus for the generally puzzled spectators. Their desultory comments as they leave—gossipy, trivial, scattered—suggest more or less all that artists can hope for when offering their work to the public. Amidst the polite chatter about Streatfield, the quality of the parking arrangements, the variety of cars present, lurks some genuine if halting attempt to fathom Miss La Trobe's purpose (233–4):

> He said she meant we all act. Yes, but whose play? Ah: that's the question! And if we're left asking questions, isn't it a failure, as a play? I must say I like to feel sure if I go to the theatre, that I've grasped the meaning . . . . Or was that perhaps what she meant? . . . Ding dong. Ding . . . that if we don't jump to conclusions, we shall think the same? . . . Then when Mr Streatfield said: One spirit animates the whole—the aeroplanes interrupted. That's the worst of playing out of doors . . . . Unless of course she meant that very thing.

Insensitive to the enormity of Miss La Trobe's creative investment in the pageant and basically unaffected by what they see, the spectators return to their separate ways, the memory of the day's entertainment already growing dim. Next year, after all, there will be yet another. Unwittingly, they constitute the final act of the pageant as they leave, for the very theme of the play is echoed in their departure. The gramophone sums it all up: 'The gramophone gurgled *Unity—Dispersity*. It gurgled *Un . . . dis . . . .* And ceased' (235).

The pageant, of course, is not an autonomous work written and directed by Miss La Trobe but part of a larger fiction created by Woolf, and its full significance can only be felt in relation to the entire novel in which it is embedded. The most important actors in the novel are not those participating in the pageant but those engaged in playing-out with—and against—each other those real-life roles they have chosen themselves. Central to the ongoing human drama taking place around the edges of the pageant is the relationship between Giles and Isa Oliver, the stockbroker and his wife, locked into a difficult marriage compounded of equal portions of love and hate. Addressing not a single word to each other in the course of the novel, they nevertheless manage to stay indissolubly lodged in each other's consciousness throughout the afternoon, fixed there by ties of anger and desire. It is the intensity of the connection between them, in fact, and the suffering exacted by that connection, which impel each to flirt with thoughts of infidelity: Giles with Mrs Manresa, the self-proclaimed 'wild child of nature,' and Isa with Rupert Haines, the mysteriously handsome gentleman farmer. And it is the intensity that brings them together at the end of the day, prepared to undertake once again the desperate, primordial struggle two souls must always wage if their love is to be perpetuated: 'Before they slept, they must fight; after they had fought, they would embrace. From that embrace another life might be born. But first they must fight, as the dog fights with the vixen, in the heart of darkness, in the fields of night' (255–6). The triumphant decision to do battle for their love, which Isa and Giles wage at the end of the novel—'Then the curtain rose. They spoke.' (256)—is as creative in its way as is Miss La Trobe's in overcoming the obstacles in the path of her completed vision. Human and aesthetic affirmation both at the end testify, in Streatfield's words, to 'the effort renewed.'

But the facile optimism of Streatfield's understanding has very little to do with the anguished reality of their relationship. If they finally begin to speak at the end, such a reconciliation does not make the isolation and despair Isa experiences during the afternoon any less painful. There is no specific reason adduced for their difficulties; they seem to be simply the result of the inevitable—and at this point greatly exacerbated—resentment generated between two people of disparate sensibility. And however much in love they are, Isa and Giles certainly have profoundly different temperaments. It is a contrast between the public and the private; the insensitive male, dealing aggressively in the external world of selling and buying, absorbed in politics and fundamentally closed to the appeal of art; the female, poetic, slightly melancholy, living close to her feelings, and finding sustenance from her own internal life in those realms of art and literature from which her husband is largely excluded. Variations, in short, on a sexual stereotype going as far back as *Mrs Dalloway*. Somewhat bullied by her husband—'Didn't she write her poetry in a book bound like an account book lest Giles might suspect?' (62)—Isa tends to channel her anger against him towards herself, seeking relief from her unhappiness in fantasies of self-annihilation. While Giles is able, in his appropriate masculine way, to release his frustrations by crushing to death a snake choking on a frog, Isa is thoroughly incapable of such direct action. Instead, she finds solace in thoughts of extinction: '"But what wish should I drop into the well?. . . That the waters should cover me," she added, "of the wishing well"' (124).

The poetry which Isa surreptitiously enters into her bogus account book resonates in her thoughts throughout the novel. Endlessly searching for rhymes and images to help define her emotional state for herself, Isa is very much a creator in her own right, though of a far more private sort than Miss La Trobe. In her isolation she is particularly sensitive to the materials of the pageant, finding in them all variety of amplification of her private feelings. It is Isa who understands that the plot doesn't matter, that 'the plot was only there to beget emotion' (109), and it is Isa who responds most acutely to the emotional content—'Love. Hate. Peace. Three emotions made the ply of human life' (111)—of the production. Her intensely personal reaction—utilizing the feelings and poetry of the play for her own purposes—suggests a function of art which is belied by the pageant's grand historical sweep. Whatever large areas of common understanding Miss La Trobe illuminates, her work is also sufficiently rich to nourish the individual subjective needs of its audience. In this, pageant and novel are one. Both are complex enough to embrace the demands not only of Isa's torment but of Mrs Manresa's contrived and callow spontaneity as well. The songs which start Mrs Manresa humming are altogether different from the fragments of poetry which make their way into Isa's consciousness, but together they indicate the great range of effect the successful work of art can command: 'They all looked at the play . . . . Each, of course, saw something different' (249).

Certainly there are no two people in the novel whose visions are more directly opposed than Giles's father, Bartholomew, and Lucy Swithin, his widowed sister. They provide yet another statement of the unity-dispersal theme scratched out by the gramophone: 'For she belonged to the unifiers; he to the separatists' (140). Lucy's faith in goodness and God puzzles Bart, whose fierce scepticism takes refuge only in the unfettered use of reason. While she spends her time (204)

> one making. Sheep, cows, grass, trees, ourselves—all are one. If
> discordant, producing harmony—if not to us, to a gigantic ear
> attached to a gigantic head. And thus—she was smiling
> benignly—the agony of the particular sheep, cow, or human
> being is necessary; and so—she was beaming seraphically at the
> gilt vane in the distance—we reach the conclusion that *all* is
> harmony, could we hear it,

Bart spends his gruffly puncturing her illusions, believing in none of the complacent visions of universal harmony offered by his sister or Streatfield. In the face of Lucy's blithe trust, Bart finds no cosmic solace at all for the simple fact of his son's unhappiness. For Bart, investing faith in anything other than purely human endeavor is sheer folly. An exchange between Lucy and Bart, reminiscent of Mr and Mrs Ramsay's weather discussion in *To the Lighthouse*, nicely sum-

199

marizes their two points of view: ' "It's very unsettled. It'll rain, I'm afraid. We can only pray," she added, and fingered her crucifix. "And provide umbrellas," said her brother' (31).

The two visions, of course, are both parts of the truth, as Miss La Trobe's pageant demonstrates. Woolf incorporates them both, just as the relationship between Lucy and Bart sustains without serious conflict the apparently irreconcilable attitudes of each: 'But, brother and sister, flesh and blood was not a barrier, but a mist. Nothing changed their affection; no argument; no fact; no truth. What she saw he didn't; what he saw she didn't—and so on, *ad infinitum*' (33).

The Bart–Lucy, Giles–Isa relationships, along with the subsidiary involvement of these four with Mrs Manresa and William Dodge, intersect continually with the pageant, each enriching the other in complex and various ways. The full significance of the pageant can only be felt when refracted through the different living beings observing its production and responding to its meaning; similarly, the muddled affairs of those functioning on a June day of 1939 take on a particular importance in the context of the stylized presentation of English history. Structuring a fiction (*Between the Acts*) around a fiction (the pageant) which presents a literary view of 'real' history provides Woolf with a suggestive form of enormous resonance and flexibility.

The title itself plays on some of the ironic possibilities Woolf establishes in the interplay here between art and life. It is a title which obviously has numerous implications, none of which necessarily rules out any other. Set right before the start of the war, it can certainly be taken to refer to the time between the two horrendous acts of the First and Second World Wars. Or, as the curtain goes up at the end on the struggle between Isa and Giles, merging their performance with Miss La Trobe's latest vision, it might suggest how they too (like the rest of us) find themselves playing roles even when off the stage; or, in a slightly different vein, how successful human relationships are deliberately crafted artifacts requiring real creative energy. However we choose to interpret the title, the centrality of illusion and the ways Woolf develops it remain a basic part of the book's power and richness.

The novel's mixture of styles, ranging from doggerel poetry to sophisticated parody, and the creative tension between the pageant and the life swirling around it enables Woolf successfully to realize her intention, stated as early as 1938, of writing a novel which would be (*A Writer's Diary*, 289–90)

composed of many different things . . . we all life, all art, all
waifs and strays—a rambling capricious but somehow unified
whole—the present state of my mind? And English country; and
a scenic old house . . . and a perpetual variety and change from
intensity to prose, and facts—and notes . . . .

The novel's densely organized verbal texture reflects Woolf's—and
Miss La Trobe's—interest in the workings of the creative imagination.
Both artists consciously play with the potentialities of language,
exploring the way words can be used not to convey information or
ideas but simply as sensual pleasures, 'rolling words, like sweets on
their tongues' (15), as well as illustrating the power of an artistic
context to endow words with meanings that go beyond any that
they might have in isolation. When Lucy Swithin points out the
nursery to William Dodge, 'Words raised themselves and became
symbolical. "The cradle of our race" (88), she seemed to say,' and
what is true here is true throughout *Between the Acts*. The book is
abundantly laced with symbolic motifs whose network of contrasts,
ironies and associations reverberates anew each time we read it.

The fish that reminds Lucy Swithin of ourselves, for example,
becomes at once the glorious silver salmon caught by Giles which first
made Isa love him, the order for fish that Isa must routinely put
through to the store in fulfillment of her domestic functions, as well as
the image, trapped 'like a fish in water' (59), by which Giles defines his
own state of oppression, to mention a few of its appearances in the
novel. And what is true of fish is also true of birds, flowers, and colors.
Generating meaning out of the clash of styles and a variety of recurring
image clusters, Woolf presides, in *Between the Acts*, over a highly
charged verbal universe.

Central to that universe is the figure of Miss La Trobe, Woolf's
most intriguing portrait of the artist. Like Lily, the painter in *To the
Lighthouse*, and Bernard, the novelist in *The Waves*, La Trobe's creative
impulses have much in common with Virginia Woolf's own. But like
the others as well, she is an independent character with an entirely
self-contained fictional life. It is fascinating, in fact, to compare her
with Lily Briscoe to see what has happened to Woolf's conception of
the artist over a period of thirteen years.

Despite Mrs Ramsay's marital obsession, Lily remains alone
throughout the novel, all of Mrs Ramsay's ambitions about her and
William Bankes having come to nothing. But if single, Lily is not in

the least isolated. Rooted in the life of the Ramsays, she is capable of maintaining nourishing friendships with a variety of people; although she cannot enjoy the only kind of relationship Mrs Ramsay understands, her unmarried state does not rule out the pleasures of other human beings. There is no terror in Lily's life, no sharp rocks on which she flounders. Her satisfaction with her work is real, and she is an accepted and respected member of the novel's human community. In Lily Briscoe Woolf has created an artist essentially at peace with herself and the world around her.

In thirteen years, however, all this has changed. The relatively easy harmony of Lily's life has given way, with Miss La Trobe, to personal and social cacophony of the most extreme sort. Her own emotional life a shambles, disliked and distrusted by the village whose inhabitants call her Bossy behind her back and cut her when they see her, Miss La Trobe endures an anguished isolation unrelieved by any human contact. Whereas Lily functions adequately in the world at large, Miss La Trobe lives entirely within the cauldron of her creative imagination. Beyond her own shaping visions there is nothing in her life: no friends, no love, not even minimal human understanding. Her ability to interpret human experience for her audience, in fact, seems directly proportional to the degree to which she has always stood outside of all conventional and familiar success. (The conception of the artist as outcast, of course, has a long and distinguished tradition, but it is something remarkably new in Woolf.) Little is known about Miss La Trobe; she appears almost a self-generated being, without roots in the past or connections in the present—which is perhaps exactly the way Woolf wants us to regard the artist (71–2):

> She was always all agog to get things up. But where did she spring from ? With that name she wasn't presumably pure English. From the Channel Islands perhaps? Only her eyes and something about her always made Mrs. Bingham suspect that she had Russian blood in her. 'Those deep-set eyes; that very square jaw' reminded her—not that she had been to Russia—of the Tartars. Rumour said that she had kept a tea shop at Winchester; that had failed. She had been an actress. That had failed. She had bought a four-roomed cottage and shared it with an actress. They had quarrelled.

Investing Miss La Trobe with a distinct sexual identity is a bold stroke which suggests how far Woolf has moved since her treatment of the artist in *To the Lighthouse*. Lily exists without any particular sexual role at all. Flourishing in her commitment to her painting, Lily seems essentially neuter, indifferent to sexual needs of any sort. Certainly she resents Mrs Ramsay's insistence on the glories of the married state, but her resentment is more in the service of defending private choice than in defining any alternate set of yearnings. Sex simply plays no part in Lily's life. Miss La Trobe, however, enjoys no such luxurious immunity from the demands of her own nature. She is very decidedly a sexual being: specifically, an unabashed lesbian. It is the collapse of her relationship with the actress, in fact, which accounts for much of her suffering: 'Since the row with the actress who had shared her bed and her purse the need of drink had grown on her. And the horror and the terror of being alone' (246). However much Miss La Trobe's lesbianism might owe to Woolf's own muddled sexual feelings, within the economy of the novel it establishes definitive proof of her estrangement from the socially acceptable, as well as a convenient cause for her rejection (247):

> The old woman looked down at the dead flowers she was
> carrying and cut her. The women in the cottages with the red
> geraniums always did that. She was an outcast. Nature had
> somehow set her apart from her kind.

Tormented by needs which are not only unfulfilled but also render her suspect in her community, Miss La Trobe has every reason to be bitter at the incomprehension and intolerance surrounding her. And yet, as she scrawls on her manuscript, 'I am the slave of my audience' (247). Whatever pain and frustration she endures in her own life, as an artist she cannot permit the merely personal to interfere with her relation to her audience or to that endorsement of the human spirit that is necessary for all great art. She is a slave not simply because it is before her audience that she must proffer her plays for judgment, but also because as an artist she cannot dissociate herself from anything that is human. For Woolf, art must always be in the service of life; and her triumph over the madness and despair that beset her personally to the affirmative vision of her work is also Miss La Trobe's. Both manage to transcend their own very real agonies in the creation of their art.

But that creation also exacts an enormous toll from both. The paroxysms of self-doubt Woolf experienced with the completion of each novel afflict Miss La Trobe throughout the afternoon as the actors mangle their parts and the spectators fail to understand the action. For the artist, no amount of personal suffering can match the pain of feeling one's creation a failure; Woolf's acute vulnerability is shared by Miss La Trobe (165):

> And the stage was empty. Miss La Trobe leant against the tree, paralyzed. Her power had left her. Beads of perspiration broke on her forehead. Illusion had failed. 'This is death,' she murmured, 'death.'

> Panic seized her. Blood seemed to pour from her shoes. This is death, death, death, she noted in the margin of her mind; when illusion fails. Unable to lift her hand, she stood facing the audience (210).

On both these occasions, the disastrous breaking of the emotional continuity of the play is averted by the sudden intervention, in the first instance, of the bellowing of cows—'The cows annihilated the gap; bridged the distance, filled the emptiness' (165–6)—and in the second by a heavy downpour of rain. Actors in an historical pageant are not limited to human beings, nor roles only to those deliberately written. Reality unexpectedly entering the pageant and coming to the rescue of illusion adds complexity to La Trobe's conception: 'The risk she had run acting in the open air was justified' (211).

Miss La Trobe's response to her pageant oscillates, much as Woolf's did to her own work, between ecstasy and despair. The possibility that she has made people see, if only for a few moments, is sufficient to justify all her effort, for 'A vision imparted was relief from agony' (117). But following every such fleeting hope comes the dread certainty that in fact, 'She hadn't made them see. It was a failure, another damned failure. Her vision escaped her' (117–18).

Although Miss La Trobe can never resolve the question, it is in the end unimportant, for she achieves another kind of unequivocal success which emerges as the novel develops. Caught up as she is in all the details of the pageant, there yet stir in the inmost recesses of her creative imagination the seeds of her next work. Before the pageant actually begins, Miss La Trobe finds herself thinking about what is to follow it: '"It has the makings ..." she murmured. For another play always lay behind the play she had just written. Shading her eyes, she looked. ... "No, I don't get it," she muttered and resumed her pacing' (78). But as the pageant unfolds, the new form begins to shape itself in her mind, so that at the conclusion of the day she hardly has time to luxuriate in thinking about what she had just finished before she is totally absorbed in what she will do next: '"I should group them," she murmured, "here". It would be midnight; there would be two figures, half concealed by rock. The curtain would rise. What would the first words be? The words escape her' (246). And going to the local inn to escape the loneliness of her empty house, the opening of her new play actually comes to her: 'There was the high ground at midnight; there the rock; and two scarcely perceptible figures. Suddenly the tree was pelted with starlings. She set down her glass. She heard the first words' (248).

What matters are not the merits of the play but the ongoing nature of the creative process itself. It is this that the novel finally celebrates above all else; Miss La Trobe's ability to continue to create in spite of the difficulties she faces constitutes a triumph of the spirit in which Woolf, in this last novel, ultimately rests. Although she committed suicide before she had revised the text for the printer, *Between the Acts* ends by emphatically proclaiming the power of individuals to create art, relationships, and life out of their own partial, disordered existences. There can be nothing exotically different about their successes, but the enterprise is no less precious for that. Isa longs for something new—'Love and hate—how they tore her asunder! Surely it was time someone invented a new plot, or that the author came out of the bushes' (252)—but when the curtain goes up on Isa and Giles, they will perform their parts with an intensity not in the least diminished by the fact that these are roles that have been performed over and over again since the beginning of time. And it is this irreducible human reality of love, hate, and peace—'Three emotions made the ply of human life'—of which Miss La Trobe's new play will consist. Woolf is careful to suggest connections between the development of La Trobe's new form and the creative struggle of Giles and Isa. Miss La Trobe's two figures alone at night on the rock necessarily merge, if only half-consciously, with Isa and Giles, alone at night in their home; and the final action of husband and wife, 'They spoke,' becomes for us part of Miss La Trobe's culminating inspiration, 'She heard the first words' (256). In their struggle to renew their love, Isa and Giles illustrate that affirmation of creative human effort central to the artistic visions of both Miss La Trobe and Virginia Woolf.

13

The Biographies;
Flush and *Roger Fry*

Flush

If a biography of Elizabeth Barrett Browning's cocker spaniel seems a
curious subject for a serious writer, it at least has the obvious virtue of
constituting an enormous release from the poetic intensity of *The
Waves*, the book immediately preceding it. Critics, Woolf notes in her
diary, frequently fail to acknowledge the need of the mind for variation, and she points out explicitly that *Flush* was taken up 'impetu-
ously after *The Waves* by way of a change' (*A Writer's Diary*, 191).
Enabling her to write in a lighter vein, it served the same therapeutic
function for her imagination as *Orlando* did following the completion
of *To the Lighthouse*. And indeed, despite its subtitle instructing libra-
rians how properly to classify it, *Flush: A Biography* is no more a
biography than *Orlando* is. Combining some of the fantasy elements
of *Orlando* with the feminist social criticism found in *The Years* (on
which she was working concurrently) and *Three Guineas*, *Flush* is its
own special blend which Woolf feared was at once 'too slight and too
serious' (*A Writer's Diary*, 191) to hold together successfully. Her
anxieties, however, were misplaced. Although certainly not one of her
major achievements, the book is a thoroughly delightful *jeu d'esprit*,
playing with serious themes in a way that avoids the twin perils of
archness and triviality.

Flush is the story of Elizabeth Barrett Browning and her escape not
only from the tyrannies of her father's household, where she is held a
captive invalid, but from the rigid oppressions of the sterile English
class system altogether. The 'dog's eye view' of the preposterous Mr
Barrett and the values of a society he embodies provides Woolf with
an effective satiric device to expose the follies of both. *Flush* also gives
us access to the bedroom and heart of Elizabeth herself, previous
knowledge of which has been limited to what she has chosen to reveal
to us in her poems and letters. His innocent canine assessment of the
206

moods and needs of his beloved mistress, as well as his own growth—paralleling and commenting on Elizabeth's—from protected, spoiled pet to an independent, sensual creature encountering experience first-hand, makes him the appropriate observer of the action.

Given to Elizabeth by an admirer, Flush soon learns the basic lesson of Wimpole Street, that all dogs are not equal. Some are high, some are low, and the two must never be confused. Looking in the mirror and seeing that he possesses the physical traits of high degree certified by the arbiter of all such matters, the Spaniel Club, and looking around him to find the purple water jug denoting rank and privilege, Flush realizes that he can never again associate indiscriminately with the mongrel friends of his youth. On Wimpole Street, distinctions are everything, and 'as long as Wimpole Street remains, civilisation is secure' (20).

For Flush, the price of such civilization is the leash; for Elizabeth, it is living the 'life of a "bird in its cage"' (47), subject to the control of a father whose sole concern for his daughter is that his commands be obeyed. For both, the existence authorized by Mr Barrett and his kind, who establish the rules for the Spaniel Club and its human counterparts, requires the thwarting of their essential natures, so that as Elizabeth lies pallidly in bed, Flush also learns to 'resign, to control, to suppress' (35) his vital animal impulses.

After four years of insulated bedroom living, Flush begins to notice a change in Elizabeth's behavior. A new animation attends the routine delivery of the postman, a new impetuousness to open a certain envelope, a new intensity in reading it. Flush senses a growing indifference to his own well-being. Hampered by his inability to read, he knows instinctively that a rival for Elizabeth's affections has emerged. On 21 May 1846 his worst premonitions are realized with the sudden entrance into the Wimpole Street mausoleum of Robert Browning. Flush is the only witness to this clandestine meeting, and to the succession of others which follows. Beset by an increasing loneliness, he nevertheless notices the happy changes in Elizabeth's health. And while her family and friends puzzle over her marked improvement, 'only Flush knew where her strength came from—it came from the dark man in the armchair' (56).

Flush's emotional turmoil—his resentment, his various jealous attacks on Browning, his desire for forgiveness—is resolved in his final accommodation to the new love that unites the three of them. Accepting Browning's permanent presence, he joins the two of them as one of the conspirators 'in the most glorious of causes. We are joined in sympathy. We are joined in hatred. We are joined in defiance of black and beetling tyranny' (70). But before any of these goals can be realized, Flush's bliss is abruptly terminated by a gang of dog thieves who steal him from Elizabeth in front of a shop on Vere Street.

The stealing of Flush (he was actually stolen on three separate occasions, but Woolf compresses them into a single incident) plays a central role in the biography, not so much for the imagined trauma it inflicts on Flush's sensibility as for the uses Woolf makes of it for the larger social and political purposes of the book. As we know from the first-hand accounts of men like Henry Mayhew, Thomas Beames, and other accurate recorders of Victorian London, the secure civilization of Wimpole Street existed side by side with the pestilential dens of the city's rookeries where, mired in filth and disease, London's poor 'swarmed on top of each other as rooks swarm and blacken tree-tops' (75). While Mr Barrett and the founders of the Spaniel Club could argue over what constitutes the proper slope of a spaniel's skull, large masses of the population lived in cowsheds, drank the same filthy water they washed in, and were ravaged by disease. Quite literally next to one another—'Behind Miss Barrett's bedroom, for instance, was one of the worst slums in London' (74)—their proximity tended not to be acknowledged by those fortunate enough to live on Wimpole Street and not in St Giles's. But even if unacknowledged, 'The terms upon which Wimpole Street lived cheek by jowl with St Giles's were well known. St Giles's stole what St Giles's could; Wimpole Street paid what Wimpole Street must' (76). Wimpole Street pets made a convenient target for enterprising St Giles's businessmen; appropriate ransom could quickly recover a lost animal. Reluctance to pay would also produce the animal, but only certain parts of it, in a package, a few days later.

Elizabeth's love for Flush, of course, makes her choice of action clear. Entrusting her brother Henry to negotiate the price with Mr Taylor, she prepares to pay whatever Mr Taylor demands for himself and his society. But from the point of view of the Barrett family and of Wimpole Street society in general, Elizabeth's uncomplicated commitment to her animal is only a part—and a negligible part at that—of the entire situation (85):

Wimpole Street was determined to make a stand against

Whitechapel. Blind Mr Boyd sent word that in his opinion it would be 'an awful sin' to pay the ransom. Her father and her brother were in league against her and were capable of any treachery in the interests of their class.

Finding the six and a half guineas that Taylor wants outrageous, Henry tells Mr Barrett who insists that it not be paid. Better a dead Flush than a compromised Wimpole Street.

Worse yet, in her battle for Flush's life against the vested interests of her father's world, Elizabeth finds even her beloved Robert to be allied with the opposition. Besieged by the abstract cries for justice, law, and the need to resist the dark forces of tyranny, and chastised for her feminine weakness by the man she loves, Elizabeth nevertheless holds firm in her belief that Flush matters more than all the weighty logic decreeing that he die to defend the glories of Wimpole Street. It is not a comfortably theoretical belief; frantic at the refusal of her family to rescue Flush, she herself orders a cab and, accompanied by a trembling servant, goes off to Shoreditch in search of Mr Taylor.

Entering the forbidden rookeries in the company of one terrified female maid was not an easy thing to do for a Wimpole Street lady, particularly when she has been assured by one of her brothers that the probability of her being murdered or robbed is quite high. And while she fails to locate Taylor himself, her expedition indicates a resolve that is sufficiently frightening to her family to move them finally to pay the ransom lest she be tempted to undertake another such trip. In addition to effecting Flush's release, the cab ride to Manning Street, Shoreditch, opens the eyes of the insulated poet to what life is like outside the protected confines of her home. Although only a brief exposure, she saw 'more while she sat in the cab at the public-house than she had seen during the five years that she had lain in the back bedroom at Wimpole Street' (91). It was not a message she was ever to forget. Her artistic imagination was stimulated in a way it had never been by the marble busts of poets littering her bedroom. For the first time, she encountered men and women who neither lie on sofas nor read books. They were to remain with her, and years later, as she sat writing in Italy, 'were to inspire the most vivid passages in *Aurora Leigh*' (92).

Focusing on the social injustices fostered and maintained by the male world in general and men like Mr Barrett in particular, on Elizabeth's defiance as a woman, and on the freeing of her imagination as a writer, the episode of Flush's kidnapping provides Woolf with an opportunity to develop all the major themes of the book. And with the return of Flush as our reliable witness, Woolf prepares us for the biography's final movement, the escape from the land of Spaniel Clubs and Wimpole Street proprieties, of 'tyrants and dog-stealers' (102), to the fulfillment of sunny Italy.

Fleeing England with the Brownings (now married) in 1846, Flush discovers, at first with some anxiety, that the 'laws of the Kennel Club are not universal' (109). Dogs roam freely in a country that seems to place no value at all on the various trappings of gentility that characterize the English. Having absorbed various of the aristocratic tenets in which he was nurtured, Flush must unlearn them all in the new joyous democracy he experiences in Italy. Flush's discovery is Elizabeth's as well. She flourishes in the sensual spontaneity and instinctive kindness of Italy and the Italians. Instead of lying in bed and sipping port, she scrambles over rocks, tosses down tumblers of Chianti, drives in a rickety fly to look at mountains and lakes: 'she delighted in the sun; she delighted in the cold' (107).

Altogether, the Italy to which the Brownings go reminds us of the Italy of E. M. Forster's novels, the land of 'freedom and life and the joy that the sun breeds' (103) that stands in sharp contrast to the sterility and mean-spiritedness of England. For Forster, the great god Pan always roams the Italian countryside, ready to bring fulfillment to the desiccated English refugees who can open themselves to accept his message; and whereas during the period of her incarceration Elizabeth is limited to the vicarious intuitions of Pan she receives through the animal presence of Flush—'Was it Flush, or was it Pan? Was she no longer an invalid in Wimpole Street, but a Greek nymph in some dim grove in Arcady?' (38–9)—now 'she no longer needed his red fur and his bright eyes to give her what her own experience lacked; she had found Pan for herself among the vineyards and the olive tree; he was there too beside the pine fire of an evening' (110–11).

In a world where 'Fear was unknown . . . there were no dog-stealers here and, she [Elizabeth] may have sighed, there were no fathers' (111), Flush and the Brownings are free to pursue their separate passions. For Elizabeth it is her relationship with her husband, the birth of her child, her writing. For Flush, responding to the call of a nature cramped for so long in a stuffy bedroom, it is love—'love pure, love simple, love entire' (112). Behaving in a happily unrespectable way, Flush embraces all aspects of life and every variety of dog he

210

encounters. His ability to absorb life directly through the senses without the distancing of the analytic human intellect permits him an understanding forbidden to novelist, biographer, or historian. Smelling and touching the texture of the world around him, 'he knew Florence as no human being has ever known it; as Ruskin never knew it or George Eliot either. . . . Not a single one of his myriad sensations ever submitted itself to the deformity of words' (125).

Even the humiliation of fleas cannot undermine his happiness. For although the solution is a brutal one—shaving off his proud coat that had always earned him the admiration of the connoisseur—he soon realizes the freedom conferred by nakedness: 'To be nothing—is that not, after all, the most satisfactory state in the whole world?' (128) Without his coat, but also without his fleas, Flush achieves the ultimate wisdom of living simply as himself—that divine state of being made possible in Italy. Flush needs all the wisdom he has acquired to endure the brief trip back to England he makes in the company of the Brownings. The gloom, the rigidity, the joylessness are as thick as ever. 'Nothing has been changed. Nothing had happened all these years,' Elizabeth understands as she prowls through the house on Wimpole Street, and Flush is not happy again until all are safely lodged on the Channel steamer returning to France. The crossing is rough, and Flush is suddenly sick on deck (135):

> 'He was ordered off the deck on purpose, poor dog,' said Mrs
> Browning. For the deck was still English; dogs must not be sick
> on decks. Such was his last salute to the shores of his native land.

Flush and Elizabeth grow old together. While she becomes fascinated with the current rage of spiritualism, with drawing-room tables that talk and move, he dozes and lies in the sun. Her visionary tendencies, her interest in '"knocking" round at all the doors of the present world to try to get out' (142), are mocked by Flush's sleepy immersion in this world, his reveling in the richness of his memory. At the end, though, feeling death upon him, Flush rushes to Elizabeth and returns her to her own past, and to the distance she has traveled since. She recalls the moment of her deep misery when Flush brought to her intimations of Pan, and the poem she wrote on that occasion (149–50).

> She had written that poem one day years ago in Wimpole Street
> when she was very unhappy. Now she was happy. She was

growing old now and so was Flush . . . . Her face with its wide
mouth and its great eyes and its heavy curls was still oddly like
his. Broken asunder, yet made in the same mould, each, perhaps,
completed what was dormant in the other.

With the two together on the sofa, the pattern of their shared life
completed, Woolf ends the biography without any fuss: 'He had been
alive; he was now dead. That was all. The drawing-room table,
strangely enough, stood perfectly still' (150).

Roger Fry

The death of Roger Fry in 1934 was a numbing loss not just for
Virginia Woolf but for all of Bloomsbury. Among the *dramatis per-
sonae* associated with Bloomsbury, Roger Fry was perhaps the most
universally loved and admired for the power and integrity of his
intellect, his passionate commitment to friendship, his complex and
deep humanity. The most influential art critic of his time (and certainly the most significant since Ruskin), who almost single-handedly
coerced England into an appreciation of modern art through his
championing of the Post-Impressionists, Fry also commanded, as a
private human being, the intense personal affection of his friends.
They found him a man of profound goodness and profound sympathy, never too busy in his fight to bring enlightenment to England
to fail to give of himself unstintingly to those around him. As both an
important public and a revered private figure, he played a unique role
for those who knew him. E. M. Forster's assessment was shared by
many: 'Roger Fry's death is a definite loss to civilization. There is no
one now living—no one, that is to say, of his calibre—who stands
exactly where he stood' (294).

Woolf's personal response to Fry is found in her diary, several days
after his funeral (*A Writer's Diary*, 224):

> I thought of him too, at intervals. Dignified and honest and
> large—'Large sweet soul'—something ripe and musical about
> him—and then the fun and the fact that he lived with such variety
> and generosity and curiosity.

The corporate esteem in which he was held seemed to make it inevitable that an immediate record of his achievements, as critic and as
human being, would be produced, though it was not clear by whom.

Woolf's early notion, already assuming the need for a biography, is of a joint effort (*A Writer's Diary*, 230):

> Ideas that came to me last night dining with Clive; talking to Aldous and the Kenneth Clarks.

> About Roger's life: that it should be written by different people to illustrate different stages.
> Youth, by Margery
> Cambridge, by Wedd?
> Early London Life . . .
>   Clive
>   Sickert
> Bloomsbury, Desmond
>   V.W.
> Later Life, Julian
>   Blunt
>   Heard and so on.

All to be combined by Virginia herself and Desmond MacCarthy. But as the project was discussed with Helen Anrep, the woman with whom Fry lived the last part of his life, and Margery Fry, one of his sisters, it gradually became an undertaking for Woolf alone. She was attracted to the idea for several reasons: not only would it give her an opportunity to express her affection for the man, but more important, it offered a new formal challenge. The critic who had written about the art of biography now had a marvelous chance to try her hand at her own, and with a subject she both knew well and admired. Armed with the support of her friends, the Fry family, and all of Fry's papers, Woolf set out to be a biographer in 1935. In 1940, her *Roger Fry: A Biography* was published.

Above all else, her portrait of Fry is a portrait steeped in love. While affection for one's subject is by no means the least of qualifications for a biographer, it does involve certain risks from which Woolf does not entirely escape. It encourages the possibility, for example, of a shaping of the material, both consciously and unconsciously, into a form that leaves certain areas unexamined, certain questions unasked. The portrait glows, but we wonder if there aren't complexities and relationships that might also have been considered in the interests of following the biographical truth wherever it may lead. And the possibilities of these constraints functioning in a variety of ways is made all the more real when the biographer is a close friend of members of the subject's family who are eager to have a portrait to cherish.

I raise these caveats not to suggest that Woolf acted irresponsibly as a biographer, glossing over dark interludes that a less committed observer might have treated, but to try to establish the special circumstances and tone of the book. Woolf does not approach her material with any of the disinterestedness of the modern biographer, intent on exploring every obscure corner of the subject's life, but with the protective concern of a friend absorbed in the task of preserving the memory of someone she loved. The distinction can perhaps best be understood by saying that Woolf has written more of an appreciation seeking to evoke the reality of the friend she knew than a biography seeking to discover and present all that might be known about a man named Roger Fry. The distinction is not meant to be invidious: Woolf's *Roger Fry* is a moving and compelling book, enabling us to experience the richness of a man whose acclaim was justly earned; that it is not necessarily the Roger Fry of his definitive biographer does not diminish her own effort, but rather sets it in a context by which we can best understand its achievement.

Working largely with his own letters and papers, Woolf takes us admirably through the different phases of Fry's life: his strict Quaker upbringing; his Cambridge years, where his father's aspirations for his son's scientific future clashed with Roger's growing passion for art; and his final emergence both as a basically second-rate painter as well as England's most distinguished art critic. She covers all the great moments of that career: his work with Pierpont Morgan and the Metropolitan Museum of Art; the two Post-Impressionist Exhibitions; the establishment of the Omega Workshops to help indigent artists and at the same time revitalize the artistic tastes of England; and at long last, near the end of his life, the offer of the Slade Professorship at Cambridge. Woolf traces throughout the book the extraordinary fertility of Fry's thought, correctly stressing the openness and range of a man who, attracted to the masters of the Italian Renaissance at the start, would also become the articulate—and notorious—defender of Cézanne and modern art. The growth from the 'shy and studious youth' (182) with his conservative Quaker origins to the fierce 'leader of rebels, the father of modern British painting' (182), taking on and slaying the reactionary forces of the cultural establishment—and doing so without compromising his integrity—is a fascinating one, and Woolf charts it sensibly and accurately. Restricting herself generally to

214

the narrative of Fry's life (though interludes of analysis and interpretation do occur), and relying heavily on quotations from his letters and other documents—sometimes too heavily, as in the slightly clotted opening chapters—Woolf succeeds in bringing the critic before us in all his power, versatility, and passion.

But 'The critic of Roger Fry as a man has a far harder task than any that was set him by the pictures of Cézanne' (294), Woolf cautions, and her words speak to her own difficulties in dealing with the more private aspects of Fry. Woolf writes with greater ease and authority about the public Fry—the lecturer, the art critic, the traveler, the writer. It is when we leave the realm of the public, however—what Woolf calls the 'granite-like solidity' (*Collected Essays*, vol. 4, 229) of external, verifiable truth for the 'rainbow-like intangibility' of personality—that she becomes curiously vague, hesitant to undertake those forays into the inner life that characterize the most searching and enduring biographies. Her reluctance, of which she seems dimly aware, is granted various sorts of theoretical justifications, generally by reference to his own thinking about the ultimate mystery of personality or art (293):

> But his influence as a human being—his own words, 'We know too little of the rhythms of men's spiritual life,' remind us of the perils of trying to guess the secret that lay behind that.

Discussing the problem of trying to put all the pieces of the man together, Woolf concludes with Fry's warning about how frail analysis is in the face of the completed work of art (296):

> It must always be kept in mind that such analysis halts before the ultimate concrete reality of a work of art, and perhaps in proportion to the greatness of the work it must leave untouched a greater part of its objective.

To try to render the impression of the man is to realize that (297)

> Those who know him best will attempt no summing up of that sensation. They can only say that Roger Fry had a peculiar quality of reality that made him a person of infinite importance in their lives, and add his own words, 'Any attempt I might make to explain this would probably land me in the depths of mysticism. On the edge of that gulf I stop.'

And Woolf always has the example of Fry himself to fall back on, for, as she writes, 'Only one subject seemed to escape his insatiable curiosity; and that was himself. Analysis seemed to stop short there' (289).

Human beings will always elude biographical versions of them, of course, and Woolf cannot be faulted for recognizing the limitations of her own attempt. But her disclaimers are symptomatic of her unwillingness to engage not so much in any large-scale efforts at synthesis as in the more mundane—and more important—detailed treatment of the texture of his emotional life, the nature of his important relationships. The causes of this reluctance, as I have suggested, are various: partly a result of both acknowledged and unacknowledged familial constraints ('The family—Now there of course I'm afraid I should have to ask you to be careful (*A Writer's Diary*, 233), Margery Fry cautions Woolf at the outset of the project); partly a result of what we can think of as the memorial nature of Woolf's purposes here, purposes which are in some ways at odds with purely biographical ones; and partly also, no doubt, of Woolf's own binding sense of propriety, her belief that there are certain private areas of self that should not be unearthed for public scrutiny. Whatever the complex of reasons, it is this part of her presentation of Fry that is the least satisfying. Complicated feelings and entanglements that an industrious biographer would labor over are treated sketchily and in generalities. This is particularly true of his tragic relationship with his wife Helen who, becoming mentally ill ten years after their marriage in 1896, was irrevocably committed to an asylum in 1910, leaving Fry with two young children. Although we are told several times of his 'splendid record of courage, patience, and devotion' (146), we never have any real sense of how he experienced these anguished years, of what his courage consisted, of what he must have felt in retrospect about his parents' concern, before the marriage which they opposed, over the state of Helen's health. We have no idea of how Fry responded to being alone with his two children. (Indeed, at no point does Woolf give us any notion of what fatherhood meant to Fry or how he dealt with the children at any time in his life.) Limiting herself to the testimony of a few letters revealing his unhappiness, added to her own almost pietistic declarations concerning his strength and nobility, Woolf fails to explore the depth and confused nature of the feelings that must have assailed Fry during this crucial period of his life.

Woolf's reticence about these years extends to almost all parts of his personal existence. The quality of his emotional life, whether with his sisters, the various women with whom he was involved (Vanessa

Bell, among others), or even Helen Anrep, remains largely unexamined. The passions and complexities are there, and often alluded to, but Woolf is finally happier following the fascinating and challenging growth of the critic than immersing herself into some of the difficulties of the private man. If 'the aim of biography,' as Woolf writes in 'the New Biography,' is to fuse the granite and rainbow 'into one seamless whole' (*Collected Essays*, vol. 4, 229), we must admit that her own work falls short of this exacting standard.

But Woolf's reticences certainly do not obscure the very real virtues of the book. In its sympathy and intelligence, it is a splendid testament to Fry. His originality, his goodness, his ability to experience the 'pure delight' (294) of people, art, and life are all captured by Woolf, and there is perhaps no finer way to praise the book than to say it makes us feel for Fry what Woolf and all of Bloomsbury felt for him. If it does not satisfy the highest claims of biography, it nevertheless succeeds in being very much the book Woolf wanted to write.

14

Social Criticism:
A Room of One's Own and
Three Guineas

A Room of One's Own

Growing originally out of two papers she delivered on the subject of 'Women and Fiction,' *A Room of One's Own* (1929) treats issues that had long been of vital interest to Woolf. *Orlando*, published a year earlier, already dealt with the difficulties of women in general—and women writers in particular in a male-dominated world. *A Room of One's Own*, in fact, lays bare most of the intellectual assumptions behind *Orlando*'s extravagant fantasy. But *A Room* is not merely a somber gloss on the marvelously irresponsible *Orlando*; it has a charm, power, and form of its own which make it far more engaging than the simple polemic some take it to be.

Part of its success is the deftness with which she avoids any taint of shrillness or heavy-handed moralizing. Although Woolf passionately deplored the various obstacles society places in the path of all creative women, she manages to protest them with a grace and wryness which prevent the book from degenerating into the narrowly didactic. Basic to her argument is the insistence that a writer who is 'harassed and distracted with hates and grievances' (88) cannot produce anything of enduring value; appropriately enough, *A Room* is in itself luminous proof of a mind which has been able to synthesize its anger and frustration into a compelling, balanced work of art. Transcending special pleadings of any sort, the book is an immensely civilized document speaking to the common humanity shared by everyone.

Like the novels themselves, Woolf's achievement here is very much a triumph of form. The 'essential oil of truth' (38) about the nature of women and their creative powers which Woolf hopes to extract cannot be obtained through the logician's straightforward plodding or the scholar's painstaking research. Her experience at the British
218

Museum, encountering the fatuous works of the male professors, testifies to the peculiar absurdity of such endeavors. Instead, Woolf devises a form whose combination of personal anecdote and public fact, of digressions and tight analysis, of hard-edged social commentary and finely wrought imaginative forays work together to convince even the most skeptical reader of the truth of her vision. Above all, it is Woolf's own mind at work which structures the book—and clinches her argument—providing us with telling examples of that 'incandescent' imagination she finds central to Shakespeare's genius. For we are finally compelled to affirm the power of female creativity less by the evidence and the logic, convincing though they are, than by the demonstration of such a creative intelligence fashioning a work of art. The famous conclusion—that women must have five hundred pounds and a room of their own if they are to produce fiction or poetry—is not as important as the actual workings of the mind that lead to it. Woolf's apparent maunderings over her theme are part of a calculated strategy which succeeds not only in exhibiting a graceful intellect thoroughly confident of itself and at home with its material, but also in drawing readers into the process by which the ideas are formulated. Addressing her audience directly about the accomplishment of Mary Beton, the persona she sporadically evokes during the course of the book, Woolf points explicitly to the rationale for the form (158):

> She has told you how she reached the conclusion—the prosaic conclusion—that it is necessary to have five hundred a year and a room with a lock on the door if you are to write fiction or poetry. She has tried to lay bare the thoughts and impressions that led her to think this. She has asked you to follow her flying into the arms of a Beadle, lunching here, dining there, drawing pictures in the British Museum, taking books from the shelf, looking out of the window. While she has been doing all these things, you no doubt have been observing her failings and foibles and deciding what effect they have had on her opinions. You have been contradicting her and making whatever additions and deductions seem good to you. That is all as it should be, for in a question like this truth is only to be had by laying together many varieties of error.

The various kinds of assaults on the truth demand a style different from the crafted, poetic intensity of the novels. Woolf speaks throughout the book in a voice admirably suited to her task. Supple

219

and informal, it moves at a leisurely pace, cajoling, musing, and following its own impulses wherever they lead. Fusing the directness of the prose-essayist with the fictive-making liberties of the novelist, Woolf creates a form which conveys not only the relevant facts but even the moral and imaginative truths that make those facts significant.

Woolf makes clear from the beginning that the subject of 'women and fiction'—the ostensible focus of the book—will not be resolved in a neat package. Her prosaic conclusion that women must be economically independent if they are ever to write is in fact offered without fanfare in the book's first paragraph. But if this wisdom can be dispatched quickly enough, the rest of the book is engaged in the more critical job of exhibiting 'as fully and freely as I can the train of thought which led me to think this. Perhaps if I lay bare the ideas, the prejudices, that lie behind this statement you will find that they have some bearing upon women and some upon fiction . . . . One can only show how one came to hold whatever opinion one does hold' (6–7). In the process of doing this, Woolf reveals an intelligence far removed from the poetic sensibility with which she has been exclusively—and misleadingly—associated. It is an intelligence thoroughly aware, for example, of the importance of money, of the degree to which 'Intellectual freedom depends upon material things' (162–3). An intelligence which has no illusions about the self-generated majesty of the creative act but understands clearly the influence that social, economic, and psychological factors exert not only on the nature, but even on the very possibility of artistic creation. She is fully aware of the way the mundane facts of physical infirmities, housing conditions, barking dogs, and crying children can intrude upon a writer's inspiration. All shibboleths attached to the sacred calling of the writer fall before a healthy pragmatism that insists on making people confront things as they actually are.

That there seems little startlingly new about any of Woolf's claims only suggests how extraordinary the book was when published in 1929. For her analysis of the explicit and implicit difficulties women, both artists and otherwise, must overcome in their quest for fulfillment and self-expression has become in its general thrust part of the unquestioned assumptions of our age. If current feminist examinations of our institutions and attitudes have moved past Woolf's treatment, nevertheless they clearly incorporate all of Woolf's basic arguments. The easy acceptance these arguments gain today should

220

not tempt us to minimize the achievement of their lucid articulation in 1929. And even when compared with the more sophisticated cultural criticism of recent years, its intelligence and imaginative elegance still make *A Room of One's Own* a work very much to be read. However rudimentary many of its arguments may appear now, *A Room of One's Own* has the inestimable advantage over its high-powered competition of having been written by Virginia Woolf.

Of the broad range of debilitating realities Woolf examines which affect women's ability to produce fiction, by far the most important is money, or more specifically the lack of it. The economic subjugation of one half of the human race by the other is by this time a dismal fact of our history acknowledged by even the most reactionary of male oppressors. Woolf's concern is not to belabor the injustice of the exploitation in itself but to demonstrate the connection between that fact and the creation (or non-creation) of literature. Although poverty, or at least the lack of financial independence is not necessarily fatal to the creative impulse, it certainly doesn't encourage it. The inability to receive a proper education, the limited opportunity to earn an adequate salary, the grinding demands of motherhood and domestic servitude—all contribute to the basic constraints not only of the material life but the imaginative life as well. For without the opportunity to think and read and experience—privileges which society has never dispensed free of charge to anybody, particularly women—the mind is deprived of the nourishment necessary for any sustained artistic endeavor. Freedom, Woolf well understands, whether intellectual, imaginative or otherwise, is by no means readily available to all; her discussion of the limited achievement of women in the arts indicates just how expensive it is.

Money, of course, confers more than freedom; those who possess it are more than likely also going to possess power, grace, prestige, and an altogether confident attitude towards themselves and their capabilities. And in the history of the human race it is the male, not the female, who has succeeded in keeping it all for himself. Woolf works out the implications of the economic inequality between the two sexes brilliantly with her fantasy, at the start of the book, of her two days spent at Oxbridge, a traditional male college, and Fernham, a college for women. Evoking the two separate ambiences with wit and charm, Woolf at the same time focuses effectively on the differences between the haves and the have-nots. The whole comparison is a splendid example of a delicately wrought imaginative structure being

221

put to serious use, and itself illustrates the method and success of the entire book.

Goading a Beadle out of his torpor by wandering on to grass reserved only for Fellows and Scholars, instantly conjuring up the guardian of the library by presuming to enter without proper accompaniment, Woolf feels at every turn the full weight of complacent tradition in which Oxbridge is wrapped. It is not merely in the prohibitions, however, that Woolf encounters a world which has never questioned its assumptions or its right to privilege. It is there also in the lushness of setting, in the massive buildings supported for centuries by nobles and merchant princes alike, in the easy confidence of the discourse and the sumptuously served meals. It pervades every thought and action, guaranteeing to any who might question that all is as it should be—and as it has always been (17–18):

> No need to hurry. No need to sparkle. No need to be anybody but oneself. We are all going to heaven and Vandyck is of the company—in other words, how good life seemed, how sweet its rewards, how trivial this grudge or that grievance, how admirable friendship and the society of one's kind, as, lighting a good cigarette, one sunk among the cushions in the window-seat.

But the partridges and the piquant sauces of Oxbridge are not found at Fernham. Here it is plain beef, with prunes and custard to follow—nothing to complain about certainly, but a sorry distance from the elegant luncheons at Oxbridge. The drabness of the fare, of course, signifies the larger fact that Fernham does not stand on the gold and silver underlying Oxbridge. If it did, if women had been able from the beginning to amass fortunes in trade and establish schools for themselves, everything would be different (32–3):

> We could have been sitting at our ease to-night and the subject of our talk might have been archaeology, botany, anthropology, physics, the nature of the atom, mathematics, astronomy, relativity, geography. If only Mrs Seton and her mother before her had learnt the great art of making money and had left their money, like their fathers and grandfathers before them, to found fellowships and prizes and scholarships . . . we might have been exploring or writing; mooning about the venerable places of the earth; sitting contemplative on the stone steps of the Parthenon,

or going at ten to an office and coming home comfortably at half-past four to write a little poetry.

But Mrs Seton and her mother never had the opportunity to do so, and from this restricted premise comes not just the lack of amenities at Fernham but the whole range of limited options financial dependency imposes upon individuals. Without the power to earn money or, in the case of Mrs Seton and her forebears, even to keep it had they been able to earn it, people are effectively disenfranchised from the full potential of life.

The enforced poverty of women is thus the essential historical consideration—hence the remedy of five hundred pounds a year—which bears upon their ability to write fiction. The call for economic equality is at the heart of Woolf's meditation on women and fiction, just as it remains at the center of all feminist writing since Woolf. But while the unadorned fact of economic subjugation is the effective cause from which all else develops, Woolf goes on to examine other features of the problem as well. One of them is the attitude of those who have the wealth and the tradition and the power towards those who don't. It has not been, as Woolf suggests, benign. People don't give up their privileges blithely, and masculine domination has bred its own perverse mythology to justify its claim to superiority. Seeking answers to the question of why women are poor, Woolf finds in the British Museum only a series of worthless books written by a variety of professors, sociologists, clergymen—experts whose main qualifications seem to be that they are not women—detailing useless facts, summarizing useless opinions, and generally documenting the argument for women's mental, moral, and physical inferiority. Common to them all is an element Woolf identifies as anger: 'anger that had gone underground and mixed itself with all kinds of other emotions. To judge from its odd effects, it was anger disguised and complex, not anger simple and open' (49).

It is the anger, Woolf concludes, of the threatened, of those who assert the inferiority of others in order to maintain their own imperiled confidence in themselves. In the grating business of life, we can sustain ourselves only by doggedly clinging to notions of our own worth, a process which is immeasurably enhanced by (52–3)

thinking that other people are inferior to oneself. By feeling that one has some innate superiority—it may be wealth, or rank, a straight nose, or the portrait of a grandfather by Romney—for

223

there is no end to the pathetic devices of the human imagination—over other people. Hence the enormous importance to a patriarch who has to conquer, who has to rule, of feeling that great numbers of people, half the human race indeed, are by nature inferior to himself. It must indeed be one of the chief sources of his power.

Such power can most readily be exerted when the assumptions are shared both by the oppressor as well as by the oppressed, and Woolf well understands the important role women have played in affirming the male ego. 'Mirrors are essential to all violent and heroic activity' (54), she writes, acknowledging not only the dependency of men upon women but also the extent to which women have been content to reflect the life-giving illusions back to their men. Although Woolf does not take women to task here for submitting to the male fantasy, her analysis clearly points the way to a feminine consciousness that is currently in the process of examining every nuance of its relationship with the masculine world.

Part of that evolving new consciousness has involved a careful scrutiny of the past to unearth hitherto unknown information about the way women lived their lives in previous centuries. In deploring the lack of any substantial historical work on this subject, *A Room of One's Own* anticipates precisely the kind of scholarship that has since begun to flourish. Woolf's speculation that the 'facts lie somewhere, presumably, in parish registers and account books; the life of the average Elizabethan woman must be scattered about somewhere, could one collect it and make a book of it' (68), has been borne out in all manner of historical investigation which seeks to resurrect women from the anonymity of their past. Woolf's barbed humility in not dreaming to suggest to the distinguished scholars that they should 're-write history, though I own that it often seems a little queer as it is, unreal, lop-sided' (68), is no longer necessary: the lop-sidedness caused by the conspicuous absence of women in history is being rectified.

But the recent developments in historiography are no help to Woolf in her quest for some understanding of the lives of women before the eighteenth century. Why were women, for example, so pervasively the subject of Elizabethan poetry, unable themselves to write any of it? Discovering nothing on the library shelves concerning what women were like or how they lived, Woolf engages in another fine imaginative excursus by creating for herself a life of Judith

Shakespeare, William's wonderfully gifted sister, to demonstrate the fate of creative women during the time of Elizabeth. Every bit as talented as her brother, Judith is of course not sent to school and not encouraged or even permitted to browse through whatever books of Will's she found. The prohibitions are not imposed out of spite but, on the contrary, precisely because the parents love her and want to prepare her for the life she will lead. Books and papers are not likely to contribute to her well-being. Betrothed by her doting parents to the son of a neighboring wool-stapler, Judith protests passionately that she doesn't want marriage. The father beats her, then begs her not to break his heart and shame him in this way. Torn between love for her father and her need to honor her own poetic gift, Judith steals away one summer's night and goes to London. But unlike Will, she is laughed at when she explains she wants to act and learn about the theater. Whereas Will could mingle with all sorts of people from every part of London, Judith has access to one. She can't act, she can't work in the theater, she can't even 'seek her dinner in a tavern or roam the streets at midnight' (72). At last, finding herself pregnant by Nick Greene, the actor-manager, Judith—'who shall measure the heat and violence of the poet's heart when caught and tangled in a woman's body?—killed herself one winter's night and lies buried at some crossroads where the omnibuses now stop outside the Elephant and Castle' (73).

The short, tragical history of Judith Shakespeare clearly owes much to the rather happier history of Orlando, down even to the inclusion of Nick Greene straight from Orlando's life as the seducer. Judith's melodramatic end, underscoring the frustrations endured by the genuinely talented woman unable to pursue the craft that obsesses her is actually less interesting to Woolf than the dilemma over style, tone, and subject matter faced by those women who do manage to write. For writers are acutely vulnerable—as Orlando's own example indicates—to the implicit and explicit assumptions of their age, to the attitudes towards themselves and their art embedded in the society about which they write. No artist can avoid being affected by the conflicts and mores of his culture (74–5):

> For it needs little skill in psychology to be sure that a highly
> gifted girl who had tried to use her gift for poetry would have
> been so thwarted and hindered by other people, so tortured and
> pulled asunder by her own contrary instincts, that she must have

lost her health and sanity to a certainty. . . . To have lived a free
life in London in the sixteenth century would have meant for a
woman who was poet and playwright a nervous stress and
dilemma which might well have killed her. Had she survived,
whatever she had written would have been twisted and
deformed, issuing from a strained and morbid imagination.

To produce a great work of art is prodigiously difficult for anybody, given the world's vast indifference to art, whether good or bad,
the temptations to despair inherent in the creative process itself, and
the countless treacheries of body, mind, and spirit to which creative
people are exposed. But for Woolf it is (or certainly was in the
immediate past) even more difficult for women, who instead of
indifference encounter outright hostility, the derision of a male world
looking with patronizing disapproval at the efforts of a decidedly
inferior species to express itself. The problem—and here Woolf moves
into the most intriguing theoretical part of her argument—is less the
damaging effects of discouragement, though they are real enough,
than the artist's need to articulate a vision that is distorted neither by
rage at the world nor a craven desire to placate it. For Woolf, the
aesthetic wholeness, the integrity of the artifact is all. The novelist
who picks up her pen riddled with hatreds and resentments, however
justified, will fail just as surely as the novelist who thinks only of what
is expected of her. In either case the book will be crippled by a burden
no novel was meant to bear; conciliation and aggression are both fatal.
The question of 'what state of mind . . . is most propitious to the act of
creation' (77) largely occupies the second half of A Room of One's Own.
The answer Woolf finds in Shakespeare: it is the incandescent imagination, purged of rancor and the concern for the opinion of others,
capable of rendering all that is private or personal into the fibre of the
work of art. Paradoxically, to say we know so little about Shakespeare's state of mind is to say a great deal about the quality of that mind
which produced his art. He eludes us in part because (86)

> his grudges and spites and antipathies are hidden from us. We are
> not held up by some 'revelation' which reminds us of the writer.
> All desire to protest, to preach, to proclaim an injury, to pay off a
> score, to make the world a witness of some hardship or grievance
> was fired out of him and consumed. Therefore his poetry flows
> from him free and unimpeded. If ever a human being got his
> work expressed completely, it was Shakespeare. If ever a mind

226

was incandescent, unimpeded, I thought, turning again to the bookcase, it was Shakespeare's mind.

For obvious reasons, incandescence has not been the common characteristic of women novelists. There has been too much bitterness on the one hand and too many pressures to conform on the other for most writers to express a vision whose integrity has not in some fundamental way been compromised by the external. For Woolf, only Jane Austen and Emily Brontë managed to resist both the temptations of their own anger and the admonitions of the kindly male professors in creating works of art free from the corruption of any foreign matter. Charlotte Brontë is traduced by her indignation at having been denied the full range of worldly experience she so desperately wanted; we feel in her novels 'a rancour which contracts those books, splendid as they are, with a spasm of pain' (110). And if George Eliot is not victimized by resentment, she nevertheless failed to shape for herself her own mode of expression, adopting instead the prose of the great male novelists with which she 'committed atrocities . . . that beggar description' (115). Only Austen and Emily Brontë were able to 'hold fast to the thing as they saw it without shrinking' (112), and to fashion a language that would permit the articulation of that vision without distortion or clumsiness. Transcending the lack of a tradition and the variety of self-indulgent emotional paths that can lead a writer astray, only Austen and Brontë, in short, succeeded in writing 'as women write, not as men write' (112).

Although Woolf does not attempt systematically to work out the differences, the distinction is crucial (132):

> But this creative power [of women] differs greatly from the creative power of men. . . . It would be a thousand pities if women wrote like men, or lived like men, or looked like men, for if the two sexes are quite inadequate, considering the vastness and variety of the world, how should we manage with one only? Ought not education to bring out and fortify the differences rather than the similarities?

To write like a woman is to explore the range of one's own sensibility without the influence of any narrowly masculine assumptions, to achieve a prose style expressive of one's own view, one that neither mirrors nor deliberately seeks to repudiate the great male models of the nineteenth century, and to feel entirely confident in one's own

227

judgments and values. Above all, it is to write without the explicit sex consciousness which has twisted out of shape so many novels of the past, to cease to see men as the opposing camp which must be catered to or railed against. That this has now become commonly possible in the twentieth century is acknowledged by Woolf in her comments on the imaginary modern novelist, Mary Carmichael. Though by no means a genius and without the passion, wit, or wisdom of her distinguished forebears, Carmichael has the advantage of not having to fight the same battles they fought. Almost entirely free of hatred and fear, her novel shows no trace of the brooding presence of masculine censure or approval. If her first book is not a masterpiece, it at least indicated that she had learned the first great lesson which will eventually result in the creation of such a work, perhaps by Mary herself, perhaps by others like her. She wrote as a woman but as a woman who has forgotten that she is a woman, so that her pages were full of that curious sexual quality which comes only when sex is unconscious of itself' (140).

It is fatal not merely for women to think of their sex while they write, but men as well. For Woolf, the purely masculine mind cannot create—or create great art—any more than the purely feminine can. The truly incandescent imagination cannot be limited by narrow boundaries but must be flexible and wide-ranging, sensitive to all manner of impulse and nuance. Woolf called this kind of harmonious, receptive mind 'androgynous,' speculating that by it Coleridge (148)

> meant, perhaps, that the androgynous mind is resonant and porous; that it transmits emotion without impediment; that it is naturally creative, incandescent and undivided. In fact one goes back to Shakespeare's mind as the type of the androgynous, of the man-womanly mind, though it would be impossible to say what Shakespeare thought of women.

'Androgynous' thus becomes Woolf's metaphor for that luminous, creative intelligence, unhindered by parochialisms and grievances, which is capable of producing great works of art. That men and women share certain psychological predilections of the other is, of course, a generally acknowledged fact. In suggesting that in the artist's mind the two strains, male and female, should work together harmoniously, Woolf is certainly not espousing any radically new psychological doctrine. Nor is she advocating large doses of androgyny as a remedy for social problems. Critics who take the term out of its immediate context to create for Woolf an 'androgynous vision' which somehow illuminates the structure and meaning of her fiction are distorting it beyond all usefulness.

If it is generally true that Woolf finds admirable the artistic sensibility that can hold its potentially disparate male and female impulses together and use both happily, at the same time her discussion of androgyny has a specific importance in the organization of *A Room of One's Own*. As we have seen, almost all of Woolf's novels end on some note of affirmation and wholeness, however transient and threatened. Having exhorted women throughout *A Room of One's Own* to write for themselves and without regard for the male bogey, Woolf found herself dangerously close to assenting to a kind of adversary posture between the sexes which she strongly opposed. Celebrating the possibility of unity, not the fact of divisiveness, Woolf's evocation of the androgynous mind serves to bring together the two sexes whose interests have seemed in opposition for most of the argument. Five hundred pounds a year and a room of one's own for women artists will in the long run be a boon to the human race as a whole, not just half of it. While special male prerogatives will have to crumble before such opportunities exist, it is a small price for men to pay. If Judith Shakespeare can somehow, by our common efforts, return to us and be permitted to express herself freely and fully, then everybody, men and women alike, will be the richer for it. In the spectacle of a taxicab going off with a man and a woman in it, which precipitates the whole meditation on androgyny, Woolf discovers a symbol for that overarching oneness of civilization she so ardently desired.

Three Guineas

Three Guineas expands some of the concerns of *A Room of One's Own* into a work of broader social implication. The darkening picture of European politics—including the specific outbreak of the Spanish Civil War—provided both the focus and the immediacy of the book. The ways in which women might prevent the horror of war is the ostensible subject, but in approaching it Woolf in fact unleashes a fierce polemic against the aberrant nexus of masculine assumptions, values, and institutions which makes war inevitable. Going beyond the cultural criticism of *A Room of One's Own*, the book excoriates the male world not merely for its attitude towards women—perverse though that is—but for its general pathology (of

229

which the attitude toward women is definitely part), its muddled priorities which celebrate the bogus and the superficial at the expense of the real and the life-giving. Woolf wrote here with the same moral passion which pervades Strachey's *Eminent Victorians*. In their mutual abhorrence of the folly of war, of the use of power of any sort, whether between nations, sexes, or individuals, and in their commitment to a civilization based on the principles of rationality and tolerance, both works are quintessential Bloomsbury documents, defining that humane sensibility for which the group is justly known. However exaggerated some of the particular parts of the attack may be, Woolf's *Three Guineas* stems from a moral vision altogether admirable in its purity.

Employing a 'didactic, demonstrative Style' (*A Writer's Diary*, 262) far more emphatic than the one used in *A Room of One's Own*, Woolf addresses the essay to an imaginary correspondent who has written asking for her assistance in finding ways to avoid war. This structure evolved from an idea initially formulated at the end of 1935 to shape the book by pretending 'it's all the articles editors have asked me to write during the past few years—on all sorts of subjects—Should women smoke: Short skirts: War etc' (*A Writer's Diary*, 262). It permits Woolf a freedom of movement and establishes a means of continuity necessary for the success of *Three Guineas*. The tightly concatenated argument is by no means Woolf's most characteristic mode of expression as a prose essayist, and the privilege we readily grant letter writers of an informal organization and even a certain amount of repetition is unabashedly employed by Woolf in responding to the query posed her.

The imaginary letter in question is written by an educated man to an educated woman. That this should happen at all is an extraordinary event which, while marking the progress women have made over the centuries, also points up the problems. When previously, Woolf comments, 'has an educated man asked a woman how in her opinion war can be prevented?' (8) Or, for that matter, asked her opinion about anything substantial? In addition to setting the proper ironic tone and introducing the theme of the nature and relationship of the two sexes, the fact that the question is asked by one educated person of another is important in defining Woolf's point of view here. For she is very explicitly writing from the perspective of what she calls the 'daughters of educated men' (12),[1] the women who have the ability to go to university, to enter the professions, to make significant intellectual contributions to society. Although Woolf is not unsympathetic to working class needs and aspirations, she also accepts without guilt the fact that she is a member of a privileged class which offers her opportunities not available to her poorer sisters. The Bloomsbury way of life was never intended to be within reach of all people; Woolf was firmly rooted in the upper middle class, and all her cultural assumptions reflect the bias. Equality for women as a whole is of course something she desires, but it is essentially the plight and potential of the daughters of educated men which concern her. And it is essentially their values—processed through the Bloomsbury refinery—and steeped in their grievances that Woolf takes on the masculine world that has appealed to her for help.

In contemplating the means by which help could be offered, Woolf starts by confronting the inescapable fact of the complete powerlessness of women. Thoroughly excluded from the centers of political and financial decision-making, barely tolerated in the professions which pay them as little as they possibly can, and in general shackled by centuries of patriarchal condescension and hostility, women would seem to be in no position at all to render assistance to a male society which has traditionally proclaimed their utter insignificance. Without access to the military authority of the armed services, the moral authority of the church, or the opinion-making authority taken for itself by the press, the daughters of educated men have no way to affect public policy. If working women were to go on strike and refuse, for example, to make munitions, that would at least hinder the war effort (24):

> But if all the daughters of educated men were to down tools
> to-morrow, nothing essential either to the life or to the
> war-making of the community would be embarrassed. Our class
> is the weakest of all the classes in the state. We have no weapons
> with which to enforce our will.

The difficulty is compounded by Woolf's insistence that the instinct

---

[1] Woolf's own footnote (265) explains the reason for this rather peculiar term:

'Our ideology is still so inveterately anthropocentric that it has been necessary to coin this clumsy term—educated man's daughter—to describe the class whose fathers have been educated at public schools and universities. Obviously, if the term "bourgeois" fits her brother, it is grossly incorrect to use it of one who differs so profoundly in the two prime characteristics of the bourgeoisie—capital and environment.'

for fighting is exclusively male, neither shared nor even understood by women. Whether it is reasonable to confine all aggressive impulses to the male of the species is an issue we shall return to later, but such a distinction is basic to Woolf's argument: 'Obviously there is for you some glory, some necessity, some satisfaction in fighting which we have never felt or enjoyed' (14). Three reasons which seem to make war so attractive to men—that it is a profession, a source of pleasure and excitement, and 'an outlet for manly qualities, without which man would deteriorate' (15–16)—are completely alien to the female sensibility. And as it is not easy to remedy what one does not comprehend, the possibility that women might contribute to the elimination of war is minimal indeed.

Despite limited hopes for success, Woolf nevertheless begins to examine the various options open to women, using the examination primarily as an instrument to expose the folly, sterility and tyranny of the male world while, in the process, defining an alternative set of values. The first general area Woolf considers where educated men's daughters might be thought to have some influence is, not surprisingly, education. If they are not able directly to exert pressure on those who issue declarations of war, perhaps they could put their energy and the money they are now able to earn for themselves (an achievement of utmost importance to which Woolf refers constantly) at the disposal of schools which will teach the young to hate war. Having seen the professions at least nominally opened to them in 1919, women now have the financial resources—meagre though they are—to bargain and choose, to decide what they want to support with their guineas, and what they want to ask in return. Should they support education or societies seeking peace?

Clearly, university education is thought to be extraordinarily important by society; witness the fact that the ruling class of England has always had it, that vast sums of money have been committed to it, and that those traditionally excluded from it, namely women, have gone to the greatest pains to obtain it. And just as clearly, university education has done nothing at all to imbue students with an aversion to war. Woolf's analysis of university structure and attitude indicates why: the same pomposities and vanities, the same love of one's prerogative and willingness to use force to protect it that lead to war are also rife in the great universities. Catering to the rich and zealously denying women access to their sacred privileges—as late as 1937 women's colleges were not granted full rights of university member-

232

ship at Cambridge—the universities promulgate the same mindless chauvinism, of sex, if not of country, Woolf finds detestable in the nation as a whole. Disinterested inquiry and a magnanimity of spirit cannot flourish in an atmosphere of combative possessiveness. Whatever their aims, such schools are in practice teaching the mentality of war.

But what of women's colleges? Perhaps they might offer the kind of education in which women could invest their guinea with confidence. Such an education, Woolf goes on in an exultant vein of calculated idealism, would teach 'not the arts of dominating other people; not the arts of ruling, of killing, of acquiring land and capital,' (62) but 'the arts of human intercourse; the art of understanding other people's lives and minds, and the little arts of talk, of dress, of cookery that are allied with them' (62). It would honor the whole person, drawing its students and teachers from all manner of people, the only criterion being a love of learning for its own sake. No degrees, no lectures, no august set of initials after one's name. Only an entire community, free from competitive strife, pursuing a common end. But such an exalted vision falls before the mundane fact that students must be taught to obtain appointments, that appointments are more easily achieved if students can put the B.A. after their names, that honors and competitive distinctions are what society cherishes above all. So the woman's college is not the simple answer; it cannot be rebuilt entirely exempt from the pestilence infecting the male bastions (65):

> the college for the daughters of educated men must also make Research produce practical results which will induce bequests and donations from rich men; it must encourage competition; it must accept degrees and coloured hoods; it must accumulate great wealth; it must exclude other people from a share of its wealth; and, therefore, in 500 years or so, that college, too, must ask the same question that you, Sir, are asking now: 'How in your opinion are we to prevent war?'

The reality, then, is that the daughters of educated men cannot direct very much influence through education to prevent war. They cannot affect the character of the male colleges, and even their own institutions are tied to assumptions they cannot fundamentally alter. Educated women themselves, of course, can express their views by refusing to teach anything that relates to war, by voicing their contempt for chapels, examinations, and degrees, by turning down any offices or honors proffered them. From the college authorities, however, they can expect little. But if the college for daughters of educated men is not the solution, it remains the only hope.

To refuse to support it is to deny women the right to an education, which in turn will prevent them from earning their livings. And to do that is to consign them once again to the private house and the patriarchal power whose values, given their complete financial dependency, the daughters are obliged, either consciously or unconsciously, to affirm. To refuse to give money to the woman's college, then, is ultimately to opt for the patriarchal view of things, which is to say, for war. Such is the grim logic which mandates financial backing for women's colleges in spite of their imperfections. Only in that way can women exert the modicum of educational influence they have at their disposal, measured out in the few guineas they have earned themselves, to bringing about the end of war.

Committing a guinea without great enthusiasm to the rebuilding of a woman's college, Woolf now turns to examine other means by which the daughters of educated men might help prevent war. Potentially more significant than the rather mild role women can play in shaping educational affairs are the professions themselves, providing women with their only real weapon, 'the weapon of independent opinion based upon independent income' (73). If the financial power of those engaged in the professions, and therefore free from patriarchal constraints, can be directly channelled into the quest for peace, it might well be more efficacious than lingering around the gates of the universities clamoring to be heard. But before Woolf considers how to harness that power in order to aid her male correspondent, she receives another letter, this time from an honorary treasurer asking for contributions—if not money then books, second-hand clothing or anything else that might be sold at a bazaar—to help the daughters of educated men in the professions earn their livings. If the request is genuine, if those women currently in the professions are in fact so poor that they must solicit contributions to keep alive, then clearly that independent opinion Woolf sought to put to work in the service of peace is not very powerful. The question is easily settled. Woolf goes straight to Whitaker's *Almanack*, that impartial authority on all facts and figures, to see what kinds of salaries are available to women, for example, in the section entitled, 'Government and Public Offices.' There, despite the claims made by philosophers and novelists like C. E. M. Joad and H. G. Wells that women are not only idle and apathetic

234

but extraordinarily well-paid in addition, Woolf discovers that women appear nowhere at all in the list of the high salaried officials: 'those to whose names the word 'Miss' is attached do not seem to enter the four-figure zone' (87). The assertion made by Ray Strachey in 1934, 'To earn £250 a year is quite an achievement even for a highly qualified woman with years of experience' (81), then, is true: women remain discriminated against and relatively impoverished, even with their admission into the various professions. Although the deadly stricture in the nineteenth century of marriage being the only profession open to women has broken down, genuine economic equality is not yet theirs. The reason for the poor pay is not a consequence of any ineptitude of women, their unfitness for responsible positions, but precisely the same reason for the determined effort of the male authorities at Oxford and Cambridge to prevent women from entering: it is the need to cling to one's own privileges and power, to keep others from participating, to maintain exclusive control over the disbursement of wealth and knowledge. It is in short the male mentality and, according to Woolf, the war mentality as well.

The weapon Woolf hoped to mobilize against war is thus not a very potent one. Without substantial money-earning power, there can be no substantial influence. But if this proved a false hope, Woolf speculates, perhaps she can best serve the interests of peace by sending her second guinea to support the women already engaged in the professions, thereby helping them 'to have a mind of their own and a will of their own with which to help you prevent war' (106).

Such a thought leads Woolf to consider the workings of the professions themselves, for if it is true, as her survey of the males in them would seem to indicate, that they 'make the people who practise them possessive, jealous of any infringement of their rights, and highly combative if anyone dares dispute them' (121), then to encourage women to enter them is only to encourage those same perverse attitudes she is trying to correct. Looked at from the point of view of the outsider, the professions breed the same brand of complacent tyranny which makes the universities so sterile. Stretching out beyond sight, the sons of educated men constitute an enormous procession, 'mounting those steps, passing in and out of those doors, ascending those pulpits, preaching, teaching, administering justice, practising medicine, transacting business, making money' (111). Marching in lock-step, they leave home at 9.30 and return at 6.30, matters safely in hand, unruffled by doubts of where they are heading or what it all means. And now that women are permitted to march at the end of that procession, the question must be asked: 'do we wish to join that procession or don't we?' (113).

The rewards of doing so are vast. To wear a wig and robes, to exhort from the pulpit, to buy and sell on the Exchange are precisely the rights for which women have been fighting. But if the price for such rights is the corruption of values, the desiccation of mind and spirit we see every day as the procession marches to and from its offices, is it worth it? Woolf's judgment of the mess educated men have made of themselves and their world causes her 'to doubt and criticize and question the value of professional life—not its cash value; that is great; but its spiritual, its moral, its intellectual value' (131). If women are to become the very things they have struggled against—creatures without humanity, drugged by an obsession with money, sensitive only to their own needs—it is far better to let the procession pass on and retain the integrity and dignity that even the poor can possess.

Dramatically stated—and even overstated—the dilemma facing the daughters of educated men is that they are (135)

> between the devil and the deep sea. Behind us lies the patriarchal system; the private house, with its nullity, its immorality, its hypocrisy, its servility. Before us lies the public world, the professional system, with its possessiveness, its jealousy, its pugnacity, its greed. The one shuts us up like slaves in a harem; the other forces us to circle, like caterpillars head to tail, round and round the mulberry tree, the sacred tree, of property. It is a choice of evils. Each is bad. Had we not better plunge off the bridge into the river . . . and so end it?

Fortunately, self-destruction is not necessary: there is a way out of the bind.

Woolf finds the answer in the 'unpaid-for education' women have been receiving for centuries. However limited access to formal education was, both famous and obscure women alike have been molded by the great teachers of poverty, chastity, derision, and what Woolf chooses to call 'freedom from unreal loyalties' (142). Biography indicates that these are the four which qualified them for the unpaid-for professions they toiled at incessantly, and while such an education obviously had its defects, it also had its virtues, for we cannot deny that these women, whatever their shortcomings, were essentially civilized human beings. To follow the dictates of these four traditional teachers of women, and to combine with them some knowledge, wealth, and a commitment to real loyalties will allow participation in the professions without threat to the self. The teachers are not demanding. 'Poverty' asks only that you earn enough money to provide independence and ensure full development of mind and body, but not a penny more; 'chastity' insists that you sell neither brain nor soul for money, that as soon as the mulberry tree begins to exert its pressure, you break off and laugh at it; 'derision' entails rejecting all methods of signifying honor and merit, holding always to the principle that fame and praise are insidious temptations to be avoided. And perhaps the most important of all, 'freedom from unreal loyalties,' a basic Bloomsbury tenet, requires 'that you must rid yourself of pride in nationality in the first place; also religious pride, college pride, school pride, family pride, sex pride and those unreal loyalties that spring from them' (146).

Guided by these teachers, women can join the procession without fear of contamination. And under such circumstances, the guinea to enable professional women to support themselves becomes a sound investment. Encouraging a life-giving presence in the long, sterile parade of the beribboned and the berobed, it is the best way for Woolf to help establish that independent, disinterested influence which might bring about the elimination of war.

Having donated two guineas to help rebuild a college and to alleviate the poverty of professional women, Woolf returns, in the last section of the book, to the original letter sent by the treasurer of the peace society recommending to her certain steps she might take to help the group realize its admirable goal: sign a manifesto pledging to protect culture and intellectual liberty, become an active member of the society herself, and finally support the aims of the society through financial contributions. Of the three, Woolf has no difficulty with the last. As she has already expressed her own judgment of how war might best be avoided by giving first to the building fund and the professional women's society, she finds no reason now to withhold a third guinea from the peace society. For its aims are essentially hers (182–3):

> To prevent war . . . broadly speaking, by protecting the rights of
> the individual; by opposing dictatorship; by ensuring the
> democratic ideals of equal opportunity for all. Those are the chief

237

means by which as you say,' the lasting peace of the world can be assured'.

The guinea, then, can be freely given, and being given in this way it celebrates that commitment to a common purpose which the entire book is about. Woolf decried the word 'feminist,' seeing it as 'a vicious and corrupt word that has done much harm in its day,' (184). What she is finally advocating is not simply the rights of women but, in the words of Josephine Butler which she quotes three times, '"the rights of all—all men and women—to the respect in their persons of the great principles of Justice and Equality and Liberty"' (185). To aspire to a narrower goal is to be guilty of that same adversary mentality of exclusion against which women have been protesting. The enemy is tyranny in any form, whether embodied in the patriarchal state or the fascist state, and with the assurance that the peace society recognizes this, Woolf has no qualms about lending her financial support.

About the treasurer's first two suggestions, she has serious reservations, however, using them both as opportunities to expose further some of the diseased tissue of the society she is trying to save from itself. Although her response touches upon various points made in the two earlier chapters, at the same time it adds important emphasis and breadth to her argument. That Woolf should imagine a woman being asked by a man to help defend intellectual liberty and culture is a splendidly ironic notion, for what segment of society has been more consistently denied both than women? Those who have until recently been denied any form of higher education, who, as Whitaker once again makes clear, are not thought capable of teaching their own literature in the university or giving advice about 'buying a picture for the National Gallery, a portrait for the Portrait Gallery, or a mummy for the British Museum' (158) are hardly in a position to urge that culture and intellectual liberty be defended. Lacking both themselves, the only way women can serve these precious commodities is to protect their own versions of them, which is to say to read and write their own language with precision and integrity. For accepting anything less than the truth while reading, or expressing anything less than that while writing—either fact or fiction, it doesn't matter—is to be guilty of the gravest kind of crime against the self. Manifestos of concern are worthless if, after signing them, women return to the desk to produce 'those books, lectures, and articles by which culture is prostituted and intellectual liberty is sold into slavery' (167). The daughters of educated men who have the ability to write must pledge themselves not to commit the 'adultery of the brain' (170) frequently demanded by our culture, both for the harm it does the author as well as the damage it wreaks upon those who read the corrupted words. In urging women artists not to compromise their visions or capitulate to the lure of success or money, Woolf is simply stressing, in slightly different language, the need to observe the wisdom of the unpaid-for teachers she previously honored. By refusing to write what others might expect, by refusing to read anything similarly tainted, women can do something more effectual than signing petitions. Perhaps even the dedication to the truth might spread, so that 'if newspapers were written by people whose sole object in writing was to tell the truth about politics and the truth about art we should not believe in war, and we should believe in art' (176). However visionary such a hope, if the daughters of educated men insist on the truth of what they write and what they read, they will at least contribute mightily to breaking 'the ring, the vicious circle, the dance round and round the mulberry tree, the poison tree of intellectual harlotry' (179) which continues to infect the culture.

One final question remains for Woolf: should she join the society whose aims she shares and to whom she has already sent her guinea? As non-controversial as her membership would seem to be, her decision most emphatically is not to. Her basic consideration in refusing to join is the importance of maintaining her difference: 'Different we are, as facts have proved, both in sex and in education. And it is from that difference, as we have already said, that our help can come, if help we can, to protect liberty, to prevent war' (188). To relinquish that difference by assuming membership in a male organization is to threaten the independence of that view and those values which are essentially all women have to offer to the cause of peace. In addition, male societies of any sort are themselves highly questionable enterprises for Woolf. However admirable Woolf finds the treasurer of this one, she cannot be confident that when all the members come together, the luminous qualities of each will not give way to some ugly corporate nature: 'inevitably we look upon societies as conspiracies that sink the private brother, whom many of us have reason to respect, and inflate in his stead a monstrous male, loud of voice, hard of fist, childishly intent upon scoring the floor of the earth with chalk marks. . . .' (191) In order to maintain whatever influence they possess, the daughters of educated men must resist any temptation to merge their identities in societies of men. Only by remaining outside such organizations can they contribute to their aims.

To the degree that it is convenient to think of people of common interest as comprising some sort of organization, Woolf imagines all the daughters of educated men belonging to an Outsiders' Society, a group which has neither treasurer nor secretary nor committee, which calls no meetings and holds no conferences. It consists solely of the daughters of educated men 'working in their own class—how indeed can they work in any other?—and by their own methods for liberty, equality and peace' (193). Though they take no formal oaths, they would all be bound by strict allegiance to the doctrines of poverty, chastity, derision, and freedom from unreal loyalties. They would also preserve an attitude of strict indifference to the warlike impulses of their brothers. By 'indifference' Woolf obviously does not mean to suggest that women ought not to be concerned about war. Rather, indifference is the only viable response to an instinct which, in Woolf's view, is completely alien to the female sensibility (194–5):

> As if it is a fact that she cannot understand what instinct compels him . . . as fighting thus is a sex characteristic which she cannot share, the counterpart some claim of the maternal instinct which he cannot share, so it is an instinct which she cannot judge. The outsider therefore must leave him free to deal with this instinct by himself, because liberty of opinion must be respected, especially when it is based upon an instinct which is as foreign to her as centuries of tradition and education can make it. This is a fundamental distinction upon which indifference may be based.

But indifference must also be based on reason. If men argue that wars are being fought to keep women and England free, the outsider must make clear that she is not free now, that her position in England for centuries has been basically that of a slave. Therefore she cannot be invoked to justify their need to kill and tyrannize. The truth she will insist upon is that 'as a woman, I have no country. As a woman I want no country. As a woman my country is the whole world' (197). It is by maintaining a calculated indifference—designed to try to neutralize the martial posturings of the male—and heeding always the lessons of their unpaid-for education that the Society of Outsiders can best serve the interests of peace and equality. It does so through the means that 'a different sex; a different tradition, a different education, and the different values which result from those differences have placed within our

240

reach' (206). While the members of the peace society can use all the public measures which their wealth and power and influence have placed at their disposal, to achieve peace the outsiders would work towards the same ends by experimenting 'not with public means in public but with private means in private' (206).

In fact, for Woolf, writing in the late 1930s, there is ample evidence that such work is actively going on in various quarters, though no attention has yet been paid it by the press. That it has thus far escaped the public glare is critical, for 'Secrecy is essential. We must still hide what we are doing and thinking even though what we are doing and thinking is for our common cause' (217). The need for such secrecy is a consequence of fear, the fear of incurring the anger of the ruling patriarchy which still does not take kindly to the independent efforts of women, regardless of how worthy their goals. The fear is justified for, Woolf claims, male resentment at the spectre of female freedom is a powerful force indeed, one to be confronted directly only at great peril. Documenting her case for the vehemence of the resentment, Woolf cites the testimony of a Professor Grensted, speaking before the Archbishops' Commission on the Ministry of Women, who argues (228–9)

> that the general acceptance of male dominance, and still more of feminine inferiority, resting upon subconscious ideas of woman as 'man manqué,' has its background in infantile conceptions . . . . These commonly, and even usually, survive in the adult, despite their irrationality, and betray their presence, below the level of conscious thought, by the strength of the emotions to which they give rise.

These strong emotions, which it takes courage to oppose, Woolf finds working throughout history to keep women in fetters, under the total control of their masters. Borrowing the term from Professor Grensted, it is this 'infantile fixation,' demanding total obedience from the helpless women which Woolf sees in the unforgiving Mr Barrett of Wimpole Street, in the Rev Patrick Brontë insisting that Charlotte refuse a marriage proposal, in Mr Jex-Blake humiliating his daughter, Sophia, for wanting to accept payment for teaching mathematics. Whether in the guise of marriage or money, it is the threat of an independent existence which is so terrifying to the men and which they must resist with all their energy. But if the nineteenth-century fathers in private were finally defeated, forced at last to relinquish their daughters from the confines of the house, the twentieth-century fathers in public continue to exercise vigilance in protecting the turf of their professions and privileges against any incursion. As long as the fixation remains strong, fear—and the secrecy it engenders—are perfectly comprehensible. The outsiders must go on toiling for peace quietly and in their own ways until such time as the public fathers understand the common interest which unites them. For the meantime, although the guinea has already been sent, the membership card will be left unsigned. It is perhaps enough at this point that Woolf's correspondent observes that 'the three guineas . . . though given to three different treasurers are all given to the same cause, for the causes are the same and inseparable' (261).

As a sustained piece of social criticism, *Three Guineas* is rather too simplistic to be totally convincing. Although it accurately depicts the massive injustice done women by centuries of sexist oppression, it loses some of its credibility in reducing all of civilization's ills to the villainy of the male. That aggressiveness is somehow a purely masculine instinct which women neither share nor even understand is an assertion that no psychologist, anthropologist, or ethologist could endorse. Driven by greeds, lusts, and the love of power, human beings of both sexes are generally highly imperfect creatures, living their lives without regard for those four great teachers of the uneducated Woolf invokes. The history of male domination is a singularly pernicious instance of a kind of exploitation that is all too peculiarly human, running throughout both sexes and all social classes at all times. To argue that women only share malignant patriarchal values when they are in a state of economic dependency on that patriarchy is, to say the least, highly dubious. Although women are by no means the problem, neither are they the solution. Thwarted at every turn by a male world which has sought to exclude them from economic power and educational opportunity, women have not necessarily been purified of all ethical dross by the oppression.

But if we cannot accept the psychological or political reality of man as the carrier of pestilence and woman as the healer or, at worst, the infected victim, such an opposition provides Woolf with a convenient means of anatomizing society's evil: it is a construction of the moralist, not the political or social analyst. And this is precisely the way the book demands to be read: *Three Guineas* is essentially a moral tract exposing the corrupt values and institutions of a culture and offering in their stead an alternative vision based on principles of justice,

242

equality, and liberty. The Society of Outsiders is obviously not intended as a realistic political hope but rather as an ideal notion of how individuals might function in society. Despite the very real masculine abuses it does document, *Three Guineas* is not in any sense a narrowly feminine protest. It is above all a protest of an extraordinarily civilized sensibility against the assumptions of a society ruled by base impulses and unreal loyalties. Its exaggerated attribution of wickedness to one half of the human race is, in part, a device that permits Woolf to develop the moral antidote with force and clarity, an enterprise in which she emphatically succeeds.

15

Literary Criticism

Throughout most of her adult life, Virginia Woolf functioned as a professional literary critic and reviewer. As Leonard makes clear in his autobiography, the Woolfs, particularly at the beginning of their careers, desperately needed the money that Virginia's journalism brought in, and starting with her first review in the *Guardian* in 1904, she continued to meet deadlines and write steadily for pay until her death. I stress as baldly as possible the professionalism of her journalistic practice as a caution to those who insist on seeing Woolf as pure sensibility existing solely within the confines of her art. Certainly the exhausting demands of the novelist's craft held the highest priority in Woolf's life, but as the five collected volumes of her essays and reviews indicate, she was also capable of inhabiting an altogether different kind of imaginative realm. Along with the therapeutic effect of the additional income, the critical writing in fact tended to provide her with needed relief from the almost debilitating intensity she generated in producing her novels. The playful, ironic, relaxed tone of her essays, with their easy accessibility, contrasts sharply with the exacting, densely saturated nature of her fiction. The two complement each other happily, giving together a rounded view of a complex mind that either one, taken separately, would not afford.

Woolf was aware that her critical prose revealed a rather different self from the one that might be inferred from her fiction. Reflecting in her diary on the difficulty of collecting her essays in a single volume (eventually published as *Common Reader*), Woolf concludes, 'Nevertheless I should very much enjoy it. I should graze nearer my own individuality. I should mitigate the pomposity and sweep in all sorts of trifles. I think I should feel more at my ease, (*A Writer's Diary*, 58). In an essay on Turgenev, she discusses the choice every writer must make between the different kinds of selves each

244

possesses. For her, Turgenev's genius lies in the fact that in his fiction he suppresses the 'I' which knows grievances, desires fame, seeks power, in favor of 'the other self, the self which has been so rid of superfluities that it is almost impersonal in its individuality' (*Essays*, vol. 1, 253). Her praise of Turgenev not only accurately defined her own fictional achievement—it is, after all, precisely that self, 'almost impersonal in its intense individuality' which speaks to us in her novels—but also points to the particular role her criticism plays in our appreciation of Woolf. For while the fiction is informed by the same kind of austere, superb impersonality she found in Turgenev, her essays possess a uniquely human flavor. The personality that remains so steadfastly outside her novels is here embodied with all of its charm, wit, quirks, and broad range of interests. The Woolf musing about life and literature through five volumes of collected writings fills out our sense of the complicated being who does not readily emerge from the pages of her novels.

As a critic, Woolf remains entirely free of any polemical commitment. She has no theory of literature for which she argues, no set of rigid critical assumptions against which she measures the fiction, poetry, and drama she discusses. For loosely descriptive purposes, the most convenient way of categorizing her critical approach would be to call her 'impressionistic,' if by that one understands simply a critic who responds to each work without limiting preconceptions, seeks to explain how it affects her and why she does (or does not) like it. Not the impressionism, that is, of a Walter Pater, who saw the text as a means of stimulating the exploration and expression of his own feelings, but rather a more eclectic, informal method which tries to determine, on its own merits, the worth of every work of art it addresses. Woolf has no serious interest in literary criticism as a significant discourse in its own right, nor any great esteem for those who spend their lives writing it.[1] The critic's role is ideally to serve the author just as the doctor serves the patient: diagnosing the difficulties

---

[1]   In her essay 'Reviewing,' written in 1939, she distinguishes between critics—people like Johnson, Arnold, and Coleridge, who deal 'with the past and with principles' (2, 205)—and that lesser breed of mortals who spend their time reviewing imaginative literature. But as this distinction is not operative earlier in her career, there is no point maintaining it here. When I refer to critics and criticism in this chapter, therefore, I refer generally to all those people and activities associated with the business of writing about literature, without investing any special meaning in 'critic' as opposed to 'reviewer.'

and suggesting the proper remedies. But for Woolf this function has been obscured by the growth and demands of the reviewing profession. Where once the author could perhaps count on several expert opinions to help him assess his own work, now there are dozens and dozens as reviewers scrape among themselves to make a living, one half of them cancelling out the other half. And as books flow in ever increasing numbers from the presses, critical judgments become more and more haphazard, each beleaguered reviewer struggling to complete one 600-word opinion before beginning the next. The result of all of this is that the artist can receive no informed guidance and the reading public is left totally bewildered. Woolf fantasizes a future in which all reviewing will be done by a 'Gutter and Taster.' The Gutter will summarize the main outline of the work, armed with scissors and paste to extract relevant portions of novel or poem, and the Taster will then affix to this some stamp—an asterisk or dagger—of approval or disapproval (*Essays*, vol. 2, 209)

> This statement—this Gutter and Stamp production—will serve instead of this discordant and distracted twitter. And there is no reason to think that it will serve two of the parties concerned worse than the present system. The library public will be told what it wishes to know—the book is the kind of book to order from the library; and the publisher will collect asterisks and daggers instead of going to the pains to copy out alternate phrases of praise and abuse in which neither he nor the public has any faith:

Even the writers themselves will come to realize that they are no worse served under this system than they are with the present one.

What Woolf finally proposes in a not altogether frivolous way is that reviewers officially abolish themselves as reviewers, writing their hurried and inadequate daily columns, and resurrect themselves as consultants and expounders, prepared to meet authors in private—and for a fee—to engage in serious discussion about their works. Reputations would thus not be slandered, library sales pandered to, or the public misled. Most important, the writers would have the benefit of the serious criticism they long for, delivered honestly and without regard for the public's scrutiny. And for such a service, Woolf concludes, writers would gladly pay, thereby ensuring the economic viability of the reviewer.

While the vision of reviewers as literary diagnosticians, catering to

246

the ills of their author-patients in private consultations, is more metaphorical than anything else, it does suggest the way in which Woolf understood the critic's mission. Recognizing the value of intelligent criticism, she nevertheless is never led to exaggerate the status of the critic or tempted herself to see the text simply as a means of permitting the critic to scintillate at its expense. Her own essays and reviews are unpretentious and at times even pleasantly casual, without the virtuoso flights of self-aggrandizement common to criticism today. If their relaxed manner keeps them from constituting what the world likes to call a 'significant body of critical thought,' they are nevertheless well worth reading, full of vitality, humor, and insight, putting us in contact with a Woolfian self every bit as real as the one she exploited for her novels.

Woolf actually published only two collections of essays during her lifetime: *Common Reader I* and *Common Reader II*, published in 1925 and 1932 respectively. The other four titled volumes—*The Moment, The Death of the Moth, The Captain's Death Bed*, and *Granite and Rainbow*—were put together by Leonard after her death. The six were subsequently turned into the standard four-volume edition, issued by Leonard, with a fifth volume, Virginia's reviews of contemporary fiction, added later. As only two groups of essays were actually fashioned into single books by Woolf herself, it makes no sense to consider at length any book separately. Essentially, I shall treat all of the essays simply as part of the whole body of non-fictional writing found in the five volumes. An exception, however, should be made for the first *Common Reader*, whose shape, themes, and scope provide a particularly good introduction to all her critical and biographical work.

Moving from the Paston letters and Chaucer to modern literature, the *Common Reader* exposes us at once to the extraordinary range of Woolf's literary interests. The inveterate habit of reading, bred in her father's library as a substitute gratification, in part, for not being permitted to go off to school, never left her: she was a bookish person in the best sense of that word, reading incessantly and widely. The Greeks, the French, Russians, English and Americans; novels, drama, and poetry; memoirs, biography, letters, and history—she devoured everything, referring to Ring Lardner and the Duchess of Newcastle with the same ease as she writes about George Eliot and Sophocles. Woolf's bookishness, however, never served the purpose of sealing her off from life but rather provided her with a means of satisfying

247

her curiosity about it. Although in her own work she was always deeply absorbed, as we have seen, with formal questions, she does not bring an exclusively technical point of view to her consideration of literature. Her interests are primarily those of the common reader she extols, the reader who comes to a book looking for insight into the way people act, think, and feel, who is eager to experience someone else's imaginative attempt to make sense of the world. The basis for her critical judgments is never narrowly professional or exotically private; she asks of literature those rather primitive questions that intelligent readers have always asked: are the characters (speaking now of novels) convincing? Are the emotions honest? and above all, is the vision of life embedded in the work of art coherent and substantial, shaping our own perceptions of things in significant ways? If these questions all smack of a nineteenth-century rather than modernist sensibility, they simply speak to the intellectual ancestry that always remained a vital part of Virginia Woolf. However radical her own technical experiments, she was, after all, very much Leslie Stephen's child. It is not the newness of her critical point of view, but rather the fineness of her intelligence and the subtle, richly human response she brings to literature that distinguish her as a critic.

Putting together a volume of essays was by no means a mechanical exercise for Woolf. The concern with form we have seen as paramount in her fiction extends even to the problem of ordering the group of disparate essays which constitute the *Common Reader*. The question of how 'to shape the book' is a real one to her: what pieces should she include, and in what order? The diary shows her toying with two roughly chronological schemes, with some difference in the specific essays to be included. Neither list includes the essay which does actually open the *Common Reader*, a point which in itself suggests that it is an essay worth looking at with some care. Although the final organization of the book is basically chronological, 'The Pastons and Chaucer' cannot claim temporal primacy as the grounds for appearing first in the volume, as it precedes Woolf's essay on the Greeks. But its position is not honorific or arbitrary, for even as it undermines the strict chronology before it begins, 'The Pastons and Chaucer' establishes the tone and the guiding critical concerns of the entire book.

It is, at first glance, a curious essay: a review of the Paston letters, four volumes of correspondence embracing the life and times of the fifteenth-century Paston family, with a self-contained short appreciation of Chaucer placed, almost like a kind of insert, in the middle. But

248

although the Chaucerian digression seems to interrupt the flow of the essay, it is in fact integral to it, turning what might otherwise have been a simple review of a volume of letters into a rather more ambitious statement about the relation of art to life. Indeed, the very form of the essay, with the lives of the Pastons framing the discussion of Chaucer, dramatizes central ideas which Woolf will return to again and again throughout this volume—and the rest of her criticism as well.

Woolf's delight in experiencing the texture of people's lives is apparent in all of her reviews of letters and memoirs and biographies. She relishes the immersion into the oddities and difficulties of other people, fascinated by the details of their relationships, their feelings, the mundane rhythm of their existences. The pleasure of the Paston volumes, for her, is above all the wealth of information it affords her about how Lady Margaret, Sir John, and their various children spent their time in fifteenth-century England. And a dificult and haphazard time it was, with the Pastons struggling with themselves, the land, and the perilous world around them. But as Woolf follows the arduous life of the Pastons, we find that Sir John, beset with all the problems of money, crops, and tenants, begins to spend less and less time agonizing over these and more and more time absorbed in the intoxications of his Chaucer. Moving from the unfinished, 'imperfect' life of the Pastons to the coherence and wholeness of Chaucer's art, Woolf enacts in the structure of the essay the significant role literature plays in life: its ability to make ordered, enduring shapes out of the chaos and impermanence of the world. The completeness of Chaucer's created world contrasts with the harried uncertainties of Sir John's and constitutes, for Woolf, one of the great claims of art. When Sir John hastens home from the fields to learn the end of the story he is reading, he is affirming the power of art which the essay as a whole celebrates.

Woolf praises those features of Chaucer's artistry which she remains sensitive to throughout all of her critical writing: his 'shaping power, the architect's power' (18),[1] his ability to confront directly all the facts of experience, exalted as well as trivial, and a joyous morality which never resorts to solemn preaching (18):

> His morality lies in the way men and women behave to each other. We see them eating, drinking, laughing, and making love,

---

[1] All references to *The Common Reader* are to the American edition (Harvest, 1953).

and come to feel without a word being said what their standards are and so are steeped through and through with their morality. There can be no more forcible preaching than this where all actions and passions are represented. . . . It is the morality of ordinary intercourse, the morality of the novel.

Most important, and what makes all of Chaucer's successes possible, is his absolute certainty of belief in himself, his perceptions, and the nature of the world around him. Chaucer possesses that 'power of conviction' (15) crucial to all great art. Characters in the *Canterbury Tales* have a coherence that is possible only when the artist 'has made up his mind about young women, of course, but also about the world they live in, its end, its nature, and his own craft and technique, so that his mind is free to apply its force fully to its object' (14). The necessity of belief for the artist remains a vital principle in Woolf's criticism; moving from Chaucer through to the twentieth century in the pages of *The Common Reader*, she chooses to close the book with a reaffirmation of the importance of conviction. In 'How It Strikes a Contemporary,' Woolf diagnoses the problem with modern literature as consisting precisely in writers' loss of confidence in themselves, their visions, and their values (244):

> our contemporaries afflict us because they have ceased to believe. The most sincere of them will only tell us what it is that happens to himself. They cannot make a world, because they are not free of other human beings. They cannot tell stories because they do not believe the stories are true. They cannot generalize.

The result is a literature gnarled by egotism of the sort she detected in Joyce, a literature which has lost the power to convince. For it is only through the certainty that 'your impressions hold good for others' (244), that you can be 'free from the cramp and confinement of personality,' as Chaucer, or Scott, or Jane Austen were. And it is only by being free that you can produce that self-contained and 'complete statement which is literature' (244).

Beginning and ending on the theme of belief, Woolf not only gives shape to the *Common Reader* but establishes as well the basic critical principle underlying her approach to all literature, whether medieval or modern. As long as the artist has confidence in his own vision, he is capable of producing significant work: 'Any method is right, every method is right, that expresses what we wish to express, if we are

250

writers' (156). Although she certainly speaks out for the legitimacy of the modern, her defense of modernist technique is not argued at the expense of what has come before; it is seen rather as another attempt, as authentic in its way as Jane Austen's was in hers, to render a coherent vision of life. Modernism is thus not a repudiation of a tradition but simply an extension of it. What matters finally is how compelling that vision is—and how successful the writer is in conveying it. And here Woolf responds to the whole range of English, European, and American literature without the constraining fetters of any single theory. Proust, Turgenev, Conrad, Defoe, Austen, the Brontës, Sterne—all are embraced by a sensibility flexible enough to appreciate the individual achievements of each novelist, however diverse they may be. It is above all the 'truth of insight'—a phrase which occurs in a number of Woolf's essays—that a great writer communicates to us, a truth which is not tied to any particular style or technique. Thus Defoe, who fashions his novels out of prosaic observation and minutely rendered, plausible character, and Emily Brontë, inventing the impossible Heathcliff and Cathy and freeing 'life from its dependence on facts' (165), both manage to deal 'with the important and lasting side of things' (95–6) in their created worlds. She revels in the sublime quirkiness of *Tristram Shandy* with the same ease as she encounters the sanity of Jane Austen, whose 'impeccable sense of human values' (144) she cherishes.

Within her broadly moral and traditional framework, which demands that a work of art be a significant vision of human experience, Woolf's great strength as a critic is her ability to engage different writers on their own grounds, searching out the 'inscape,' to use G. M. Hopkins's term, of their own individuality. The self, for Woolf, is a 'streaked, variegated' (*Essays*, vol. 4, 161) thing, capable of all kinds of odd manifestations, and one important role of the critic is to help others understand those different manifestations as they reveal themselves through works of art. 'Whether you are writing a review or a love letter, the great thing is to be confronted with a very vivid idea of your subject,' she writes in a short essay on Poe (*Essays*, vol. 4, 42), enunciating a working principle that remained very much hers throughout her life. The contact she makes with texts is always concrete and immediate, not abstract or filtered through some larger social, literary, or psychological purpose. Her impulses as a critic can be likened to those of Sterne's sentimental traveller who 'wishes to seize the essence of things,' (*Essays*, vol. 1, 97) and realizes they can be found not necessarily 'at broad noonday in large and open streets, but in an unobserved corner up a dark entry' (*Essays*, vol. 1, 97).

It is important to recognize the breadth of her literary interests and the varied, flexible nature of her critical approaches, for Woolf has all too often been taken as a rigidly polemical modernist, insisting on the hegemony of the modernist vision. The reasons for this misapprehension of Woolf rest largely on the popularity (and partial misunderstandings) of two essays, 'Modern Fiction' (1919) and 'Mr Bennett and Mrs Brown' (1924), which have by this time become almost obligatory anthology pieces of modernist criticism. Reading the two outside the context of the rest of her work, and assuming they embody all of Woolf's ideas about fiction, it is easy to see how the distortions came about. Perhaps the most famous passage—and undoubtedly the most quoted—in all of Woolf is the 'shower of atoms' paragraph in 'Modern Fiction.' Arguing for the legitimacy of novelists attempting something other than conventionally realistic works, Woolf reminds us that life does not generally present itself in thirty-two neat chapters, containing the proper amounts of comedy, tragedy, and love interest (*Essays*, vol. 2, 106):

> Look within and life, it seems, is very far from being 'like this.' Examine for a moment an ordinary mind on an ordinary day. The mind receives a myriad impressions—trivial, fantastic, evanescent, or engraved with the sharpness of steel. From all sides they come, an incessant shower of innumerable atoms; and as they fall, as they shape themselves into the life of Monday or Tuesday, the accent falls differently from of old. . . . Life is not a series of gig lamps symmetrically arranged; but a luminous halo, a semi-transparent envelope surrounding us from the beginning of consciousness to the end.

Such a metaphoric declaration was never intended as a binding prescription for novelists to follow, or a theoretical scheme which would find Dorothy Richardson, say, or James Joyce, to be better than Walter Scott or Thomas Hardy, but rather a halting effort by which she seeks to define, 'in some such fashion as this . . . the quality which distinguishes the work of several young writers, among whom James Joyce is the most notable, from that of their predecessors' (*Essays*, vol. 2, 106–7). While it certainly suggests some of the differences in technique and vision between the modern novel and its Edwardian ancestors, it can hardly be said to describe the fictional worlds of Joyce or Woolf herself, nor to constitute any of the assumptions behind her critical methodology. It is instead part of a struggle to gain respectability for writers who had initially offended by their oddness—among whom it is fair to include Virginia Woolf—and never represents a bias she held to in her own criticism. Her aim is always to embrace, not exclude; modern literature is not necessarily more insightful than what has come before, but it is surely not less. 'Everything is the proper stuff of fiction' (*Essays*, vol. 2, 110): Defoe's conventions are as revealing about life as D. H. Lawrence's.

Similarly, the generational split between the Edwardians and Georgians she describes in 'Mr Bennett and Mrs Brown' appears far more theoretically compelling than Woolf ever really thought it to be. As Samuel Hynes has shown, the essay developed out of an intense feud Woolf was waging with Arnold Bennett, a feud that had more to do with an ego abused—Woolf having been criticized by Bennett for faulty characterization in *Jacob's Room*—than with any principled literary disagreements.[1] Determined to answer the affront, Woolf gradually fashioned an essay which roots her personal vindication in a larger conceptual framework: it is not that the Georgians are unable to create character or catch life—in this case, Mrs Brown—but rather that the outmoded Edwardian conventions no longer provide the appropriate tools to do so. Putting Mrs Brown on the train to Waterloo and surrounding her with Bennett (and, to extend her case, H. G. Wells and Galsworthy, too), Woolf shows how all three fail to render the essential spirit which is Mrs Brown's. It is the failure of an artistic generation, necessitating the radically new efforts of the Georgians who can apprehend Mrs Brown only by renouncing the inadequate methods they inherited from their predecessors. Although the argument correctly points out the change of sensibility and technique which begins to distinguish Georgian from Edwardian fiction, 'Mr Bennett and Mrs Brown' remains more of a fully orchestrated personal answer to Bennett's criticism than a critical model exploring one age's response to another.

While 'Mr Bennett and Mrs Brown' is probably the best-known instance of Woolf's dressing up in theoretical trappings intensely individual assertions concerning her own values and techniques as a writer, it is by no means the only one. Indeed, most of her speculations about modern literature are of this sort. When Woolf appears to theorize, that is, she is invariably being most personal, providing us

[1] See S. Hynes, *Edwardian Occasions* (Oxford University Press, 1972), 24, 37.

with ways of understanding her own work rather than equipping us with a means of dealing with others. A good example of this is 'The Narrow Bridge of Art,' an essay reflecting, among other things, on the absence of any kind of vital poetic drama in the modern world. Woolf finds the constricted, fragmented present with its ironies, its isolation, its tawdriness to be inimical to poetry. Poetry does not have the flexibility to capture 'the sneer, the contrast, the closeness, the complexity of life' (*Essays*, vol. 2, 226). If the age cannot be grasped by a genre 'which has never been used for the common purpose of life' (*Essays*, vol. 2, 223), it will be left to prose to interpret the world for us. Woolf then goes on to describe some of the features of the new prose that will emerge (*Essays*, vol. 2, 224–5):

> And it is possible that there will be among the so-called novels one which we shall scarcely know how to christen. It will be written in prose, but in prose which has many of the characteristics of poetry. It will have something of the exaltation of poetry, but much of the ordinariness of prose. It will be dramatic, and yet not a play. It will be read, not acted. By what name we are to call it is not a matter of very great importance . . . . It will resemble poetry in this that it will give not only or mainly people's relations to each other and their activities together, as the novel has hitherto done, but it will give the relation of the mind to general ideas and its soliloquy in solitude.

What Woolf is doing here, of course, is not detailing the hypothetical nature and form of the new novel but actually beginning to fashion, in language strikingly similar to what she uses in her diary, her rough conception of *The Waves*. A diary entry of 1927, the year 'The Narrow Bridge of Art' was written, makes clear the entirely subjective impulses behind the larger theoretical formulation of the essay: 'Why not invent a new kind of play,' she notes, jotting down a series of different voices and actions which might be relevant to it. 'I think it must be something on this line—though I can't now see what. Away from facts; free; yet concentrated; prose yet poetry; a novel and a play.' (*A Writer's Diary*, 104).

Her advice in 'A Letter to a Young Poet' on how the young artist should properly relate to the modern world outside him speaks clearly to the relationship she aspires to in her own novels, particularly *The Waves* (*Essays*, vol. 2, 191):

254

What I mean is, summon all your courage. . . . Let your
rhythmical sense wind itself in and out among men and women,
omnibuses, sparrows—whatever comes along the street—until it
has strung them together in one harmonious whole. That
perhaps is your task—to find the relation between things that
seem incompatible yet have a mysterious affinity, to absorb every
experience that comes your way fearlessly and saturate it
completely so that your poem is a whole, not a fragment; to
re-think human life into poetry and so give us tragedy again and
comedy by means of characters not spun out at length in the
novelist's way, but condensed and synthesized in the poet's
way—that is what we look to you to do now.

Despite such an exhortation, it is fair to say that Woolf never in fact
asks for these things from writers she discusses in her essays and
reviews. She is content to create herself the kinds of works she talks
about without assaulting others for their failure to share her vision. In
general, her best-known critical statements about the nature of modern literature primarily constitute attempts at self-definition, rather
than providing an instrument of practical analysis to approach individual writers or texts.
No such distinction exists in her writing on women and fiction, a
subject in which she was, for obvious reasons, passionately interested
all her life. Here the theoretical and practical are one, the larger
philosophical concerns establishing a coherent focus for her examination of specific writers. Woolf's involvement in the feminist cause, if
not as radical as contemporary polemicists pretend it to have been, was
nevertheless a real and abiding commitment. As *A Room of One's Own*
and *Three Guineas* indicate, Woolf saw clearly the kinds of explicit and
implicit oppression under which women had suffered for centuries,
and she deplored then, much as people deplore now, its crippling
psychological, social, and economic consequences. The effect on
women writers, of course, was primarily to prevent them from pro-
liferating. Art flourishes when people have the time to attend to it. A
room of one's own and the leisure to occupy it are the necessary
conditions of art; women's historical failure to gain access to such
things is the most obvious fact in any consideration of the subject of
women and literature. But beyond the sheer physical difficulties
which the culture has always put in the path of aspiring women
writers, Woolf perceives a more challenging problem. For if the

woman does indeed find her way to free herself from domestic burdens so that she can write, the question then remains as to what and how she shall write. The first pitfall to be avoided is the temptation of trying to write as a man would write in order to earn the approbation of the ruling male literary culture. Advocates for androgyny notwithstanding, Woolf makes clear again and again that men and women see things differently and should therefore write about them differently. The woman who either consciously or unconsciously tries to adopt for herself a masculine style or point of view is doomed to triviality as an artist, a pathological condition Woolf sees as more prevalent in the eighteenth and nineteenth centuries than now. But equally as destructive to art—and far more insidious because subtler—is the temptation of writing in a parochial and shrill way as a woman, of permitting the special pleadings of sexual identity to influence one's work (*Contemporary Writers*, 26):

> The women who wished to be taken for men in what they wrote were certainly common enough; and if they have given place to the women who wish to be taken for women the change is hardly for the better, since any emphasis, either of pride or of shame, laid consciously upon the sex of a writer is not only irritating but superfluous.

This is not a plea for androgyny, but for art. Sexual differences are an inescapable result of there being two sexes—'The first words in which either a man or a woman is described are generally enough to determine the sex of the writer' (*Contemporary Writers*, 26)—and the challenge to the writer, male or female, is to produce work which is not deformed by any narrow sexual insistence. If you cannot escape the particular perspective of your sexual identity (to attempt to do so, indeed, would be fatuous), you can at least escape 'the tyranny of sex itself' (*Contemporary Writers*, 25), be it of the oppressed or the oppressor. For Woolf this is exactly what great artists manage to do. She finds Jane Austen more satisfying than George Eliot, and Emily Brontë more compelling than Charlotte precisely because Eliot and Charlotte compromise their art in various places by expressing feelings particular to their position as women which are not thoroughly absorbed in the texture of their novels. Indignation and resignation in presenting these values are both inimical to the integrity of a work of art. It is the genius of Austen and Emily Brontë that they rise above all base claims on their art to meditate on life without the distortions of personal grievance.

Woolf sees a writer's commitment to any cause, then, whether personal or political, as potentially fatal to the finished work of art. Didacticism of any sort is anathema to her; novelists must never permit undigested strains of feeling to deform their visions. This is an entirely defensible critical position with a long and distinguished tradition behind it. At the same time, it must be recognized that it is a position with certain inescapable political implications. Woolf has not been well served in recent years by her cultic admirers who insist on finding in her a radical social thinker firmly committed, in her imaginative and critical writing, to all manner of admirable goals. Whether it is good or bad to be a radical social thinker (and I make no judgment on the subject), it should be obvious that whatever else Woolf was, she was surely not that. Neither in her novels nor in her assessments of other writers is she concerned with what can broadly be thought of as social issues. This is not to argue that she was insensitive to injustice, poverty, and the like, but simply to point out that her work focuses on other sorts of things. In a review of E. M. Forster's *Aspects of the Novel* in 1927, she chides Forster for seeking to protect life in the novel at the expense of art. Forster's view of Henry James, for example, that he 'pursued the narrow path of aesthetic duty' (*Essays,*, vol. 2, 53), but in so doing sacrificed a large portion of human life, is attacked by Woolf as an inadequate understanding of the relationship between 'life' and the novel: 'It is the humane as opposed to the aesthetic view of fiction' (*Essays*, vol. 2, 55). And although Woolf's criticism is by no means the narrow, life-denying approach to literature for which one should properly apologize, it is clear that her work never wanders far from what are finally aesthetic considerations.

To attempt to make her another kind of critic is to distort her work. In 'The Leaning Tower,' a paper originally read to the Workers' Educational Association of Brighton in 1940, she speaks with great impatience of the writers of the 1930s—Auden, Isherwood, Spender, Day-Lewis, MacNeice and company—and their battle with the middle-class culture which spawned them. It is not a battle Woolf views with much sympathy. The English writer, for Woolf, has always enjoyed special advantages that cannot easily be rejected. Woolf claims the Auden generation is essentially self-indulgent and puerile, trapped by its own callowness into abusing the very system by which it has profited. The difficulties of such a position necessitate the worst kind of self-deception: 'The bleat of the scapegoat sounds loud in their work, and the whimper of the schoolboy crying "Please, Sir, it was the other fellow, not me"' (*Essays*, vol. 2, 171). Unable ever to leave the tower of privilege they occupy, they remain mired in self-contradiction, 'and their state of mind as we see it reflected in their poems and plays and novels is full of discord and bitterness, full of confusion and of compromise' (*Essays*, vol. 2, 172).

Woolf sees their efforts to escape the isolation of their privileged position and to bring about social change as not only futile—'How can a writer who has no first hand experience of a towerless, of a classless society create that society?' (*Essays*, vol. 2, 175)—but equally as important for her purposes, responsible for their bad art. It accounts for the haranguing, for the shrill didactic tone of their work. The preacher has been allowed to replace the artist, and the result is bad prophecy and even worse poetry.

While some of her reservations about the tone of their work unquestionably make sense, the virulence of her attack, her accusations about the destructiveness and emptiness of their writing speak to an animus that transcends mere critical disagreement. If detectable grievance of any sort—as we saw in her treatment of women writers—represents a serious aesthetic impurity for Woolf, the assault on class and privilege mounted by the poets of the 1930s was particularly difficult for her to endure. For although in her paper to the Workers' Association she seems to include herself among those of her deprived audience who never had the advantages of the tower occupied by the male poets—'But we are not in their position; we have not had eleven years of expensive education' (*Essays*, vol. 2, 171)—she in fact shares precisely the same perspective as those with a tower seat. Denied an expensive formal education by the rigidities of sexual bias, Virginia nevertheless experienced, as Leslie Stephen's child, the same kind of rarefied life as that led by the Oxford and Cambridge poets. And certainly her point of view, literary and otherwise, was shaped by that experience. The primacy of the aesthetic for Woolf clearly grows in part of the special existence that was hers not only as a Stephen but also as a Woolf. I state this not as a crippling flaw of the sort endlessly stressed by F. R. Leavis, but simply as a fact which must be accepted if we are to appreciate her work in its totality. If it accounts for the unpleasant fastidiousness, for example, of her objection that women writing out of a sense of injustice 'bring into women's writing an

258

element which is entirely absent from a man's, unless, indeed, he happens to be a working man, a negro, or one who for some other reason is conscious of disability' (*Essays*, vol. 2, 144), it also helps us to understand the non-polemical nature of her criticism, the range and ease of her learning, her commitment to art.

The aesthetic grounds of her censure of the Auden group, then, represent only a portion of her full response to them. In rejecting the institutions and culture which nurtured them, they were striking directly at Woolf's security, and her judgment of their work is by no means an example of disinterested literary criticism. Their immersion in politics was not only uncongenial to Woolf, but threatening as well. It was, above all, not what artists properly did. Activism and art do not mix.

Her repudiation of the 1930s' poets, however, does not suggest she was blind to the inequities they were fighting against. She, too, saw the chasm between the rich and poor, the restricted opportunities England offered many of its citizens. The difference is not in the vision but in the methodologies of the solution. Anticipating a future in which the income tax will dissolve all class distinctions, Woolf sees no need for concerted social action. Classes and towers will shortly be odd vestiges of the past. In the meantime, what can best help bridge the remaining barriers of class is not political rhetoric but literature (*Essays*, vol. 2, 180):

> We have got to teach ourselves to understand literature. Money is no longer going to do our thinking for us. Wealth will no longer decide who shall be taught and who not. In the future it is we who shall decide whom to send to public schools and universities; how they shall be taught; and whether what they write justifies their exemption from other work.

The possibility of a just and classless society can thus be enhanced by learning to read the books the public library system now makes available to all people: 'We can help England very greatly to bridge the gulf between the two worlds if we borrow the books she lends us and if we read them critically' (*Essays*, vol. 2, 180). And Woolf ends her paper with an exhortation to the workers not to unite but to take possession of the culture from which they have so long been excluded (*Essays*, vol. 2, 181):

> Let us trespass freely and fearlessly and find our own way for

ourselves. It is thus that English literature will survive this war and cross the gulf—if commoners and outsiders like ourselves make that country our own country, if we teach ourselves how to read and write, how to preserve, and how to create.

In quoting this essay at some length, I do not mean to reduce it to farce—though some of its assumptions are extraordinary—but simply to show how firmly rooted in a particular class Woolf remained all her life. Not that education and literature don't matter—they obviously do. Seeing the public library system working in league with the income tax to bring about social change, however, suggests a degree of insulation from political reality which clearly defines a rather special class point of view. It is not a point of view which trivializes her criticism, though it certainly serves to establish its limitations. While it may seem ungenerous to end on a note of limitation, Woolf at this point needs to be rescued more from the uncritical fervor of her supporters than anyone else. The extravagant claims made for her, the obligation imposed on her to provide prophetic wisdom for a multitude of social and sexual causes threaten to obscure her real achievements altogether. Above all else, her achievement was primarily—and happily—literary. She writes for the common reader, not the common man (or woman), and does so with uncommon elegance, wit, and sensitivity. It was finally to the cause of literature that she devoted herself, and it is for this that we should properly admire her.

Suggested Reading

While there is an enormous amount of secondary critical literature growing up around Virginia Woolf and Bloomsbury, the best introduction to both remains, with a few notable exceptions, the assorted non-fictional writings of Woolf herself as well as the various reminiscences of her contemporaries. The notable exceptions are Michael Holroyd's exhaustive two-volume biography of Lytton Strachey and Quentin Bell's equally thorough treatment of his aunt, Virginia. Both provide detailed views of Bloomsbury life, establishing the necessary biographical context within which we can appreciate the achievement of Woolf, Strachey, and all of their friends. Although Bell is far more reluctant than Holroyd to discuss his subject's literary work, nevertheless his book is essential reading for anyone curious about Woolf. Along with the dispassionate accounts of the biographer, there are a host of fascinating autobiographies which help us understand the period as well as the people. While no view is altogether satisfactory—and many, indeed, conflict with one another—taken together they constitute a vivid picture of what Bloomsbury was like. The most relevant of these are Leonard Woolf's five volumes (*Sowing*, *Growing*, *Beginning Again*, *Downhill All the Way*, *The Journey Not The Arrival Matters*); David Garnett's three (*The Golden Echo*, *The Familiar Faces*, *The Flowers of the Forest*); John Lehmann's *The Whispering Gallery*, *I Am My Brother*, *The Ample Proposition*; and although they bear on Bloomsbury less directly than the others, the interested reader should also consult the first two volumes of Bertrand Russell's three-volume autobiography, as well as Osbert Sitwell's five: *Left Hand*, *Right Hand*, *The Scarlet Tree*, *Great Morning*, *Laughter in the Next Room*, *Noble Essences*. Clive Bell's *Old Friends* gives a protagonist's view of his Bloomsbury compatriots and John Maynard Keynes analyzes the values and origins of the group in his essay 'My Early Beliefs' in *Two Memoirs*. Roger Fry's letters, edited by Denys Sutton, put us in touch with the thinking of one of Bloomsbury's most respectable citizens, while two of its most authentic exotics, Carrington and Lady Ottoline Morrell, have also left letters and diaries: *Carrington*, edited by David Garnett, and *Ottoline* and *Ottoline at Garsington*, both edited by Robert Gathorne-Hardy. Vita Sackville-West, Woolf's friend and onetime lover, wrote a brief autobiographical fragment that remained undiscovered until her son, Nigel Nicolson, came upon it after her death. The story of Vita's unusual marriage with Harold Nicolson and her relationships with, among others, Virginia, is told in Nigel's *Portrait of*

261

a Marriage. For a general overview of the many complex relationships in Bloomsbury, David Gadd's *The Loving Friends* provides an adequate summary.

The most important contributions to our understanding of Woolf's mind and art have come from Woolf herself. *A Writer's Diary*, the one-volume abridgment Leonard made of the diaries she kept over the course of her entire career was for many years the standard source of information about the evolution of her novels and her views of her own art as well as that of others. It is still perhaps the most useful single-volume introduction to her work that we have. Several years ago Anne Olivier Bell started on the project of editing the complete text of the whole diary. Thus far three volumes, covering up to 1931 have been finished. Two more are planned. Similarly, Joanne Trautmann and Nigel Nicolson have been putting out a complete edition of Woolf's letters. Four volumes, of an anticipated six, have already been published. When completed, the letters and diary together will provide an extraordinary wealth of insight into Woolf. With the recent publication of Woolf's hitherto unpublished autobiographical writings in *Moments of Being*, edited by Jeanne Schulkind, as well as some previously uncollected critical essays in *Books and Portraits*, edited by Mary Lyon, there is no reason why the indefatigable reader should not be thoroughly familiar with almost every part of Woolf's life.

Clive Bell: *Old Friends*. Chatto & Windus, 1956.

Quentin Bell: *Virginia Woolf: A Biography*. Hogarth Press, 1972; Harcourt Brace Jovanovich, 1972.

Carrington: *Letters and Extracts from Her Diaries*, chosen and with an introduction by David Garnett. Jonathan Cape, 1970.

Roger Fry: *Letters*, ed. Denys Sutton. Chatto & Windus, 1972.

David Gadd: *The Loving Friends*. Hogarth Press, 1974; Harcourt Brace Jovanovich, 1974.

David Garnett: *The Golden Echo*. Chatto & Windus, 1953; Harcourt Brace, 1954.

The Familiar Faces. Chatto & Windus, 1962; Harcourt Brace Jovanovich, 1963.

The Flowers of the Forest. Chatto & Windus, 1962; Harcourt Brace Jovanovich, 1963.

Michael Holroyd: *Lytton Strachey: A Critical Biography*. Heinemann, 1967–8; Holt, Rinehart & Winston, 1968.

John Maynard Keynes: *Two Memoirs*. Rupert Hart-Davis, 1949; Augustus M. Kelley, 1949.

John Lehmann: *The Whispering Gallery*. Longmans, 1955; Harcourt Brace, 1955.

I Am My Brother. Longmans, 1960; Reynal, 1960.

The Ample Proposition. Eyre & Spottiswoode, 1966.

Ottoline Morrell: *Ottoline: The Early Memoirs of Lady Ottoline Morrell*, ed. by Robert Gathorne-Hardy. Faber & Faber, 1963.

Ottoline at Garsington: Memoirs of Lady Ottoline Morrell, 1915–1918, ed. By

Robert Gathorne-Hardy. Faber & Faber, 19 ; Alfred A. Knopf, 1975.

Nigel Nicolson: *Portrait of a Marriage*. Weidenfeld & Nicolson, 1973; Atheneum, 1973.

Bertrand Russell: *The Autobiography of Bertrand Russell: 1872–1914*. Allen & Unwin, 1967; Little, Brown, 1967.

    The Autobiography of Bertrand Russell: 1914–1944. Allen & Unwin, 1968; Little, Brown, 1968.

Osbert Sitwell: *Left Hand, Right Hand*. Macmillan, 1945; Little, Brown, 1947.

    The Scarlet Tree. Macmillan, 1946; Little, Brown, 1946.

    Great Morning. Macmillan, 1948; Little, Brown, 1947.

    Laughter in the Next Room. Macmillan, 1949; Little, Brown, 1948.

    Noble Essences. Macmillan, 1950; Little, Brown, 1950.

Leonard Woolf: *Sowing: An Autobiography of the Years 1880–1904*. Hogarth Press, 1960; Harcourt Brace Jovanovich, 1960.

    Growing: An Autobiography of the Years 1904–1911. Hogarth Press, 1961; Harcourt Brace Jovanovich, 1961.

    Beginning Again: An Autobiography of the Years 1911–1918. Hogarth Press, 1964; Harcourt Brace Jovanovich, 1964.

    Downhill All the Way: An Autobiography of the Years 1919–1939. Hogarth Press, 1967; Harcourt Brace Jovanovich, 1967.

    The Journey Not the Arrival Matters: An Autobiography of the Years 1939–1969. Hogarth Press, 1969; Harcourt Brace Jovanovich, 1969.

Virginia Woolf: *Contemporary Writers* (London: Hogarth Press, 1965).

    A Writer's Diary, ed. by L. Woolf. Hogarth Press, 1965.

    The Diary of Virginia Woolf, ed. Anne Olivier Bell, vol. 1, 1915–1919 (Hogarth Press and Harcourt Brace Jovanovich, 1977); vol. 2, 1920–1924 (Hogarth Press and Harcourt Brace Jovanovich, 1978); vol. 3, 1925–1931 (Hogarth Press and Harcourt Brace Jovanovich, 1979).

    Letters, vol. 1, 1888–1912 (Hogarth Press and Harcourt Brace Jovanovich, 1975), vol. 2, 1912–1922 (Hogarth Press and Harcourt Brace Jovanovich, 1976); vol. 3, 1923–1928 (Hogarth Press and Harcourt Brace Jovanovich, 1978); vol. 4, 1929–1931 (Hogarth Press and Harcourt Brace Jovanovich, 1979).

    Moments of Being: Unpublished Autobiographical Writings, ed. by Jeanne Schulkind. Chatto & Windus, 1976; Harcourt Brace Jovanovich, 1976.

    Books and Portraits. ed by Mary Lyon. Harcourt Brace Jovanovich, 1977.

Index